STUDIES OF A LITTERATEUR

STUDIES OF A LITTERATEUR

BY

GEORGE EDWARD WOODBERRY

Essay Index Reprint Series

91985

BOOKS FOR LIBRARIES PRESS

FREEPORT, NEW YORK

First Published 1921
Reprinted 1968

LIBRARY OF CONGRESS CATALOG CARD NUMBER:
68-26486

PRINTED IN THE UNITED STATES OF AMERICA

NOTE

The author has collected in this volume besides articles that were contained in his earlier books some papers of later years, for consent to reprint which he cordially thanks their various original publishers. These papers are "Bacon's Essays," The Century Co., New York, 1900; "The Brontë Novels," Harper's Bazar, 1899; "Shelley's Poetry," D. C. Heath & Co., Boston, 1908; "Shelley's 'Cenci,'" D. C. Heath & Co., Boston, 1909; "Sydney's 'Defence of Poesie,'" The Merrymount Press, Boston, 1908; "Shakespeare's 'Midsummer Night's Dream,'" George D. Sproul, New York, 1907; "Rupert Brooke," John Lane Co., New York, 1915.

CONTENTS

STUDIES OF A LITTERATEUR

ILLUSTRATIONS OF IDEALISM

I. PATER ON IDEAL ESTHETICISM

The heart of Pater's "Marius" lies in his thought about the ideal, and it is in the nature of all such thought to make a peculiar demand upon the reader. Its wisdom is felt to be, as it were, sacerdotal, and requires a conscious preparation of mind in him who would know of it; its vision is supernal, and disclosed only when some spiritual illumination has been sent before. So runs a Platonic doctrine of election and grace that has been held as rigorously in literature as in theology. This aristocracy of idealism — its exclusiveness, its jealousy of any intrusion of the common and worldly within the company it keeps, its sense of a preciousness, as of sacred things, within itself — is incorporate in every fiber of Pater's work; and he makes the demand natural to it, not only implicitly by an unrelaxing use of such esthetic and intellectual elements as appeal exclusively to the subtlest faculties of appreciation in their highest development, but explicitly also by the character of his hero. Marius, before he became an Epicurean, was molded for his fate; his creator demanded an exceptional nature for the esthetic ideal to react upon in a noble way, and so Marius was born in the upland farm among the fair mountains to the north of Pisa, and was possessed from boyhood of the devout seriousness, the mood of trustful waiting for the god's coming, which is exacted in all profound idealism. *"Favete linguis!* With the lad Marius there was a devout effort to complete this impressive outward silence by that inward tacitness of mind esteemed so important by religious Romans in the performance of their sacred functions." Marius was born one of the choice natures in whom the heavenly powers are well pleased; and emphasis must be given to this circumstance because it follows that the ideal life which he lived, deeply meditated though it is, is really an individual one. Marius is not typical, nor even illustrative in any broad way of the practice of esthetic morals; and yet, since he is not national, nor local, nor historic, in his essential self, since he is more than an enlightened philosopher, and yet less than the enlightened Christian, since his personality approaches the elect souls of other ages, other sentiments and devotions, and yet is without any real contact with them, he is typical and illustrative perhaps of something that might be. This confusedness of impression springs from the fact that Pater, while he imagines in Italy, always thinks in London; he has modernized his hero, has Anglicized him, indeed, and nevertheless has not really taken him out of the second century. It was a bold thing to attempt. It was necessary for his purposes as an evangelist of ideal living, and perhaps within the range of moral teaching it is successful; but the way in which it was done is a main point of interest.

A Roman Epicurean, one suspects, was not unlike the proverbial Italianated Englishman. The native incompatibility between the distinctive Roman temperament and the light-hearted gayety of Greek sensuousness was similar to that between the English and the Italian character in the later times; the perfection of Marius by means of a Greek ideal may run parallel with English culture under the southern influences. There was, too, in Roman character a trait or two which bring it near to qualities that lie at the base of our own stock. Even in the Italian landscape there are Northern notes such as Pater mentions when Marius, in his walks to the coast, sees "the marsh with the dwarf roses and wild lavender, the abandoned boat, the ruined floodgates, the flock of wild birds." We are told, also, that "poetic souls in old Italy felt, hardly less strongly than the English, the pleasures of winter, of the hearth, with the very dead warm in its generous heat, keeping the young myrtles in flower, though the hail is beating hard without." This note of Marius's home-life and the love he had for it, with his particular regard for "Domiduca, the goddess who watches over one's safe coming home," and with the ideal of maternity that grew up in his memory of home, — this peculiarly English note is struck in the opening and is dominant at the end. Certain other characteristics ally this Etrurian boy with that nobler strain of English blood, the Puritan strain as it was in Spenser. His instinctive seriousness, his scrupulosity of conscience, his inheritance of a certain somberness from the stock that adorned the Etruscan funeral urns, his attachment to places and awe of some of them as sacred by the touch of a divine power, his sense of invisible enemies about his path, his rigorous self-discipline in preparation for certain hereditary sacred offices, a deadly earnestness at times, — as when he gazes so fixedly on the rigid corpse of his friend Flavian, — such are some of the traits that define his nature as essentially rather Northern than Southern, and provide a ground of special sympathy and understanding for us.

The second device by which Marius is modernized is by giving to him a power which, for one who runs as he reads, makes the character incredible. He is said to be affected sometimes in a way the opposite of the experience which many have who, on seeing a new place, seem to have been there before: Marius feels, in the most marked of his experiences, something that shall be, — he has always a prescience. Thus, in the cadence of Flavian's verses he hears the music of the Latin hymnology; in the sight of his second friend, Cornelius, who displays and puts on his armor of a Roman knight in the dusty sunshine of the shuttered country-house, he foresees the Christian chivalry; in the faces and groups of the worshipers in Cecilia's house he discerns the serene light and streaming joy of Giotto's and of Dante's vision, and looks on the Madonna and the Child that Raphael first painted. In all this there seems an unreality; in the Puritan Roman, the Cyrenaic Christian, there is a sense almost of conscious artifice, as if one were being befooled. And yet, as for those Northern notes of landscape, custom, and character, scholarship can give chapter and verse for them; and as for the gift of prescience, — well, if it were impossible for Marius to have it, in a sufficient measure at least, then the theory of ideal living which he held to was at fault. And this Marius, so constituted, his creator places in an Italy over which the romantic desolation, which we know, was laying its charm of dreamful decay, and in a Rome which, then as now, was the huddled deposit of religions.

The intellectual conviction on which Marius conducted his life was simple and common enough, as must be the case with every theory capable of being made a principle of living. The world is what we think it, and our part in existence is the fleeting moment of present consciousness. What shall be done with this moment? Economize it, said Marius, in dissent from the Stoic who said, "Contemn it." Economize it; make the most of the phenomena that arise in it, and see, so far as it depends on you, that these phenomena, both of sensation and idea, as they arise, are the most valuable possible to the moment; and so your experience — in other words, your life — will be the fullest and most refined. Above all, do not forget the main thing in this doctrine of economy, which is that the worth of experience depends, not on what it is at that moment in its detached and transitory phase, but on what it will prove in memory when it takes its place permanently and in relation to the whole of life. In such a scheme, receptivity, the most alert and varied powers of taking in impressions, is the one aim of cultivation. Here, too, much depended on the nature of Marius, this time on the side of his Southern endowment. An impressibility through sensation was his gift, his talent; and especially he was susceptible to what the eye observes: he was one of those who are "made perfect by the love of visible beauty." This is the point of union of his life with the esthetic ideal, and makes the story of it a pathway through scenes of loveliness not unlike, in a certain mild beauty, the frescoes on ancient walls. The narrative is pictorial, almost to the point of decoration, and moves always with an outlook on some fair sight. From the landscape of the villa where Marius was born — among those delightful Etrurian hills whence one looks to the marbled rifts of Carrara gleaming above olive and chestnut slopes, and gazes off through the purple sea-valley of Venus's Port, the noblest gateway of the descending sun — to the last throttling earthquake morning, a beautiful visible world is about us, and exercises its attractiveness both in nature and in humanity. The one end of Marius was to appropriate all this, to choose the best of sensation and its most nearly connected emotions, and to live in that. To do this involves a secondary talent, a gift of insight, a power to perceive relative values, which in reality means a faculty of moral discrimination; and just here one may easily fail to see whence Marius derived this.

Why was it, for example, that he, being so attached to sensation and the emotions that cling closest to it, rejected voluptuousness, with all its forms of beauty and joyfulness, as a thing essentially not beautiful nor joyful? What was it that kept him, the comrade of Flavian, who represents the pagan surrender to this life, pure, — so pure, indeed, that with his visionary sense he foresaw in chastity an ideal that was to be, and foreknew its coming beauty? A mere interpreter of character, an analyst, would say, that Marius obeyed in these choices his own nature, — that Puritan nature whose compulsion is always strong. He venerated his own soul and cherished its early instincts, and this was his salvation. But one might also give another explanation, which would seem more harmonious with the purpose of the author; one might say that what is moral is in its outward manifestation so clothed with beauty, visible beauty, that the man who looks for beauty only, the noblest, the ideal beauty, will find therewith the highest, the ideal good. It is essential to such a seeker that he shall look with his own eyes and be frank with himself; shall "look straight out" and acknowledge what he sees; and this Marius does, thereby prefiguring in a way and practically making that "return to nature" which is the continually recurring necessity of all sincerity. If virtue does in fact wear this outward loveliness — and who would deny it? — why may not the lover of beauty have truly seen the new and springing forms of goodness, recognized them, and taken their promise into his life? In other words, was not that prescience of Marius merely a power of clear and honest seeing of the elements of beauty and ugliness there before him?

That this is Pater's view of the matter is indicated most definitely by the contrast which he continually insists on between Marcus Aurelius and Marius, and which he brings out clearly in the attitude of these two toward the gladitorial shows. In the amphitheatre Marius is conscious of the Emperor, the strenuous Stoic, as "eternally his inferior on the question of righteousness." The young Epicurean has a "decisive conscience on sight" which is indubitable, — that conscience which, in its condemnation of the great sin of an age, is the touchstone of the select few in it, and makes them on the side of the future and aware of its excellence to be, when "not to have been, by instinctive election, on the right side was to have failed in life." Aurelius, we are told, made the great mistake: *Vale, anima infelicissima!* is the last word of our author to him on the eve of the persecutions. And the reason is, that the Stoic was truly blind; he had paltered with his senses until they lied to him, or spoke not at all. Marius saw the deformity of the evil, and, while rejecting it as something he might not see and live, chose the good by its beauty, and so selected in the midst of that Roman corruption the Christian elements in whose excellence the Church would triumph and be made fair.

There may be some surprise in perceiving in the
evangel of estheticism a morality of this height, a concentration of attention on the beauty of austerity, an
exaltation of a noble Puritanism toward which the
Cyrenaic ideal may lead. When this is understood, however, one finds it natural enough that the pervading tone
of this history of an ideal life is really religious; idealism,
when it is living, cannot be otherwise than essentially
religious. Nevertheless, it is a bold thing to put the
question, as Mr. Pater implicitly does, whether an attention to the beautiful, to visible beauty, may not only
be equivalent to moral discrimination and a safeguard
of virtue, but also a mode of solving the ultimate religious questions of deity and man's relations to it. Marius
does arrive at an intimation, perhaps a faith, that a pro-
tective divine companionship goes beside him, and at an
emotion of gratitude to that unseen presence.

Two points only, in this wide branch of the speculation, can be dwelt on now. He says toward the end that
he thinks he has failed in love; and here he touches on
one weakness of his ideal, for it is only by love, as he
perceives, that any reconciliation between the lover of
beauty and the multitudinous pitiful pain which is so
large a part of the objective universe can be obtained.
The second weakness is perhaps greater. In his ideal
there is both doubt and isolation; the subjective element
in his knowledge, the exclusive reliance on his own impressions, the fact that in metaphysical belief the world
is only his world, and in actual living the experience is
individual, — all this holds in it a basis of ultimate incer-
titude. True and real for him it no doubt is, but is that,
indeed, the necessary limit of knowledge and life? In
effect, too, his creed is Protestant; independently of the

necessary element of doubt in it, it has the isolating force inevitable to the believer who will accept only the results of his own examination by exercise of private judgment. This position is unsatisfactory; and it seems to allow the rationality of that principle of authority by which an individual life obtains correction for its idiosyncrasies, cancels the personal error, and at the same time lets in upon itself the flood of the total experience of humanity summed up and defined in the whole body of the elect. Though stated here in terms of the Stoical philosophy, this is the Catholic conclusion. Or, if Marius does not quite assent to this, he does accept it in a half-hearted way as an hypothesis which is worth making since it reunites him to mankind. There is, it may be observed, a tendency toward Catholicism throughout the religious speculation. Another note of it, for example, is the attraction felt by Marius in the ritual of worship, as the perfection of that ceremonialism to which, in his boyish worship of the old gods, he was devoutly trained.

After all, at the end one still states the promises of this esthetic ideal, even when working on so unusual a nature as Marius's, interrogatively. Marius's life does not set it forth with convincing power. For one thing, it is not a vital life, but a painted one; and there is an inconsequence in the series of pictures, — they do not seem to follow one another by any iron necessity. It would be foolish to complain that a life avowedly only receptive and contemplative of the beautiful is inactive. Marius does nothing except at the end. Yet, within such limits, one never sees how beauty affected Marius or developed his soul, and though he is said to have got much from companionship, one sees love operant in him very seldom, and then it is a very silent and unexpressed love. He repeats his own epitaph, — *tristem neminem fecit*, — and it was true; but all his life seems negative, and continually one asks, How did he really live? and gets no answer. His whole life was a *meditatio mortis*, — that is all that is told us.

A sense of failure, or rather of incompleteness, oppresses one at the end of the narrative. Even granting that the success Marius is said to have achieved — one is never quite sure that he did — by that exquisite appreciation of beauty and impassioned contemplation of its ideal forms, was, in fact, his; yet of what worth was it, — what did it mean to either God or man? The Northern idealist, the Puritan, cannot dispense with some serviceableness as essential to any high living. One should not push the point too far, however, Independently of all that has been said, any one who cares to think on counsels of perfection for man's life will find profound and original thought about the ideal elements still at hand in modern days for use, and many wise reflections, sown in this history. It is a rare work, and not carelessly to be read. Some exquisiteness of taste, some delight in scholarship, some knowledge of what is best worth knowing in the historic expressions of man's aspiration, and, above all, that "inward tacitness of mind" the reader must bring to its perusal. What of it? Have we not the highest authority for casting our pearls where Circe's herd cannot come?

II. A GREEK TRAIT NOTICED BY DR. WALDSTEIN

One distinction between the Greeks and ourselves may be expressed by saying that our culture as a people rests upon literature, on the printed word, while that of the Greeks based itself rather upon observation, on the thing seen. The divergence of intellectual mood thus induced between ancient and modern is profound, and affects the whole higher life. In reflecting upon this classical trait, however, something is to be guarded against. It is well known that the illiterate, generally speaking, think in images, and that this power or habit of visualization, sometimes thought to be characteristic of the poet, be it observed, usually falls into disuse in proportion to the increase and continuity of exclusively literary culture in the individual, until the point is reached at which a man thinks without having a single image definitely projected upon the mind's eye; his mental processes are, in fact, as colorless and formless as algebraic calculations. Mr. Galton's experiments in this matter are still fresh in our memories. Now it is not to be inferred that this was always the case, nor indeed that the intellect of highest development may not in the past, at least, have habitually thought in images, as the unlettered do to-day; and in Greece it appears that the picture language of the mind, as one may call it, held a place more important than with us, and perhaps equivalent to our own idea language. The Greek, as every one knows, peopled the earth with presiding geniuses, of more or less exalted rank, from Oread and Naiad, to the great Zeus of Olympus. These forms we call imaginary, and to our thought they are always tenuous; the point to be remembered is that, when the Greek spoke of Athene, an image came before his mind, and one not hypothetical and consciously symbolical, like Liberty with her cap, but definite, real, and awful, like the statue on the pediment or in the temple. The Greek mind leaned on these images as our mind does

on the alphabet in all mental life; hence the poetry and
the art of the age had a certain ease and naturalness,
an intimacy with things seen by the eye, not equaled
in the work of later times, except possibly in Italy.
Dr. Waldstein points out that the most striking expression of this plastic necessity, inherent in Greek thinking, is the doctrine of Platonic ideas. To the moderns,
however tolerant they may be, there seems always a
childishness, a grotesque quality, the more marked because of Plato's splendid and rich endowment, in the continual insistence in his philosophy on the "ideas" of the
table and the flute,— the table without any definite
number of legs, the flute without any particular quality
of sound; and the case is not much helped, even if one
perceives, as Schopenhauer shows, that the doctrine is
essentially accurate in truth, and wholly intelligible, since
it is merely the modern statement of the subjectivity
of time and space put conversely. Notwithstanding these
admissions, our minds still find the Platonic ideas
awkward to deal with. But that Plato, at the end of his
abstrusest speculations, and at the threshold of one of
the greatest generalizations of the human intellect, fell
back upon the image-forming faculty, and insisted on
particularizing the universal by means of a mystery
or fiction of thought, is a crowning proof of the per-
vasiveness and inner mystery of the plastic spirit in the
culture of his civilization.

This trait of the Greeks has been dwelt on, in the
present instance, less for itself than for its bearing on the
idealism of the art of Phidias, of which the marbles of the
Parthenon are the greatest examples. Of course Dr.
Waldstein, who knows the value of this supreme achievement of the idealistic temperament in man, is himself

an idealist, and when he has occasion to analyze the monuments treats at more or less length of the theory of idealism. He distinguishes at once two kinds of physical representation, the portrait and the type, and affirms an analogous difference in representations of the spirit that animates the stone, — the man as he is, and the man as he ought to be. He observes, too, that the Greeks were fortunately supplied with subjects of sculpture in which both the physical and spiritual perfection of man were proper elements, and, indeed, requisite; namely, the heroes and the gods. The higher life was the theme of their art in its greatest excellence, not as a possible but as an actual existence. This of itself was a valuable help to them, for centers of imagination were thus determined for them and given a certain validity; whereas among the moderns art is felt to be in its essence a mode of subjective creation, having no reality except in thought. The resulting sense of uncertainty, the weakened faith in such emanations of man's brain, almost inevitable for the contemporary poet or artist, is one cause of the recoil of our imagination from the ideal, and of the attraction of realism for our writers, and perhaps of our content with a literature and art that will have fact for its province. "Let us have facts," is the cry; "of truth — that is, the relation of facts — who can be certain? Let us represent men as they are; of men as they ought to be who has any observation?" And even within these limits of the new school it is said, furthermore, that attention is to be paid to the individual; not to man as he is, but to this·man, taken at random, as he is. The type is too general to be depicted, too far removed from actual seeing, too much an abstraction of the mind. It is plain that at the root of the difficulty felt by the realists who theorize in this way lies the conviction that the further the literary or any other representative art gets from the special fact, trait, or passion in its particular manisfestation, the more vague, doubtful, pale, rubbed-out, — in a word, the more generalized, — it becomes, and hence loses sharpness, vigor, and illusiveness. But with the Greek the case was clearly quite otherwise. There was no loss of individualization in the type, whether of physical or of spiritual perfection. This Theseus or that Hermes is ideal; both are generalized from men, but they suffer no loss of vitality thereby. The idealism of Athens did not fade out in abstraction, but embodied the permanent elements of harmonious beauty in body and spirit, in forms "more real than living man." The habit of thinking in images, or with fixed associations of images with general notions, was one reason for this success, undoubtedly; but before concluding that the literary and rationalizing culture of our day forbids us to hope for a similar blending of the type with individuality, let us remember that as with Phidias, so with Shakespeare: Hamlet is at once the type and the man. The poet born cannot turn aside, on this hand, into science, as the realists do; nor on that hand, into philosophy, as the allegorists do. To him that ideal art alone is possible in which the two are united in the expression of permanent and universal truth through selected facts.

Nevertheless, it may be urged, the Greeks passed rapidly from the idealistic to the realistic stage. And in connection with this one observes the happiness with which Dr. Waldstein identifies the elements of likeness between the Greeks and the moderns, just as he opposes their differences to each other. The most admirable example is an inquiry into the esthetical qualities of the Hermes of Praxiteles, and in the course of it he delineates the characteristics of the age of Praxiteles and parallels them with the traits of the time just subsequent to the French Revolution. In doing this he incidentally describes the common spirit in Shelley, Musset, and other representatives of an art, not of the noblest, but not of the worst either, of the interval after the great age, yet before the marked decadence. It may be said that the English never had an age of the Phidian kind; in European culture that is to be sought, if at all, in medieval art. The Praxitelean age, however, was reproduced in essence in the first generation of our romantic period. A certain pathos, felt in view both of the world and of one's self, is perhaps its dominant quality, and with it go a sophistication, a self-consciousness, a reflectiveness, a slight yet not complete abstraction of the spirit from the object before it, illustrated by the expression of the head of Hermes in relation to the infant Dionysus on his arm. It is the mood of one whose spontaneous joy has been disturbed forever by thought. In such work one sees that the objective character of art, as it was in Phidias, is yielding to a new impulse; that the hold of the imagination on the divine and the eternal is slowly relaxing. At last, idealism went out in Greece, and, either in the shape of the portrait statues, or of such sculptures as those of Pergamon, realism came in to be the be-all and also the end-all of art.

Why was it, one asks, that the plastic nature of the Greeks did not preserve them, if the image-making faculty did in fact count so much in their development? How did they come to lose the ideal forms that sprang in the mind of Phidias when he thought of beauty and virtue?

One cannot say that idealism failed, for its triumph in the Parthenon marbles marks the highest point ever reached by the imagination in embodying its vision. It died out, and one says in explanation that the attention given to technique at last led to a disregard of the idea; or that the mere ability to reproduce details exactly was a temptation to apply art to deceptive imitation of the seen instead of to an illusive expression of the unseen; or that the age had lost the great ideas themselves, the perception of beauty and virtue, the belief in them and honor for them, and hence necessarily declined upon the things of this world, — that is, upon what is seen by the bodily eye rather than in the realm of thought and spiritual insight: and of these explanations perhaps one is as true as another, for they are all descriptions, from different standpoints, of what actually occurred. It is impossible, however, that in view of this history, and of the similar course in the development of medieval painting, one should not ask himself whether the rise and defense of realism among us mean that literature is to follow in the same track, and die, as sculpture and painting died, until a new age shall set the wheel turning again; for if the history of the arts teaches anything, it is that the ages of idealism are the ages of power, and those of realism the premonition and stiffening of death.

III. THE PERGAMON MARBLES

THE development of the Greek genius in sculpture, after it had passed its first maturity in Phidias and his immediate successors, presented the same characteristic signs shown in the history of other modes of artistic expression in other nations. A reasoned conception of the ends and means, a trained appreciation of form, a complete mastery of technique, were inherited by the sculptors of Pergamon. The purpose being defined and the tools perfected, no originality was allowed them except in style; and consequently their work, like the last dramas of Shakespeare, or the creations of Browning or Carlyle, exhibits an excess of subject, an effort to put the utmost of muscular action, of narrative import, of allegorized truth, into their marbles. And yet, in connection with this intensity, as it is called, it cannot fail to be observed that their sculpture (herein touched with the decadence) breathes the self-glorifying spirit of triumphant skill, rather than the overmastering idealism of the earlier patriotic and religious motives. In their pictorial composition and landscape backgrounds, also, one is tempted to discern the harmful influence of that so vaguely known school of painting that flourished in the preceding period, and to piece out by conjecture our fragmentary conceptions of its manner. It is complained that modern sculpture is too pictorial; almost as soon as the art was recovered in Italy it fell into the same error, particularly in relief work; but in Greece the profuse use of color on the marble, as ground and also for direct decoration, together with the employment of metals and jewels as additional adornment, must have brought the two arts so closely together that the transference of modes of treatment was inevitable. The striking thing is that painting, then as now, seems by its greater compass to overpower its more hampered rival.

Besides this tendency to overtax the power of expression by the weight of subject, and this pride in mere technique in close association with a humiliating imitation of a different art, these Pergamon sculptures display other marks of being essentially quite modern. Their realism is especially noticeable. The Greeks of the elder time, it must be acknowledged, were remarkably fortunate in that their realistic spirit fell in with an actual existence which itself appealed to the imagination in many ways. In the Athenian prime the life that taught Sophocles and Agathon was heroic or idyllic, and needed hardly a touch to exalt its elements into the most imaginative idealism. When Plato could not write a dialogue without making a drama, nor Aristophanes compose a comedy without breaking into the sweetest lyric song, nor Phidias chisel a flying fold except for eternity, a presence was upon the earth and a spirit in men that made realism not less trustworthy as a guide to sculptors than is the "Look into thy heart and write" as a maxim for poets like Sidney. But when the barbarians broke in from the north upon Asia Minor, and the luxury of oriental manners and the fantasies of oriental mind stole upon the old order and changed it, to study the real was not necessarily to achieve the beautiful. The barbarians chiseled by the Pergamon sculptors are very different from those that once adorned the Parthenon: they are fierce, ugly, portrait-like, studied from the life. The giants, too, by the same artists are not even altogether human, as in the older reliefs, but many are monstrous: conglomerates of snaky folds and Titanic limbs and ox necks, finny wings, pointed ears, horns, and such Egyptian and Assyrian confusions. For this debasement of the type, few will consider the wonderful finish, the minute and successful imitation of fur, scale, and stuff, a compensation. So, too, the representation of mortal agony is, in these works, carried to an extreme of truthfulness that is upon the verge of the revolting. This new bent of realism which, ceasing to select from the beautiful in life, now takes these three directions, — toward the portraiture of types not noble, toward the close copying of accessories not important, and toward the reproduction of shocking aspects of existence, — this essential difference between the art of Athens and of Pergamon, it would be but too easy to parallel in more than one province of our own intellectual life. These remarks, although they were not meant to point such a moral, incidentally illustrate how misleading is the word "ancient" when applied to the Greeks. Wherever approached, they are as level to our own times in thought and deed as any of the so-called moderns; and though their language, in its former dialect, is dead, its golden words always fall upon our ears as if from the lips of some wiser contemporary. In looking on these recovered marble fragments, just as in reading the "Antigone" or "Alcestis," the centuries seem meaningless.

SOME ACTORS' CRITICISMS OF OTHELLO, IAGO, AND SHYLOCK

AN actor of genius, at the moment of impersonating (either in imagination or in fact) a character of Shakespeare's, is probably nearer to the dramatist's creative mood than any one else can get, except possibly the poet born. He may, to use a phrase of Booth's, in speaking of this mode of coming to an understanding of Shakespeare, "hit it" by the mere force within that bears him naturally on. Or, to take the case in which his sympathy with the *rôle* is imperfect, he may perceive wherein he is defective more clearly by his conscious failure than by any analysis. Again, the difficulties that arise from not knowing how Shakespeare put the play on the stage may not be solved rightly, it is true, by the moderns; but the conclusions of the acting fraternity on these matters are much more worthy of weight than those of men unacquainted with the practical working of that "business" which is a sort of cement for the scenes. Support could be found from many quarters for what Dr. Furness says in behalf of actors as useful critics; but without further reasoning, one may invite attention to some considerations in regard to Othello suggested by quotations from memoirs of the profession and other records, and especially from Booth's annotated acting-copy, extracts from which, although not made with any view of publication, may be found in the Variorum edition of the play.

Mr. White, in his satirical essay upon "The Acting of Iago," expresses the opinion that all the modern impersonations are inadequate, and that the fault springs from a radical misconception of the character. Theatrical companies are made up, every one knows, with an actor for each of the varieties of human nature which are usual in a play; so far as character is concerned, they enact types. Iago, of course, falls to the lot of the "heavy villain," whose aim, in stage life, is to do his wickedest always, everywhere, and in as many guises as possible; he is continually pointing to the mark of Cain on his forehead, so that there shall be no mistake about his identity. "I think," says Booth, — and the criticism holds all the meat of Mr. White's essay in a nutshell, "the light-comedian should play the villain's part, not the 'heavy-man,' I mean the Shakespearean villains." In consonance with this is his reiterated advice to his Iago to think evil all the time, but not to show it; to be the prince of good fellows, inexhaustible in *bonhomie,* genial, jovial, gentlemanly, — the friend and pleasant companion whom every one liked, whom Desdemona trifled with, and Cassio respected for his soldiership, and Othello trusted as a man as faithful in love as he was wise in the world. "A certain bluffness," Booth says "(which my temperament does not afford), should be added to preserve the military flavor of the character: in this particular I fail utterly; my Iago lacks the soldierly quality." So far, certainly, Booth does not differ from Mr. White in his conception of the bearing, the outward manner and sensible aspect, of the Venetian liar. Let us look at it from Mr. White's point of view: "Edwin Booth's Iago is not externally a mere hardened villain, but a super-subtle Venetian, who works out his devilish plans with a dexterous lightness of touch and smooth sinuosity of movement that suggest the transmigration of a serpent into human form. And in his visage, and, above all, in his eye, burns the venom of his soul. . . . But even Edwin Booth's Iago, although much finer and more nearly consistent with itself and with the facts of the tragedy than any other that is known to the annals of the stage, is not the Iago that Shakespeare drew." But what is it that is lacking? Mr. White paints Iago as the popular flatterer, the sympathetic sycophant, the gay, easy-going, pleased and pleasing fellow; and, so far as the side shown to the world is concerned, this is Booth's conception, and (allowing for the defect of soldier-like frankness which he feels in himself) it is his impersonation. Why is it not, then, Shakespeare's Iago? Mr. White is ready with his answer: Because Shakespeare's Iago would do no harm, except to advance his fortunes; he had no malice; he was merely selfish, utterly unscrupulous as to his means of obtaining what he sought, ready to win his gain at any ruin. Now, it is clear that the evil which Mr. White has just said burns in the actor's eye is not mere selfishness, not the cold light of calculation simply, with no more rooted passion; it is just what Mr. White says Iago did not have, — it is malice. So one gets the hint; and on searching the remarks of Booth to see what indications there are of his conception of the essence of Iago's soul, the spring of his motive, the changing emotions that enveloped his thoughts at their birth, one perceives at once that, while Booth would have Iago outwardly amiable, he has not the least idea of reducing the dye of villainy in which the character has been steeped by those of old time. Inside, Booth has no doubt, Iago was a spirit of hate, and he knows at what moments of anxious interest, at what crises of the temptation and the plotting, this will gleam out in the expression of the eye, or in those slight tell-tale changes which are natural to the most self-possessed man, and are significant to us only because we are on the watch for them. By observing, consequently, with what passages he connects this devilish malignancy of nature in Iago, one can judge, as between him and Mr. White, what justification he has for making Iago cruel as well as selfish, and revengeful as well as ambitious. Mr. White's theory is that Iago wished to supplant Cassio, and ruined Desdemona in order to accomplish this end; that he used his suspicion of Othello's intimacy with his wife almost as an after-thought, to bolster up his purpose with an excuse; and that, having chosen his method with perfect indifference to its morality or its humanity, he overreached himself and failed. This view may gain upon one by its plausible and emphatic setting forth, just as pleas for Judas Iscariot or any other client of a clever devil's advocate may do, but only momentarily; for when one attempts to adjust the speeches of Iago, word by word and line by line, to this conception, especially with such notes of direction and caution as these of Booth's to the actor, echoing the text, as they do, through all modulations of suspicion, suspense and suppressed passion, the idea of an Iago without malice simply dissolves, and leaves not a rack behind. In reality, this new notion of Mr. White's is only the old story that Iago is motiveless, which has disturbed so many critics, and given occasion to such marvelous explanations of his villainy. The disparity between the moral causes and the mortal results, between the errors and the penalties of the victims, has been widely felt; the attempt is consequently made to ascribe a cause for the catastrophe that shall justify it to the reason; and naturally one writer has over-accented and exaggerated one element in the play, and a second writer another element, and so on; but Mr. White bears away the palm from all in his assertion that Iago did all the mischief just to get on in the world, and that the only reason it was so great was because of the unlimited power for harm in the union of ability with utter un-scrupulousness in a man's makeup. Shakespeare gives the key-note of the action in the very first words Iago utters, unheard except by his own bosom. What was the first thought on his lips then? "I hate the Moor." And perhaps in that most difficult moment of the *rôle*, the climax of Iago's fate, the elder Booth was right in making the expression of this intense enmity dominant in "the Parthian look which Iago, as he was borne off, wounded and in bonds, gave Othello, — a Gorgon stare, in which hate seemed both petrified and petrifying." In this matter the actors seem to carry it over the editor, who, indeed, was in that essay a better social satirist than Shakespearean scholar; and, to our mind, the conception of Mr. White is too harmonious, also, with the intel-lectual power and the delight in its exercise so marked in Shakespeare's and in Booth's Iago.

There is more scope for different interpretations in Othello's case than in Iago's. Othello, it is obvious to any one of the least insight, is a character in whom temperament counts for so much more than anything else as practically to possess the whole man; his actions pro-ceed directly from his nature; his doubts and suspicions act at once upon his heart, and are converted into emotion

of the most simple and primitive type almost instanta-
neously; his mental agony itself tends to become blind
physical suffering; he does not think, — he feels. It
is in the expression of temperament that the actor is
left most free by the dramatist, is least shackled by
words, and oftenest relies upon other modes of utterance,
of which (we too easily forget) language is only one.

In Othello, consequently, who is the creature of his
temperament, the actor influences the character to an
unusual degree; and as the range of feeling is from the
lowest notes of tender happiness to the explosions of
unlimited despair, the way in which the actor conceives
of feeling, his ideas of what makes it noble, and of the
manner in which a grand nature would express it, affect
the play profoundly. A certain bent has been given to
the stage interpretation and also to criticism, by the
notion that Shakespeare meant to exhibit in Othello a
barbaric passion, the boiling up of a savage nature, the
Oriental fervor and rashness, the dæmon of the Moor-
ish race. Yet nothing is plainer in Shakespeare than
his utter disregard of historical accuracy; he never depicted a race type, except the Jewish. If Theseus is an
Athenian, or Coriolanus or Cæsar himself a Roman,
then Othello may be a Moor; but it is most comfortable
to the facts to regard them all as simply ideal men, who
take from their circumstances a color of nationality and a
place in time, but who are essentially all of one race.
The view of those actors who give Othello a ferocity of
emotion because he is a Moor, or of those critics who
discern in the violence and brute unreason of some play-
ers in this part something to praise on the score of
Othello's birth under a hot Mauritanian sun deserves no
sympathy. The Oriental touch in the impersonation

ought not to go beyond such slight signs and tokens as
the crescent scimitar, — of which Booth says, "It is harmless," — if we are to keep to Shakespeare's art as something better than a costumer's. Othello does not exhibit one extravagance that requires to be excused by
the reflection that it is natural to an alien race, though
not to the English. But within the limits of the character
conceived as merely ideal, there is a fine opportunity
for difference among actors, and they have availed themselves of it. To indicate it by a word, Othello's passion
seems to have been the cardinal thought of Kean, irresistible, compulsive as "the Pontick Sea," impressive
by its main force and elemental sweep; Fechter, whose
conception of nobleness of nature was a poor one, sank
all the heroic in the melodrama to which the situations
lent themselves; and Booth, giving far more distinctness
to Othello's suffering so that his revenge becomes hardly
more than an incident in the course of his own soul's
torture, reveals the scene of the tragedy at once as in
Othello's breast, where the spirit of evil is feeding on a
mighty but guileless heart. It is not Desdemona's death
that is the climax, — that is mere pity; but the tragic
element finds its conclusion in Othello's last speech and
stroke. The intensity of Kean or the ideality of Booth,
working upon the tragic temperament in each, must produce Othello with a difference: one tempts to excess in
ferocity, the other in pathos; but either is consistent
with the text. After all, it is with great actors as with
poets, — their creations partake of their own nature,
in all heroic and ideal parts; but if, as is thought, sympathy is the best revealer of the inner meaning of works
of the imagination, certainly the disciplined and habitual
enacting of great *rôles* by actors of genius ought to be a

source of light and knowledge regarding them, notwithstanding the allowance that is to be made for the "personal error" of individuality.

It is a striking quality in the immortality of "The
Merchant of Venice" that it has survived a change in the
public mind in its attitude toward the Jewish people.
To the Elizabethans, and Shakespeare among them, the
Jew was hateful. It may well be questioned to what
extent Shakespeare himself, with all the tolerance that
his understanding of the springs of human nature gave
him, felt the pity in the dramatic situation of Shylock
that a modern audience must feel. Booth's conception
of Shakespeare's creation is too direct and natural not
to justify itself to the student, — " 'an inhuman wretch,
incapable of pity, void and empty from any dram of
mercy.' It has been said that he was an affectionate
father and a faithful friend. When, where, and how does
he manifest the least claim to such commendation? Tell
me that, and unyoke! 'T was the money value of Leah's
ring that he grieved over, not its association with her,
else he would have shown some affection for her daughter,
which he did not or she would not have called her home
'a hell,' robbed and left him. Shakespeare makes her
do these un-Hebrew things to intensify the baseness of
Shylock's nature. If we side with him in his self-defense,
't is because we have charity, which he had not; if we pity
him under the burden of his merited punishment, 't is
because we are human, which he is not, except in shape,
and even that, I think, should indicate the crookedness
of his nature." Booth goes on to justify this traditional
conception by an easy argument against the notion of
"the heroic Hebrew," the type of the vengeance of a

persecuted race, whose wrongs justify its acts. He refers to the "dangerous 'bit of business'" when Shylock whets his knife. "Would the heroic Hebrew have stooped to such a paltry action? No, never, in the very white-heat of his pursuit of vengeance! But vengeance is foreign to Shylock's thought; 't is revenge he seeks, and he gets what all who seek it get, — 'sooner or later,' as the saying is."

This characterization is not too vigorous, nor does it go too far. We may find it not only in Shylock as Shakespeare drew him, but reflected also from Antonio. It is in Antonio personally that the attitude of the medieval Christian toward the Jew is found. The unexplained melancholy of Antonio, his fidelity in high-minded friendship, and the dignity of his bearing under the cruelty to which he is exposed have obscured to us the other side of his character as the Rialto merchant. We see more of Bassanio's Antonio than of Shylock's: the man who had interfered with the usurer in every way and personally maltreated him, and was as like to do the same again; the proud, hard-hearted, and insulting magnifico whom Shylock hated for himself. Antonio is every whit as heartless to the Jew in the hour of his triumph as Shylock was to him when the balance leaned the other way. His cruelty is lacking only in the physical element; it is not bloody, but it goes to the bone and marrow of Shylock's nature none the less. There is no sign that Shakespeare saw any wrong in all this. It was thus that the Christians looked upon the Jews, and they thought such treatment right. Shakespeare differed from others — from Marlowe, for example, in his delineation of the Jew of Malta — in one point only: he was able to take Shylock's point of view, to understand his motives, to assign the reasons with which revenge justified its own motions; in a word, to represent Shylock's humanity. The speeches he puts into the Jew's mouth are intense and eloquent expressions of the reasoning of that "lodged hate" in his bosom; they are true to fact and to nature; on our ears they come with overwhelming force, and it is impossible to our thoughts that Shakespeare could have written them without sympathy for the wrongs that they set forth with such fiery heat. But when from this it is argued that Shakespeare, in writing this play, made a deliberate plea for toleration, and carried it as far as the necessities of his plot and the temper of his times permitted, then it is needful to remind ourselves of what Booth calls "the baseness of Shylock's nature." Shakespeare did represent him as base, with avarice, cunning, and revenge for the constituent elements of his character; he did not hesitate to let the exhibition of these low qualities approach the farcical, as he would never have done had he thought of the Jew as in any sense heroic. Shylock had suffered insult and wrong, but there was nothing in him individually to excite commiseration. From beginning to end he shows no noble quality. Modern sympathy with him apart from the pity that tragedy necessarily stirs, is social sympathy, not personal; it is because he is an outcast and belongs to an outcast race, because every man's hand is against him and against all his people, that the audience of this century perceives an injustice inherent in his position itself, antecedent to, and independent of, any of his acts; and this injustice is ignored in the play. The feeling which Shylock, as a person, excites, and should excite, is nearer that which Lady Martin describes as her experience: "I have always felt in the acting that my desire to find extenuations for Shylock's race and for himself leaves me, and my heart grows almost as stony as his own. I have seen his fiendish nature fully revealed. I have seen the knife sharpened to cut quickly through the flesh, the scales brought forward to weigh it; have watched the cruel, eager eyes, all strained and yearning to see the gushing blood welling from the side 'nearest the heart,' and gloating over the fancied agonies and deathpangs of his bitter foe. This man-monster, this pitiless, savage nature, is beyond the pale of humanity; it must be made powerless to hurt. I have felt that with him the wrongs of his race are really as nothing compared with his own remorseless hate. He is no longer the wronged and suffering man; and I longed to pour down on his head the 'justice' he has clamored for, and will exact without pity." Upon this matter Spedding admits of no reply. "The best contribution," he says, "which I can offer to this discussion is the expression of an old man's difficulty in accepting these new discoveries of profound moral and political designs underlying Shakespeare's choice and treatment of his subjects. I believe he was a man of business, — that his principal business was to produce plays which would draw. . . . But if, instead of looking about for a story to 'please' the Globe audience, he had been in search of a subject under cover of which he might steal into their minds 'a more tolerant feeling toward the Hebrew race,' I cannot think he would have selected for his hero a rich Jewish merchant plotting the murder of a Christian rival by means of a fraudulent contract, which made death the penalty of non-payment at the day, and insisting on the exaction of it. In a modern Christian audience it seems to be possible for a skillful actor to work on the feelings of an audience so far as to make a man engaged in such a business an object of respectful sympathy. But can anybody believe that in times when this would have been much more difficult, Shakespeare would have *chosen* such a case as a favorable one to suggest toleration to a public prejudiced against Jews?"

The omnipresent devil's advocate has several times come to Shylock's defense with a legal plea. Those who could find something to urge in extenuation of Judas Iscariot had an easy task in showing that the Jew of Venice was more sinned against than sinning. The decisions of the young doctor who came armed with the recommendation of the learned Bellario have been overruled in every court of appeal. The bond itself is declared invalid, inasmuch as it contained an immoral proviso in the article that sought Antonio's death; the attempt to defeat it, its validity having once been granted, by denying the right to draw blood and requiring the exact amount of a pound of flesh to be cut out, is characterized as a wretched quibble, and set aside on the ground that a right once allowed carries with it the minor rights to make it effectual; the denial of the original debt for the reason that it had been tendered and refused in open court is declared a gross error, such tender having no other result than to destroy any claim for interest subsequently. But not to mention all the grave reasons alleged to break down the reputation of the Court of Venice and show the illegality of its judgments, it is clear that on legal grounds the case was very badly managed, and in the event the Jew met with no better fortune than was the lot of his race before an unscrupulous and hostile tribunal everywhere. Nevertheless, the disputants upon the other side, who allege the substantial justice of the decisions rendered, do well to remove the discussion out of the plane of legality. There is much that is weighty in their argument. Shylock must be regarded as standing, after the nature of Judaism, for the law as a thing of the letter; this is the justice which he demands, not real, but literal; and if, by a still more strict interpretation of the letter of the bond than he had thought of, his claim was defeated, the audience will acknowledge the relevancy of the new point that is made, and will enjoy the spectacle of the Biter Bit, in which there is always an element of comic justice. As to the quibble involved, that belongs to the nature of literal interpretation always. Thus the matter is not without defense even on this level. But what really pleases the audience is not the method, but the fact, of the Jew's defeat; and in the fact, however brought about, lies the ethical element, the victory of real over illusory justice, of equity over legality, of the right over the pretense of right. Shakespeare was not expressly philosophical; but there is little straining of the facts of the case in the view that in the discomfiture of that "law" which the Jew invoked, in the signal defeat inflicted on the letter of the bond, there is a suggestion of the conflict between Judaism and Christianity, the literal and the spiritual, the law and that justice with its elements of mercy into which the law develops, which is one of the great phases of historical civilization. Whether Shakespeare put it there is immaterial; but that a modern audience finds it there, and that it was at least dimly present to an Elizabethan audience, is hardly to be questioned. The idea is a simple and ancient one; and in it is to be found whatever ethical meaning the play may have.

But it ought to be always remembered that the primary

endowment of Shakespeare was the artistic temperament: he was a poet first, and everything else afterwards. To say this is the same thing with saying — though it must be stated briefly — that the ethical principle in him was a necessity of the imagination, not of the understanding; was vision rather than inference; was a part and not the whole. One can no more imagine life truly without ethics than he can imagine mass without cohesion; a creative genius, consequently, a man of imagination all compact, does not necessarily start from ethics in molding his works, but it is more likely that the moral principle which his works must contain as a part of their reality will be secondary and derivative. Shakespeare is ethical because he imagined life truly; he did not imagine life truly because he had thought out, in Lord Bacon's manner, the general principles of morals.

LATE VICTORIAN VERSE: BROWNING, SWINBURNE, TENNYSON

In old times, when, if legends say true, to be a poet was to wander in the guise of a divine beggar amid the isles of Greece, or to ride as a troubadour in the lists of Love's court, or to sit, snowy-bearded, in the minstrel's corner of some baron's hall, following the Muses was rather a sort of angelic gypsying than a profession; or, if the phrase seems light, it was the career merely of a blessed mendicant. In the classical age, manuscripts had already brought about some modifications in the habits of the strollers, and the printing press at last effectually put an end to all that. Poetry, divorced from song to the popular comprehension, turned into literature; and, with the many changes involved in and accompanying this, it came about that, instead of winning bread perhaps the more readily by waking some familiar strain, now the poet had to make a new song to get a new alms. Publishers, too, took the place of musical instruments as the necessary complement of the text; and, not to speak it profanely, since by common report poets have found them by no means "easier to be played on than a pipe," the calling has no longer that fine indifference to mortal circumstance which gave it character when the favorite of the gods was honored of all men. Yet in the old notion that the poet was inspired of heaven, and to give him food was an obligation

both of religion and courtesy, there was this truth, —
the perception that the high gifts of the spirit have no
relation to reputation or livelihood, or any of the respecta-
bilities, the forms and shows, of the world, but are separate and apart; and there was also this of good as well, —
that the poets, though the best of them shared in the
weakness of our nature, were kept somewhat by this
fiction of the *sacer vates* from any degradation of the
art to routine uses. But did not Homer sing for his
supper, and Spenser for a place at court? — this one
for his laurel, that one for the gold beaker, and that
other for some laughing Lalage? Let it be so; the old
tradition, the idle fancy, serve to set in bolder relief
the book-making, money-getting, reputation-sustaining,
in a word the professional poets, of the modern time;
for, if it be not altogether a new thing, certainly to a
greater degree now than ever before do the acknowledged poets, the "kings of song," exercise their power
out of mere habit, because they have always made verses
and published them at tolerably regular intervals.

The three leading poets of England in their later
years gave the world evidence, one cannot say of their
genius, but of their craft; and the volumes taken together are a fair test of what may be called professionalism in poetry, under the very best circumstances of
native talent, cultivated art, and wide knowledge of the
affairs of men. Two of the authors were old men, and
the third was no novice in life: with the former, if at all,
we might expect

> "long experience to attain
> To something of prophetic strain,"

and with the latter was associated for many years that power of youth which, in poets, seems independent of time. Browning, Tennyson, and Swinburne are names so deeply graved in the memory of men that it would require very excellent work indeed to make them more lasting. It will hardly be thought that these late poems can add to their fame, and therefore none need grudge the friendly liberty if one who is less a critic than a looker-on, in our literary republic, treats them not so much for what they are as for what they illustrate; nor need any find disparagement in comparisons of old with new, odious as such methods of examination are, for to mark a difference will not, in this case, be to suggest a fault. Professionalism in poetry may be worth as frank discussion as professionalism in athletics, for example: it is not in the breed of sporting-men alone that our civilization diverges from that which flowered and seeded in the games of each Olympiad.

On the first pages of "Ferishtah's Fancies" there is a difference to be noted. Instead of invoking any Muses or other gods, as in the days when the world was young, Browning, in a wholly modern way, addresses the reader, and hands him a bill of fare, literally speaking. It is a handsome bill of fare, faultless in technique, with a certain piquancy of its own in the way of rhyme, — "Italy" with "Spit ally," for instance, — and of a roughened, acrid meter; it is written over, too, with epicure viands, and seems almost to exhale odors of appetizing cookery; in fact, it is a receipt for preparing ortolans (apparently after the manner of the Maison Delapierre, Gressoney St. Jean, Val d'Aosta), and it is used in the old-fashioned Scriptural way as a parable, of which the interpretation runs, "Reader, you have in these poems

a dish of ortolans *à la Italienne;* if you know how to eat
those you will know how to read these. Robert Browning, *prandens.*" We have not dined at Gressoney on the

> "some dozen luscious lumps,
> Or more or fewer, —
> . . . heads by heads and rumps by rumps,
> Stuck on a skewer,"

but we understand the similitude, and have read by the
help of our second-hand knowledge of the ortolan roast,
as the poet petitions. This prologue, we thus discovered,
was really in excellent taste, — was an artistic necessity,
indeed; for Ferishtah, the dervish, whose wisdom is here
preserved, poetized, or rather preached, after this manner,
in parables, and out of such occupations as eating apples
or cherries, or cutting up melons, or sowing "a bean-
stripe," drew the honey of sound moral reflections. One
might say, if he had the courage to make such a sweeping inference as would denote a member of the Browning
Society, that in this prologue the master struck the key-
note of these poems by showing how the highest philosophic thought, the eternal lessons of God's being and
man's duty, reside in the commonest and most trivial
objects and affairs of daily existence. You have but to
look at your plate when dining, and lo, there is truth!
That suggestion is perhaps a trifle esoteric for these
pages: such, however, was Ferishtah's method, and hence
there is a propriety in his English sponsor's attempt to
do likewise, though one cannot help thinking he would
have orientalized more successfully if he had chosen
some simple thing, like a cherry, or an apple, or a melon,
as Ferishtah does, rather than an epicure's dish. But
indigestibility, after all, seems an essential part of the

matter, in both ortolans and verses, to his own stomach. It takes a very sophisticated poet — no warbler of native wood-notes wild — to describe himself, even half in jest, as Apollo's caterer.

In attending thus to the prologue at considerable length we have really been writing with a side glance at the poems themselves. They consist of the moralizing allegories in narrative, familiar as an Eastern form of literature, supplemented by short lyrical pieces, which usually give an emotional echo of the truth which has just been elaborated in a purely rational way. How Browning reasons in verse is well known; since Dryden no one has done it so well, at least in point of intellectual as distinguished from literary form. It is thoroughly understood, too, that his disquisitions are more highly prized by seekers after instruction than by the lovers of mere poetry. The thought is of course conservative, and it deals principally with modern problems (ancient, too, for that matter) of theology and religion: evil, prayer, anthropomorphism, asceticism, truth, and the like. Criticism of the substance of this does not belong under poetry, since there is essentially no appeal to the esthetic faculty, but only to the reason; and this can be said more unreservedly than is usual even with Browning's work, for in his later books there has been none so exclusively intellectual in its interest as is the present one. And here, incidentally, we come upon a feature of professionalism in poetry, — upon what, in default of better terms, we may call a substitution of routine in execution for a living art. So a lawyer has a certain amount of office work which is dispatched by the help of formulas and legal blanks; or a clergyman writes a sermon, perhaps, when he is tired, by the help of other

formulas and theological blanks. The characteristic of
such work is that it is done mechanically. A poet, if
he has been well trained, has the same resources, not
only in the poetical blanks of verse-form, the set terms
of his distinctive vocabulary, the fixed style of various
manners, dramatic, elegiac, narrative, but more subtly
in the very form of his customary thought. To come to
the case in hand, Browning has, as a practised crafts-
man, obtained a certain command which makes it impossible for him to fall below a definite and high excellence in expression, and thus he is always both facile and
sure; but, beyond that, he has also developed habits of
reasoning, so that his intellect is a mold, and, no matter
what goes into it, always gives out the same form of
thought. In other words, there is something fairly to
be described as mechanical in his thinking as well as in
his handling: there is an intellectual routine in his works,
— the hardened, ossified form of what was once a fluid
and vital art. Students of his poetry perceive at once
that the subjects, the themes, of the present volume are
accidental; he would have written as well, as profitably,
on any other matter of intellectual interest, and he
would have said essentially the same thing. "Ferishtah's
Fancies" is, without any disrespect or disparagement,
merely a poetic blank filled in. As in the case of other
professions, the value lies in the filling in; sometimes
its worth is more, sometimes less. What it is in
this case will depend largely on the patience
and religious prepossessions of the persons to whom
the paper comes. Merely as a professional poem,
however, "Ferishtah's Fancies" is a fine illustration
of routine thinking; and truly, in the present
dearth of inspired thought, men have reason to be grate-

ful that it is so excellent, — to recur to the prologue, "excellent i' faith — you cannot feed capons so."

In Swinburne's "A Midsummer Holiday and Other Poems," the mechanical element, one need hardly say, is limited to the verse-forms, the vocabulary, and the style, and is, in fact, with difficulty to be distinguished from the mere mannerism of his hand. The facility of Swinburne, the flow and sonorousness of his lines, are so overpowering that frequently one has to read them over, and by a distinct and painful effort neglect the emphasis and cadence in order to get at the idea; and in this last volume the double reading is as necessary as ever. The confusion of sense by words, as heretofore, has now and then a comical touch, as, to take a striking example, in the line,

"Your good little glad grave smile";

or in the attack on the method of modern biography (by means of private letters), that enables all to

"Spy, smirk, sniff, snap, snort, snivel, snarl, and sneer";

one would as lief read the dictionary as lines like that so far as poetic charm is concerned. But these are the familiar traits of one who is, notwithstanding, our most passionate and musical poet. The range of his new verses is much more varied than Browning's; but it is curious that the series of lyrics which gives the title to the volume is somewhat similar in form to the parables of Ferishtah, since it consists of a number of descriptions of seaside views, each of which concludes with an emotional echo of the scene in the final stanzas. After this group comes the ode to Victor Hugo, with a foot-note list of the works

alluded to in the text, as if that would make the poem
more intelligible to one who was unfamiliar with them
beforehand; and the usual variety of elegiac, infantile,
and political effusions fills out the book. Swinburne's
memorial stanzas are among the best of his work, and
those on Mazzini do not fall below the standard they
ought to reach to do honor to such a man. So, too, though
he has written more finely of children than in the "Nine-
Year-Old Ode," and has put forth more stirring political
verses than any of these in which he sings the crusade
against the peers, — "O Lords, our Gods," — there is
a sweetness and freshness in the former, a fervor and
scorn in the latter, which show that the force of his
genius is by no means spent. The line called out by
the Tennyson peerage, —

"Stoop, Chaucer, stoop; Keats, Shelley, Burns, bow down, —

opens with the majesty of one of Milton's sonnets.

Nevertheless, the volume as a whole owes much of
the pleasure it gives to the pleasure it recalls. The level
of the flight is not so high as it was, though the grace of
the movement, the bend downward, the slow circlings,
the strong upward soaring, attest the same eagle of song.
There has been much aspersion on Swinburne's genius,
but one might as well deny the beauty of the leopard's
skin because of its spots. In remarking, therefore, that
this last volume is somewhat tame, in comparison with
what has come before from his pen, we do not mean to
join in the common censure of him as a mindless, babbling
versifier, nor to point even by implication at the fact that
the worship of childhood seems to have displaced that
of womanhood, in his poetry; but there is a lack of
vigor, a lassitude of the imaginative faculty, a paucity

even of fancy, in which he was once so affluent. It is
seldom, indeed, in these pages that one sees in the way
of mere fancy such a faëry touch as in the sonnet "On
the Death of Richard Doyle": —

"Let waters of the Golden River steep
The rose-roots whence his grave blooms rosy red";

though in this one poem there are other lines as delicately
done. It is much more seldom that there is any brief
lyric burst to recall the chorus singer of the "Atalanta"
and the "Erechtheus." Swinburne's genius depends on the
imagination primarily, as Browning's does on the intellect, and the imagination will not work mechanically;
even when it seems to do so, as in Moore's oriental
poems, or in Young's religious meditations, or in Wordsworth's ecclesiastical sonnets, it is hardly worthy of the
name, and the region of its exercise by these poets is far
from Swinburne's demesne. It involves a much more
severe drain on a man's genius to write imaginative poetry periodically than reflective poetry; and while Swinburne has written as many volumes, perhaps, as
Browning, in spite of his fewer years, he has not been
able to keep the same level of excellence in his own work
that Browning has maintained; and the facility that he
has as a master in the profession, instead of assisting
his make-believe, has really been of the fatal kind that
smooths the Avernian descent. If there must be a new
book of verses each year, an imaginative poet has little
opportunity to select; he must print nearly all he writes
that reaches respectability. It is under this necessity
that in this volume, as in nearly all the previous ones,
is included so much that is not distinctively either good
or bad; but in the case of lyrical poetry, not to be excel-

lent is to fail. Professionalism favors mediocrity in a
man by cultivating content with what he is usually able
to work out day by day, instead of discontent with all
save what he can achieve at the full height of his nature
in some fortunate moment; and hence for the true lyrist
it is a snare. So far as this volume is the utterance of
self-stirred genius, it is worthy of the shelf where the
"Laus Veneris" is; so far as it is the perfunctory handi-
craft of a professed poet, it should have straw and
stubble for its resting-place.

Tennyson has been so faithful to his art that no one
could harbor the thought that he has ever written except
from the inner impulse, or published except in the per-
fectest form of which he was at the time capable. His
drama "Becket" is finished with painstaking care, and
if it fails of the immortality of "In Memoriam" it will
be because the author is not a dramatic poet. In his
early verse he gave no sign of having in him the capacities of a playwright, and as his genius rounded out and
put forth power in the various provinces of poetry there
was no indication of his being one of Elizabeth's men.
It was felt to be hazardous when he gave the world
"Harold" and "Queen Mary"; and now, though "Becket"
is stronger, finer, more instinct with manliness, than
were the earlier two, it is not certain that, had he begun
thus, he would have won fame by this road. Distinction,
certainly, he would have gained. "Becket" is in a sense
a powerful play, with beauty and a touch of humor
(so meant, at least), and a certain roughened realism in
some of its character details; it has incident, situation,
dialogue and monologue, passion and pathos, an extraordinary variety in mood, sentiment, and setting, and
yet it does not make on the mind an impression either

of character or of poetry at all comparable to the least
of Shakespeare's plays, or to the best of some smaller
men than Tennyson, who breathed Shakespeare's air.
Becket himself is a great subject; there is none finer,
and it has attracted poets of large ambition before this;
the men, the scene, the events, seem built for the purposes of tragedy. But a man of dramatic imagination
does not need all this help from history; he can take a
nameless Italian *novella,* and make its tale of more consequence to humanity than all the lives of all the Arch-
bishops of Canterbury. "Becket" is wonderfully perfect
in its handling, in its phrase, its contrasts, its subordina-
tions to the essential unity, its management of groups,
its strokes of climax, — in all things that art knows of
and can create; and being so perfect as it is in these ways,
one wonders why it should not impress the mind as
much as some plays infinitely inferior to it in mere construction. Tennyson has mastered the theory of the
drama; and we are told that if we do not enjoy his
creations in this province of poetry, if we do not value
the self-suppression which has not allowed one quotable
line to stand out from others, and similar virtues dear
to the theorist, we are wrong. Perhaps that is just the
trouble. Shakespeare has so spoilt us that we will have
no drama that is not romantic, that does not enchain
us by a thousand wefts as well as by one main event. If
Tennyson were a born dramatist, he would not have
cared to inquire whether he fulfilled the academic ideal
of what a drama should be. He would have written one,
and shamed the schools. "Becket" has the perfection,
the color, composition, and incident of a fine historic
painting; it has the dignity of a noble narrative told
in tableaux; but it has not the spirit of the life itself.

It is cold, limited, literary. It is presumably a part of the plan that there should be, as we have said, no quotable line, nor any fine passage that sings itself into the memory by its mere beauty. The attention is concentrated upon the action, and hence it may be expected that on the stage and to the eye the drama would be more effective. But this severe simplicity, this merciless pruning of all the graces of poetic expression, require the genius of another race to appreciate it. It was not Shakespeare's way. It is as certain as any such thing can be by internal evidence that Tennyson had no call to write this work except the ambition natural to so finely endowed a mind. There is more of England's heart in the song of Sir Richard Grenville's fight, more of man's life in "Rizpah," than in the whole of "Becket."

Nearly all the poems in "Tiresias and Other Poems," when published separately in periodicals, were from time to time greeted by the popular press as the Laureate's latest inanity. Yet a book of like finish and strength would bring any unknown poet into the front rank without a dissenting voice, and this one itself will adorn the company in which Tennyson's name will secure it a place for a period to which the criticism of our age can assign no limit. The art of the master, the perfect control of modulated language for poetic ends, pervades the whole; some great themes, so treated as to develop the wisdom of great ideas, are here; and, more conspicuous in the lesser verses, the grace, ease, and sureness of an exquisitely refined mind make an element of pleasant attraction. The lack of recognition of these things on the part of the public suggests that the decline of poetry is not wholly the fault of the singers. It is not without justice, however, that the rude general decision is recorded against Tennyson's old-age work; that the people refuse, and will continue to refuse, these latter-day poems.

For one thing, it is exceptionally limited in its appeal, — the outgrowth, in many parts, of his personal relations as a man and as an Englishman. It opens with a tribute to his friend, Fitzgerald, a charmingly natural copy of epistolary verses, familiar, reminiscent, with a touch of humor and also of the soberness of life's closing day, — the greeting of an old man to the friend of his youth who has aged with him. It was sent by his son's hand, and inclosed the poem "Tiresias," written long ago; but before the missive arrived the host was dead. And so a third copy of verses follows, memorial stanzas, appreciative, somewhat pathetic, calm, and mild. The whole is a threefold sheaf upon his friend's grave. "The Charge of the Heavy Brigade" has likewise its prologue of a rhymed note of dedication to General Hamley, commemorating a visit from him, and an apologetic epilogue replying to some "girl-graduate" who would have the lyre struck only in praise of peace; and dangling from this is still another stanza, repelling the commonplace reproach that songs are not deeds. The group, taken together, is rambling matter. Then there are some prefatory stanzas for his brother's poems, not without a stroke or two on the higher chords, but how different from the childhood tablet in honor of the same love in "In Memoriam!" And, later, there is the inscription written for Lord Dufferin's Tower, at his request. As one reads these various bits, the memory revives in him of the old-style days when a poet used his art in every-day intercourse with agreeable acquaintances, and handed about the manuscripts: they belong to the leisure moments of a cultivated life, and

their place is with the personal records, the letters and
acts of courtesy, of their author; they are the courtli-
ness of literature. Others, besides those mentioned, have
their source in the lettered life: the tribute to Catullus,
a lovely poem; that to Virgil, with a Roman magnificence
and amplitude, — a poem for whose perfection no critical praise suffices. The audience for such pieces as
these must be small. They presuppose a special taste,
a rarity even of modern culture. If the poet would
take all hearts with him he must steer his lonely bark to
other seas.

To be treated as a friend and a scholar by Tennyson
is not a hard lot, though the public are barred out. To
be treated as Englishmen is something which we have
no shadow of right to object to. If the Princess and the
Queen were nearer to us, the lines in which the residence
of the young wife with her mother is turned into a
curious astronomical vision might seem more than merely
court business; and if the changes of English political
life appeared more dangerously revolutionary than our
experience of democracy allows, the ferment of popular
distrust that disturbs some of the poems might be
thought less unfortunate. Tennyson's patriotic verses
hitherto have celebrated deeds and principles which
touched us through their native nobility, or some
community with our own civic life or our historical sympathy with England's past; but in the present
volume he deals mainly with political moods, and now
and then exhibits signs of irascibility with the young
democracy, as if he were tempted to drop into plain,
outright denunciatory prose. The temper of this portion is most simply shown in the lines to the Duke of
Argyll, who is idealized as representing the element of

order in change, — to speak unpoetically, the brakes on
the wheels when the curve of progress discloses a down
grade; and this conservatism has been unthinkingly
associated with the poet's elevation to the peerage.
Tennyson, however, was always a conservative in this
sense. His well-worn phrase about "the red fool-fury
of the Seine" measures his English hatred of Celtic
politics. The idea of Liberty, and of the people which
is her charge, impresses his imagination, and the distress
of the lot of the English poor has enlisted his sympathy;
but he was never so full of the divine rage that he would
pour out the Flood and make the past an antediluvian
memory, nor of the divine hope that he would sing the
New Song before the millennium was in fact established
at Westminster without disturbance in Lombard Street.
The past glory of England, which has been so largely the
illumination of his genius, has a deeper hold upon him
than modern ideas; and from early days he exhibited
the aristocratic temper of an idealizing nature and the
repugnance of a sensitive mind to the coarse thumb of the
mob — see with what fierceness it breaks out here in the
splendid vigor of "The Dead Prophet." There is no
change of accent in his later utterances about Freedom that we can discern. The "dark ages of the popular
press" were probably a topic of conversation years ago
with his friend Carlyle. The only difference is that when
he names Liberty here, he immediately begins to think
about her sister, Order, and he is very anxious that
the latter should not be discriminated against. For him
the great civil principles seem to have descended from the
ideal, and to have got confused with temporal measures;
so that even when he sets out to write a sort of imperial
chorus, "Hands All Round," for the mother country, the

conquered provinces, and the colonies to join in, it becomes, instead of a triumphal hymn of greatness, a plea for the integrity of the combination and no retreat on the frontiers. The secret of the weakness of poetry of this kind is that it springs from prudential considerations which lie in the region of the practical judgment and of shifting circumstances, too narrow and changeful to serve for ideal motives. These odes, or stanzas, or blank verse are as truly occasional pieces as if they were written for a banquet of the Whig peers. The four lines of General Gordon's admirable epitaph are worth whole octavos of these poems.

The remainder of this volume is addressed really to the public, and to the whole of it on both sides of the water. Attention has been most attracted by the two poems which are concerned with questions or aspects of religious faith, "Despair" and "The Ancient Sage." The latter consists of two parts in different measures, interwoven: one in which the youthful disciple develops the pleasurelessness of life on an atheistic theory, the other in which the wise and metaphysical old man makes a running commentary on the first. It is a beautiful work of poetic contrast, and an example of the fascination of a flawless style. In "Despair" the treatment is less didactic, and the ballad form, in which Tennyson has always exhibited his dramatic power most successfully, helps. In substance it is meant to light up in a lurid way the darkness of a sect-creed on the one hand, and of a science-creed on the other, and between the two the man goes crazy. In both of these pieces, and in detached passages elsewhere, the hostility of Tennyson to the materialistic tendencies in the science and speculation of the age is pronounced, and has been

commented on not so much because of the thing said
as of the temper of the saying. His words have less the
rush of poetry than the violence of controversy. But
one must remark that, as in matters of state, so in matters
of faith, this conservatism is no new thing; since he
came to his belief, in "In Memoriam," he has steadily
become more settled in his reliance on a divine
element in the universe in intimate relations of Providence to man. With this we are concerned
only as it affects his poetry, and that is really
a small matter; for the comparative failure of
such work as "Despair" to take hold of the public
is not due to its jealous attitude toward so-called modern
thought, but to an artistic defect. The ballad, as has
just been said, is Tennyson's best dramatic form. In
it his force gets swing. In the present case, however,
in order to justify the passion which was compelling
expression, he was obliged to create exceptional incidents
and a situation too plainly invented for set purposes.
The imagination is not taken captive, does not believe
the alleged basis of fact, but, on the contrary, the reason
detects an artifice. If the supposed case be voluntarily
accepted as real, the vehement declamation becomes
natural, and the poem great; but for the public the
imaginative acceptance must always be involuntary, and
hence arises the tremendous power of passion in poetry
when it is evolved from the common things of our experience. A similar reason is to be assigned for the weakness among the people of the two ballads which deal
with domestic infelicity, of marriage in one case and of
betrothal in the other. There is in both these a seeming
tampering with the facts for the sake of effect: an obvious
over-emphasis of a sea-landscape in one, where the poetic

passion is brought to its focus in the midst of a storm
by the novelist's *deus ex machina* of having two deaths
happen in the distant places at the right time; and in the
other an equally obvious over-emphasis of a mood with
which sympathy must be imperfect, because the facts
that might sustain it are practically suppressed. The
dramatic power of Tennyson is so intense that it needs,
for its working, a situation of rare emotional capability,
and at the same time not too strange, such as he had,
for example, in the marvelous ballad of "Rizpah."
His grasp in these last poems is so strong that he seems
to crush what he touches.

Much better are the two ballads not yet mentioned,
— the pieces in dialect that belong to what is sometimes
called *genre* work. Together with the idyl, "Balin and
Balan," and the "Tiresias," and the battle lyric of the
Heavy Brigade, they are the distinctly poetic work of
the volume, unadulterated by any admixture of religion,
politics, court compliment, temporal occasions, public
or private, or even personal friendship not lifted into
universal meaning. The Irish ballad is, after the lines
to Virgil, the most perfectly wrought poem in the volume; and the English ballad, though without the typical
power of the earlier characters that have used Tennyson's
dialect, has a rustic interest of the Dutch interior kind.
For the sake of completeness, let it be said that "Balin
and Balan," of which the morality is profound, suffers
by being made the body-piece of this volume; in its
place among the great idyls, its low relief and simple
action will find their artistic necessity. It is unjust to
judge an incident of the frieze as if it were a figure of
the pediment.

That the volume is less than the last one, which gave us

"Rizpah," "Grenville," and "Columbus," may be readily
granted, as that was less than its predecessors. Time
has counted, no doubt. "Old age hath yet his honor
and his due"; and instead of the charm and might of
manhood we have the ease, the less exacting art, the
more fragmentary and less selected thought, of less vigorous years. There is delight and profit in this last collection as in all that went before, and the alleged
conservatism of the peer proves a familiar thing, — not
that of a convert, or that of a declining life, but that of
the poet who has always been impressed by the values
that a great national past has established, and who
fears that the builders of the new future will care less
for the beauty and righteousness which he has spent
his life in praising.

"Locksley Hall Sixty Years After" — "this dramatic
monologue," as Tennyson describes it in his dedication — met with little justice at the hands of the
public. Just how much the poet meant to convey by this
explicit assertion of the dramatic character of so important a composition is uncertain. It is easy to give
too much significance to a slight thing merely because it
is unusual; but may it not be that Tennyson set that
exact phrase across the head of his poem to warn his
critics and readers against too close and definite an
identification of himself with the old man who pours
forth his gray thoughts with such iron vigor, with the
passion, the elevation, and something of the possession of
a prophet saying his last? If Tennyson had any such
apologetic purpose in view, he failed to make his meaning plain. The reception given the poem illustrated once
more, unfortunately, the degree to which public regard
for him had lessened. Certain phrases and moods of the

new "Locksley Hall" were seized upon at once, not without a trace of ill-natured satisfaction, and scattered broadcast as a proof, if any more were necessary, that the noble lord was a Bourbon among reactionists. Against this tide of opinion the poet could not bear up; and it is much to be feared that a really great composition of the poet who stands without a rival in his age is generally regarded as evidence of dotage.

This prejudice of the public and the hasty judgment which it made possible are the more to be regretted, because the poem offers difficulties enough to the reader without any addition from outside. It is hard to understand at once, and to follow all its turns and episodes. It requires to be read many times, to be familiarized, in fact, before the general mood of the speaker, the sequence of the incidents and their bearing, and the flow of the ideas about society and human life disclose their harmony and combined power, and move as rapidly in one's mind as on the page. This is partly because of the breaks, the changes, the incoherent or incomplete phrases, that belong to the dramatic structure of the poem. It is, indeed, dramatic in a severe and strict sense, and so truly is the experience of the old man its centre that in reading it one must let all thought of approval or disapproval go, and identify himself with this stern Nestor. It will be time enough to say he is foolish and garrulous, and overestimates the size and prowess of his old companions in the days of their youth, when one has mastered the experience of these Sixty Years, which is woven in this shifting web of memories, reflections, and maxims. But the difficulty of the poem is not merely verbal: the monologue is abrupt in its transitions as well as in its expression; thought breaks in on emotion, some picture

of the past comes back, a fact of the boy's life to whom
he is speaking recurs to point the old man's world-
knowledge, or the landscape before them catches his
eye, or the general fate of the world pushes aside all
other interests. Altogether the work is very intricate,
very full of events, overflowing with thought; it com-
presses, indeed, within its limits not only the career of
the speaker, but several individual lives connected with
his, and the general life of the world in his generation.
The sweep is thus long and wide, and Tennyson employed, moreover, his most compact and rapid style;
with every couplet there is a step taken and an effect is
gained, and it is a strong head that can keep the pace
when the poet is at once so intense, so profound, and so
dramatic. Most of the lines are, of course, plain, but
there is often one that does not yield its thought or
picture, and particularly its relation to the rest, unless
the mind lingers upon it; and on the other hand, the idea
or the image is often so brilliant, and made as it were
at a single casting, that it stands out too much by itself,
and one forgets the story that is being told and the total
mood that is being developed. It is not superfluous to
dwell thus a little at length on the difficulty in the mere
reading of this poem, if it reminds us that poetry is
not always as easily intelligible as a sneer at it is; and in
this case Tennyson has certainly suffered by a lack of
that attention to which his labors have given him the
right. One ought to remark, furthermore, that there is
no real obscurity in the poem, but only a speed and
vividness to which one must first accustom his mind, as
he does his eyes to a strong light.

But all this, it may be said, is merely prefatory. What
of the poem itself? Is it not a pean of the counter-rev-

olution, a negation of one of the most stirring hymns of progress ever written, a kind of recantation of the poet's youth? We are not disposed to seek any shield for Tennyson in the notion that this is a "dramatic monologue," and not the expression of personal views; be the facts what they may, the tenor of the new "Locksley Hall" is in consonance with too much of his later work to allow us to doubt that in its social, political, and artistic views it represents its maker with practical fairness. It may be admitted, too, that the Sixty Years have made a difference in the heart of the young man whose musing bivouac has become so famous. Hope belongs to the twenties, and it is not unnatural to find the clouds taking on their traditional "sober coloring" at fourscore; the question is not whether there has not been change, but whether there has been through all the changes loyalty to the one aim, — whether the voice at eve is or is not "the voice obeyed at prime." In what respect, then, is it held that this poem fails of the mark set by the old one so long ago? It does not fail in the ideal of personal duty, of which the manly English pattern is celebrated in the boy's father's death and in the squire's long life, and is inculcated very nobly by the man in his direct advice to the boy; and it is to be observed that all is definite and practical now, whereas the old poem was essentially vague. It does not fail, either, in the appreciation of worth as the stamp of manhood, and the assertion that it is independent of rank, to be found often among the people in its most noble and useful forms; and this position, commonplace as it is, is stated with marked emphasis, and in no half-hearted or reluctant words. In point of humanity, certainly nothing can be advanced against it, for the

condition of the poor in modern life has never been set
forth in lines of more burning shame than here. It is
true he denounces Zolaism; but in "the years of April
blood," of which he once wrote, he would surely have
done the same. So one might go through the whole poem,
to find that the words are those of wisdom; unless, indeed, some doubt should arise with regard to the couplets which seem aimed at the doctrine of government by
suffrage, and in these he does not so much protest as
express doubt and hesitation. The fact is that in
particulars most persons of sense and judgment will
agree with this poem; but at the same time many of
them, who are still possessed of the hopefulness and
energy of life, will feel a certain unfriendliness in the
mood of Tennyson, a certain cold and grimness, which
has in it just a shade of despair. This does pervade
the poem, and finds definite expression in the sense of
how little is accomplished toward reforming the world
in any one age, how much of personal error there is in
individual life, how often in the life of nations there
are periods of decline and failure, and in like commonplaces, which gather more weight and meaning in proportion as one grows in experience; and especially it
is to be remarked that, in defining the characteristics of
the present age, the poet dwells upon what makes for
danger and sorrow and all things evil, to the exclusion
of the other half of the horizon. The poem, so far as
it goes, is just and sound, and it touches upon great
phases of the general life in a thoroughly humane, wise,
and righteous way; but it is an imperfect view, — imperfect even for old age; and if we are asked wherein
its great deficiency lies we should be forced to answer
that the speaker, whether he be Tennyson or only a

character of imagination, lacks faith, both in the over-ruling of Providence and in man himself. We have found it impossible to reconcile the general drift and temper of the poem in regard to society with the acknowledgment of the divine power, which is one of its leading traits. Such a subject, however, is to be touched with a light hand; and we have already said enough to explain our judgment that this new "Locksley Hall" is a really great poem, which must in time recover from the odium under which it lies, and take a high place among the works of its author. In detail it is crowded with beautiful English scenes and with noble poetic images; its workmanship, though difficult, is in the grand style of art; and in ethical power it exceeds the earlier poem, because its passion is not that of a selfish and heated youth, but is identified with the uncertain tragedy of impersonal humanity in the mass. Since "The Revenge," Tennyson has written no work of this lofty kind.

A LITERARY PORTRAIT OF ROSSETTI

Mr. Sharp draws a portrait of Rossetti, the lineaments of which he says any one could see in "The House of Life":

"Those who have never met or seen him, or who had never heard of his personality, would discern a man with an acute, even painfully acute, sensibility, with a passionate love of the beautiful, with a habit of morbid introspection and a tendency to succumb to morbid impulses, with an occasional passion and vehemence, startling in its suddenness, and, while of an essentially spiritual nature, forced by bent of genius into a poetic expression wherein sensuous images and symbolism are preëminent."

This single sentence has the compactness of final criticism; it describes all that is essential in Rossetti's personality. In this man of keen senses and brooding mind and almost ascetic aspiration, there was a strange blending, and at times apparently a confusion, of the artistic and poetic faculties. This fact contributes much to give his work its peculiar charm and to make it a critical puzzle. Mr. Howells once said that Rossetti should have "painted his poems and sung his pictures." The phrase indicates the sense of imperfect expression that one usually feels in contemplating his work of either kind. He charged his pictures with ideas they could not express without the commentary of the sonnet he so frequently annexed to them, and he filled his poems with color and visions they could not present without the illustration he so seldom gave. The pictures will not be apprised at their worth unless the observer can carry out their mental suggestion with poetic feeling, nor his poems unless the reader has powers of vivid visualization. This union of the two faculties would hardly have been possible, certainly would not have been so fruitful of good results as it was, had not Rossetti been a mystic. A mystic he primarily was, a man who cared less for the object or the thought than for its vague and often arbitrary suggestions; who used things and ideas not for their current value, but as coins stamped with his own image and superscription; tendering them for the original and self-derived worth he gave to them. Necessarily he dealt much with symbols, the only refuge for a mystic who desires to indicate his meaning to others. If he wished to bring before the mind the Temptation of the Flesh, he painted a luxurious woman or he sang of "Eden Bower," but in either case Lilith is more than she seems, she stands for something else. If in his work one sees or hears mention of a dove or an apple, one must ask, not what it is, but what it means, for he is almost certainly using a sign-language.

Again, like mystics in general, he does not rest in his idea, but is ever either elaborating it or passing to cognate ideas that it has suggested. The peculiarity in Rossetti's case is that, because of his sensuous susceptibility, he chooses his symbols from the things of the senses, using what is most significant to himself to express what is highest, and therefore displaying the spirit through the flesh. This drew on him the unfortunate review that so much embittered his life, in which he was branded as one of the "Fleshly School." The pur-

ity of his mind cannot be questioned. One proof of it is
the fact of his suppressing or modifying the passages in
his poems most objected to, when he came to a truer
knowledge of his common audience, so much more alive
to his physical than to his spiritual meaning. As he is
not to be ranked with the "Fleshly School," neither is
he to be put among the so-called Neo-Pagans, for even
less than they had he anything classical in his genius.
He was original in the sense that he was a medieval
man "born out of time"; but this phase of his character
is given in Mr. Sharp's own words:

"It is true the beautiful was the ideal of the Greek
artistic mind, and also that the beautiful was the aim
of Rossetti in his dual vocation — but how different the
conceptions of beauty! The former looked to light,
clearness, form, in painting, sculpture, architecture, to
intellectual conciseness and definiteness in poetry; the
latter looked mainly to diffused color, graded to almost
indefinite shades in his art, finding the harmonies
thereof more akin than severity of outline and clearness
of form, while in his poetry the Gothic love of the
supernatural, the Gothic delight in sensuous images, the
Gothic instinct of indefiniteness and elaboration, carried
to an extreme, prevailed. . . . His classical work can
be so called only in a restricted sense, first, because
his sympathies were not Greek, but Gothic, and because
his creations typify the mysterious yearning of life, the
brooding and hope and despair and resignation of a
certain type of womanhood; not the joy *in* life, the
exultation of physical being, the spiritually untroubled
Greek ideal. Penelope, Pandora, Proserpina — these as
they appear to us through the medium of Rossetti's
subtle and beautiful art are not the Penelope and Pan-

dora sung of and painted from time immemorial, the Proserpina who wandered in fair girlhood in the bright sunshine along the warm, sweet-scented Sicilian fields; but through the eyes of *this* Penelope all womanhood that dreams and yearns for a scarcely definite yet apprehended ideal love seems to look forth; in the eyes of *this* Pandora lie prophetic gleams of all she, typical of woman, can let loose upon the world, as she opens the casket from whence wing, in circling and evasive flight, passions and delights and joys and sorrows; and in the face of *this* Proserpina, queen of the dark realms, as she passes along the corridor in her splendid but desolate palace, there broods the regret and the passionate longing of all women who look into the past, and see that it is full of light, and that its day can never dawn again."

This not only marks Rossetti as romantic, symbolizing, and mystical, but it also indicates well and accurately the special character of his pictures to such as have never seen them, and helps to an understanding of the fascination they possess over men in whose minds, as in his, beauty and thought are not disjoined. Mr. Sharp, however, notwithstanding such eulogy as is implied in the above passage, has no disposition to become responsible for Rossetti's defects by approval of them. In both arts, it must be confessed, Rossetti's command of technique was far from perfect. In painting he did not draw well, never having learned how, and his continual repetition of the same face in successive pictures was a weakness. In poetry he did not know nature; and all must notice in his verses the paucity of natural facts and the lack of feeling for them; what few there are, being such as strike an artist's eye rather than stir a poet's heart. Did any man of equal poetic endowment ever remark to a friend that it was "wonderful how much a bit of nature helps," or ever write to an acquaintance, as Rossetti does, in a letter here given, for "a feature or incident characteristic of the glen at nightfall," to put in his poem, when he had just spent some time in the place referred to? His treatment, too, is frequently literary, as distinguished from natural, depending on study or inspiration at second-hand. An analogous fault appears in his diction, in such a line as

"The embowered throstles' urgent wood-notes soar."

His choice of form was by no means instinctive, and was sometimes far from right, as noticeably in "The White Ship" and the beryl song of "Rose Mary"; he occasionally sank into bathos in wholly meaningless though fine-sounding lines; his music is monotonous, his ear for dissyllables is very defective, and his rhymes, now and then, are incomprehensible. Nearly all these blemishes Mr. Sharp notices; but the claim that, in spite of them, he makes for Rossetti as a remarkably original, exceptionally endowed, and influential mind, is valid.

MARY WOLLSTONECRAFT

No one can read many memoirs without being impressed by the lavishness of nature in creating fine ability, and by the richness of life in attractive and honorable character. None of the inevitable ravages of time is more deplorable than its wresting the recollections of these from the memory of the living world. It is therefore at all times a pleasant task to recall to mind those who have wrought out, more perfectly than others, the worthiness of which all human life is capable; and the task is peculiarly grateful when it may serve to set in a fairer light the acts and words of a beautiful woman, to whom the world has ungenerously refused her due of gratitude. Mary Wollstonecraft was such a woman. The story of her life is the story of the earliest vindicator of the right of her sex to larger freedom and to the opportunity for higher mental and moral accomplishment than had been its lot; it is the story, too, of the first Englishwoman who cast herself solely upon literature to win her bread; and besides these extrinsic sources of interest, it is in itself a story of such trial, fortitude, affection, and pathos that it may be told in some detail, with the hope of awakening the compassion of those to whom the exercise of sympathy is not an unwelcome pain.

"Fatigued during my youth by the most arduous struggles, not only to obtain independence, but to render myself useful, not merely pleasure, for which I had the most lively taste — I mean the simple pleasures that flow from passion and affection — escaped me, but the most melancholy views of life were impressed by a disappointed heart on my mind." In these words Mary Wollstonecraft summed up justly her early life. It was led, indeed, in such vulgar surroundings that her enemies, exaggerating its wretchedness, used it to palliate her faults as if it had been almost an initiation into vice. She was born at Hoxton on the 27th of April, 1759, into a drunkard's home; her maiden years were spent in the daily presence of domestic misery wrought by men's faults or vices. Soon after she was twenty-one years old her father's family, never united by very loving ties, was broken up. She was received into the home of her friend, Fanny Blood, which was made wretched, like her own, by a father's drunkenness and was disgraced by a sister's frailty. There she became dear and serviceable, but she was withdrawn from this temporary refuge by the troubles of a sister, whose husband's violence was driving her insane and at last forced her to desert him. The sisters opened a school, for Mary had had considerable experience in teaching, but after a brief success they got into financial difficulty, in the midst of which Mary was summoned to Lisbon to attend her old friend Fanny. After a hard winter voyage, she arrived only in season to comfort her friend's last days. Oppressed with her loss, she immediately set sail for England. Ill health and low spirits not unnaturally filled her mind with morbid anticipations of an early death, but the letters in which she records these are softened by patient piety, and lighted up by helpful affection for those with whom kinship or acquaintance bound her. The school came to a lingering end in debt, and she was forced to go to Ireland and take on herself the unwelcome task of teaching Lord Kingsborough's children, "literally speaking wild Irish, unformed, and not very pleasing." Fatigued by the domestic bickerings, unmeaning laughter, and boisterous spirits of a set of silly females, — so she describes her life, — she won the affection of her charges, and thereby lost her situation through the mother's jealousy.

In the fall of 1788, therefore, by the advice of Mr. Johnson, the book-seller, who had published her first unsuccessful pamphlet two years before, she gave herself to the individual pursuit of literature in London, but with much hesitation and secrecy for fear of ridicule. She was thus the first woman of distinguished ability to rely for support solely on services to the reading public. Her work, of course, was hack work; but in the intervals of drudgery she wrote two books that are still remembered: one only because it was illustrated by Blake; the other the "Vindication of the Rights of Woman," published in 1792, at the time a notorious volume, which was the fruit of Rousseau, the French Revolution, Tom Paine, and her own bitter experience, and which earned for her such evil report that nearly forty years after her death the "Gentleman's Magazine" spoke of her as "grossly irreligious, indelicate, and dissolute," — with what degree of justice will be seen.

During these years her relatives burdened her time and drained her purse; nearly all of her numerous family partook in large measure of her hard-earned bounty. The glimpses we get of the members of this family, most of whom were sordid and ungrateful, are not pleasant; but if we wish to see what masks life wore to this fine-natured woman, we must look at things which we would gladly avoid. Let this picture of her father, however, given in a letter from her sister in 1791, be enough: his red face convulsed with ill-humor and every unamiable feeling, his hair gray and dirty, his beard long, his body worn to a skeleton, and clad in clothes not worth sixpence, coughing, panting, continually falling. It is no wonder that with such letters in her hand, with the irremediable misery in life thus brought home to her, Mary Wollstonecraft was often in low spirits; no wonder that melancholy views of life were impressed upon her mind. What had life given her but a difficult, precarious subsistence, hard won by continual effort, amid scenes of misery, frivolity, and disgust? But at last her day of trial seemed to brighten: she became well known in London literary circles; cultivated and agreeable men and women became her friends, and in the fall of 1792 she determined to join Mr. Johnson and the Fuselis in a six weeks journey to Paris, and to avail herself of the opportunity of entering society there, which the recent translation of her "Vindication" assured her; but, her less adventurous companions being frightened (perhaps, at the September massacres), she embarked alone in December.

France then exercised over her the same fascination which set the heart of the youthful Wordsworth in a flame. France was the home of her principles, the spring whence she had drawn no small part of her literary culture, and to France she looked as the source of intellectual light and the hope of political liberty. She arrived in Paris at a great moment in the Revolution. The preceding month the convention had issued that incendiary decree declaring any nation which might rise

against despots thereby the sister of France. Soon she
saw the king pass under her windows on his way to trial,
sitting with more dignity than she would have expected
from his character, in a hackney coach clustered about
by National Guards, who seemed to deserve the name.
That night, as she sat alone in her chamber writing, on
lifting her eyes from the paper, she saw eyes gleam
through a glass door opposite her chair and bloody hands
shaken at her; in so many frightful shapes, she says,
had death taken hold of her fancy. And on going to bed,
she adds, "for the first time in my life, I cannot put out
the candle," — one of myriad women's tremors amid
those events. The king's head was quickly off; the
shadow of the oncoming terror fell upon France, and
underneath it — ordinary human life continuing undisturbed by the throes of the republic — her own tragedy
drew nigh. Her position as an Englishwoman was full
of danger; retreat to her own country was cut off, and
she found protection among the Americans. On the fall
of the Gironde, in which party she counted her French
friends, she lost her heart to one of these Americans,
Gilbert Imlay, formerly a Revolutionary soldier, a land
agent in the back settlements, and a sensible writer upon
the Western Territories, but now a fortune-seeker in
Paris.

It was a strange love-mating: this woman of extraordinary beauty and eyes the most meaning that Southey
ever saw, of conversation that delighted Coleridge, of
mental vigor rare if not first among women of her day,
of a full and refined sensuous endowment, sensitive,
responsive, compact of fancy, imagination, sentiment,
and passion, — a woman, too, acquainted with the world,
and indulging no illusions concerning manly heroism, —

and this gold-greedy adventurer, sensual of life, yet with a better nature dying under the blight of what he deemed the exigencies of the world.   In whatever way it came about, Mary Wollstonecraft accepted him as her lover in the spring of 1793, governed only by affection, as she afterwards wrote, and in the rectitude of her own heart "careless of vulgar precautions," or, in more intelligible words, of a marriage ceremony.

There is no need to seek a possible excuse for her in the danger which would have attended the necessary declaration of her being an Englishwoman, had she been married in due form, in illustration of which the case of Lord Nelvil and Madame D'Arbigny in "Corinne" has been fitly cited; there is no reason to believe she would have desired formal marriage had she been within the shadow of St. Paul's.   With that rash extinction of all forms in their animating spirit characteristic of radical reformers in that age, she believed that affection and choice constituted marriage.   Having seen in the only home she had known from childhood the misery of legally compelled unions after the husband had been false to all his duties, it was as easy for her to fall into error in her time as for women to avoid it in our time.   She must stand by her mistake; she looked for permanent association; Imlay in a legal document called her his wife; and there the matter rests.

The story of their life together is told in the most touching private correspondence of which the sanctity was ever broken.   In reading it one cannot avoid a feeling of intrusion.   It sprang from the long separation of the lovers, due to Imlay's business, which first took him to Havre and then to London.   In it may be read, in words alive with love or grief or scorn, — words fiery,

impulsive, direct, sincere, unchecked, — how peace and
fragrance and freshness filled the morning of their new
life, and gave place to anxiety, distrust, contempt, and
despair; how she quickly found out that she had "more
mind than he, because she could find food for love in
the same object for a longer time," and that (with her
unsexed plainness of speech), while the way to her senses
was through her heart, "there was sometimes a shorter
cut to his"; how the hope that she could revivify that
better nature, which she saw sometimes striving to master
his "commercial face," so that at the last she and virtue
might conquer, faded out; how the birth of her child —
that Fanny whose fate is familiar to all who know Shelley's life — brought the warmth of hope, to be followed
by a keener chill; how she upbraided that greed for
money which kept him from her; and how, at last, her
essential nature, lost in affectionate ecstasy for a time,
reasserted itself, and let loose her scorn upon his sensuality and threw off his protection for herself and her
child.

In marriage, when love fails, duty steps in; but she
had no place for such duty in her system. "The little
girl and I will take care of ourselves; we will not accept any of your kindness, your distant civilities, — no,
not we. . . . Do not suppose that, neglected by you,
I will lie under obligation of a pecuniary kind to you!
No; I would sooner submit to menial service. I
wanted the support of your affection; that gone, all is
over!" She had been now two years in France, and
this was the result of it, — love, motherhood, desertion;
she had looked forward to "as much felicity as the world
affords."

Meanwhile, the dark eclipse of the Terror was waning; and, the human heart being unable to endure a constant rack of emotion, Mary Wollstonecraft, in the pauses of her grief, had written an account of the Revolution, valuable now as being the work of an eyewitness, and remarkable for its sober judgment. She had not yet broken irretrievably with Imlay, and in the spring of 1795 she returned to London, to reconciliation and a distrustful pleasure; she even submitted to take part in his despised business, and, with a maid and her child, set sail for Norway to attend to his embarrassed affairs. From this time the old correspondence begins anew, with scanty hope from the first, and sadder and more bitter at every writing. In spite of mental distress, the sea and the mountains brought back her health, braced her muscles, she says, and covered her ribs; but neither health nor her delight in the novel grandeur of nature about her could make her forget her wound. The facts remained, and when, on her return, she met them she could not face their blank stare. "Let my wrongs sleep with me," she wrote to Imlay; "soon, very soon, I shall be at peace." One night in November, having first drenched her clothes by standing in the water, she leaped from Putney Bridge into the Thames. She called this "one of the calmest acts of reason," although by it she deserted her friendless child. What would she have said, could she have forecast the years, and seen the body of that child, influenced how much by her mother's example none will ever know, floating lifeless in the waters of that same river? Some passing boatmen rescued her, and recalled her to a hated life, to new farewells to her old lover, and to her former struggle for an independent living in London, the city for which she now felt a repugnance amounting to horror.

Her life resumed its accustomed ways; time and labor poured out healing, and having done her duty toward Imlay, she was at last enabled to be just to herself, and to cast out of her life the remembrance of unworthiness. Meanwhile her descriptive letters from Norway and Sweden were published, and she reentered London literary society, where honor was still in store for her. There she met William Godwin, the almost forgotten philosopher, who once earned fame in more than one stroke for English liberty. At first Godwin was not pleased with Mary Wollstonecraft; he had heard that she spoke slightingly of him, and he thought she took too large a share in the conversation, because he wished to hear Tom Paine talk. Repeated meetings modified his impressions, and gradually friendship, rooted in mutual regard, passed unobserved into the affection that binds man and woman indissolubly. Which was before or which was after, which was the toil-spreader and which the prey, said Godwin, it was impossible to know; and he who believed marriage should be abolished, and had published his opinion and the grounds of it where all might read, married her. Perhaps Mary Wollstonecraft had herself some experience from the social disrepute into which in a slight degree she had formerly fallen. Certainly this was in Godwin's mind, for he wrote to a friend that he submitted to the ceremony only in order to secure the social position of the individual; and having done that, he held himself no otherwise bound than before. They were married in March, 1797, and led a peculiar wedded life; for Godwin had some bachelor-bred notions among which one was that members of a family should not live together continually, for fear of becoming tired of each other's

society; and consequently he took lodgings apart from
his wife, where he spent a considerable portion of
his time. Sometimes they walked together in the morning, but frequently did not meet until dinner, after which
it was not unusual for them to separate for different
social assemblies. Their life was happy; but this late-
found content was not to last. On the 30th of August
their daughter Mary was born, and, after a painful
illness, the mother died on the 10th of September, leaving Godwin to the task of writing her memoir and editing her unfinished works. Afterward, in the novel of "St.
Leon," he drew her character as it was revealed to him
in their private life.

Her life, here described by its simplest human elements, gathered dignity and luster from the character
of her thought. She was an enthusiast in a cause which
she served with all her powers, — with novel, tract, and
dissertation; in nearly everything she wrote, she had the
elevation of her sex most at heart. Should any look into
her volumes for radical views, however, they would find
little to reward them; the rights of woman which she
vindicated were few and primitive, and words which,
coming from her, were novel and vigorous have become
commonplaces upon our lips. Women, as she observed
them — and there is only too much in the memoirs and
romances of that age to bear out her description — were
feeble and foolish creatures, moving in a mean and
narrow sphere, without an aim except to get married,
without a motive except to better themselves, with no
conception of conquest except what voluptuous promise
might win over men's eyes; in her eighteenth-century
rhetoric, "Taught from their infancy that beauty is
woman's scepter, the mind shapes itself to the body,

and roaming round its gilt cage only seeks to adorn its prison." Under this ideal of women's life, decreed alike by Rousseau and the English clergy, the bent of the education of women was, in her own words, to make them alluring mistresses, and the result of it was empty-headed or faithless wives, unfit to bear or rear children, and unable to retain their husband's attentions.

Against this system Mary Wollstonecraft protested; but the reform she proposed went no farther than that her sex should add to the person of a woman the character of a rational being by the acquisition of virtue and knowledge, through the exercise of that reason of which the perfectibility was her surest ground for looking forward to an immortal life; and the utmost privilege she asked was an equal opportunity with men to develop those mental and moral capacities which are the immortal part of humanity. To become the companions, rather than the toys, of man; to win the honor of his respect rather than the homage of his gallantry; to set their minds on making happy, healthy, and chaste homes; to discharge the duties of wives, sisters, and daughters; to be worthy of a life to come, — these were the simple and inoffensive aims which Mary Wollstonecraft set before women. She uttered no radical views upon marriage, which, on the contrary, she professed to respect as the foundation of almost every social virtue.

Perhaps, in her own day, her book, which is essentially an appeal for the education of woman, founded on the social value of such a reform in its effects upon family life, would not have been so censured, had she not urged her opinions with a plainness of speech which would be offensive, were it not that such freedom was usual in books of the kind, and necessary, as she thought, for her cause. There is reason to fear, however, that while she possessed that delicacy which shows itself actively in perception and thoughtfulness, she lacked that other delicacy of reserve which shows itself in reticence. She bares her thoughts, and they are sometimes such as women seldom put even into veiled speech. Her novels, which are simply moral essays, cannot be freed fom the blame of opening in too rude and blunt a way the hideousness of some parts of human life; her characters are like persons in a hospital, brought together to illustrate the disease of humanity, not to exhibit its normal nature. In composing these half-finished works she was filled with the purest philanthropic spirit; but certainly in feminine delicacy as well as in literary art she was at fault.

Two subsidiary points in her "Vindication" ought not to be passed over: one of them is her advocacy of day schools for both sexes, in opposition to the academical system, which she denounced in unmeasured terms as giving rise to institutions where the relaxation of the junior boys was mischief and that of the senior vice; the other, deliberate avowal of the benefits of woman suffrage, as follows: —

"Though I consider that women in the common walks of life are called to fulfill the duties of wives and mothers by religion and reason, I cannot help lamenting that women of a superior cast have not a road open by which they can pursue more extensive plans of usefulness and independence. I may excite laughter by dropping a hint which I mean to pursue at some future time, for I really think that women ought to have representatives instead of being arbitrarily governed, without having any direct share allowed them in the deliberations of government.

But as the whole system of representation is now in this country only a convenient handle for despotism, they need not complain, for they are as well represented as a numerous class of hard-working mechanics, who pay for the support of royalty when they can hardly stop their childen's mouths with bread."

From the opinions already spoken of it is clear that Mary Wollstonecraft was not wholly irreligious; but she was not orthodox. She expressly rejected the doctrines that man introduced evil into the world, and that men will be punished hereafter for purposes of vengeance. She clung only to the being of God and the hope of immortality; submitting all else to the test of reason, she found skepticism or ignorance her portion. In lesser matters, she thought piety sometimes indicative of villainy; she distrusted the value of private and public charities; and she especially reprobated the forced religion of the public schools which made a youth "receive the sacrament of the Lord's Supper to avoid forfeiting half a guinea, which he probably afterward spent in some sensual manner." She called the observance of Sunday in the decorous London streets stupid, and thought the gladness she had seen in France of a Sunday was a "sentiment more truly religious"; then she goes on to give us a glimpse of country manners: —

"I recollect in the country parts of England the church-wardens used to go out during the service to see if they could catch any luckless wight playing at bowls or skittles; yet what could be more harmless? It would even, I think, be a great advantage to the English if feats of activity — I do not include boxing matches — were encouraged of a Sunday, as it might stop the progress of Methodism and of that fanatical spirit which

appears to be gaining ground. I was surprised when I
visited Yorkshire, on my way to Sweden, to find that
sullen narrowness of thinking had made such a progress
since I was an inhabitant of that country. . . . Besides,
many of these deluded persons, with the best meaning,
actually lose their reason and become miserable, the
dread of damnation throwing them into a state which
merits the term; and still more, in running after their
preachers to promote their salvation, they neglect the
interest and comfort of their families; so that in proportion as they attain a reputation for piety they become
idle."

Apparently, therefore, her own early and trustful
piety had been destroyed; or, rather, when its speculative
basis has been undermined by her mental growth and
her reading of the French philosophers, it was transformed into a humanitarian religion similar to the advanced Unitarianism of our own days.

Leaving on one side that fund of observation which
in her important works attracts the student of history
and manners, and displays the largeness, justness, and
penetration of her mind, these were the opinions she
thought out and sought to make prevail. A liberal woman
who speaks out her whole mind is nearly certain to
give offense; for liberality implies a disposition to tol-
erate condemned views and to introduce new practices,
both of them actions inconsistent with that bearing which
the ordinary man admires in woman. For this reason
she gave offense in her own day by originating and
advocating opinions which are now so familiar that we
forget they ever were original, and can hardly believe
there ever was any necesssity for advocating them. Her
work and life, therefore, are a tide-mark of opinion, and

are valuable on that account, even if they possess no other virtue for us; they reveal the great ebb of convention and prejudice in our century, the advance our time has made in lines of civilization more important than material progress, — in the ideal of life, and the opportunities granted by legislation and public opinion for the attainment of that ideal. The causes which she served are now living, and many of them are advanced in victory probably beyond her hope; the abuses she denounced are dead or languishing. There is only one act of hers which will meet with universal blame, and that was an error in conduct for which her early experience and the support of contemporary speculation plead forcibly. The race has found the institution of marriage too essential to social safety to allow any attack upon it to be passed unquestioned. She, by her conduct if not by her pen, set herself against this, and was consequently overborne and trampled down, her name slandered, and the virtue that was in her lost sight of; for, in such cases, the ordinary man is incapable of discriminating between acts which result from defective theories and those which result from moral depravity rooted in licentiousness and sensuality. Excepting this error, it would be difficult to find in her life anything more blameworthy than rational and active liberalism.

Posterity has passed her by, for she performed no notable act and produced no great literary work. She exercised only a contemporary influence; but, like the character of forgotten ancestors shaping in some degree our own acts and thoughts, her work lives in the great body of public opinion, which in respect to the themes she treated is so much more elevated and pure than it was a century ago. She lies among the undistinguished dead; but it is a grateful task to recall the names of those who have contributed to make human life more clean and more beneficent.

The circumstances of her life and the character of her opinions it is easy to tell; but there is comparatively no record of the woman whose feminine charm and beauty are lost to memory, except so far as the applause of her friends and the loveliness of her portraits reveal them. She was courageous, enduring, and loving in life, as well as original, liberal, and fearless in thought; she united the charities of daily ministry to her friends with the graces of a mind cultivated by literature and acquainted with philosophy; she was as open to human emotion and sympathy as to the loveliness of nature, her joy in which, before the days of Burns and Wordsworth, was her refuge and comfort; in her struggle with life she neither lost nor harmed the most admirable qualities of womanhood. One is tempted to link her name with that of George Sand; in many ways she suggests the great French-woman; vast as was the difference in their genius, they belong to the same order of women. Her name, never-theless, will remain obscure; and the last memory of her will be, that over her grave in old St. Pancras church-yard Shelley wooed and won the daughter in bearing whom she died.

> "For One then left this earth
> Whose life was like a setting planet mild,
> Which clothed thee in the radiance undefiled
> Of its departing glory; still her fame
> Shines on thee."

A WORD FOR PEPYS

As one glances over "Pepys' Diary," not for the last time, and lingers on some whimsicality, or piece of gossip, or other *révélation intime* it may be, he escapes the guilty consciousness of eaves-dropping just by the very awfulness of the joke Pepys played upon himself in being his own sole confidant, and thus blabbing more than the tiring-women of the whole century. Here under our hands we have in cold type "the perpetual aside" he whispered in his own confidential ear, and the humor of the situation is something not approached in comedy. How could it be unless the screen scene in Joseph Surface's drawing-room could be made a whole play? This dramatic situation, this continued discovery of Pepys behind the circumspect worldliness with which he sheltered his peeping soul, is a main element in the humorous fascination of the diary; one feels almost as if he were himself among the laughing gods who see this same comedy of "What Fools these Mortals Be" playing everywhere on the broad stage of the world, and there is a taste of divine felicity in the spectacle. If one cannot apply to the diary the classical definition of a good book, — "the precious life-blood of a master-spirit, embalmed and treasured up on purpose to a life beyond life," — it is a classic, nevertheless, and keeps the plebeian vitality of a very honest, vain man and a true Briton, though possibly he would rather have been condemned to a second death than pos-

sess an immortality of such very extraordinary pub-
licity as Fortune has given him. Be that as it may, he
has added cheerfulness to history and given humaneness
to our thoughts of the feeblenesses of our kind. The
most cynical, seeing how fairly well this inconsiderate
diarist turns out in the confessional of his least-breathed-
on thoughts, must feel less certain of the sight men would
see were the curtain lifted from the bosom of the pas-
ser-by. Pepys was one of the most English of his race;
he was the British islander, and circle within circle, the
Londoner, just as Voltaire was French, Gautier Pari-
sian; he had the defects of his nativity, broad, deep,
well-marked defects, visible as far as you can see a
scarlet coat, and he had foibles and eccentricities of his
own, and cranks of many varieties, but his good nature
and his contracted view carry them off; one no more
thinks of criticising him than the ideas of old Sir Roger;
and with all these appurtenances of humor, he had sound
and sterling qualities of business, integrity, public spirit,
intelligent and active curiosity, and, in a certain sense,
traits of a liberal mind and some humane tastes, so that
any reader may well pray that, should the discretion of
his own silence ever be turned by some flank movement
of posterity, and the conscienceless editor come in on the
rear of his thoughts, he may cut as respectable a figure
as the highly honorable Mr. Pepys, who was garrulous
of his follies only to himself, and when his lock was
forced was found to have been addicted only to Lilli-
putian wickedness. Everything about him was on a petty
scale, it is true, except his diary; but the size of that
makes amends for the littleness in other things.

Of all the wandering loves of Fortune, this, which has
made Pepys immortal, is the strangest vagary. How

many laureled heads of Davenants and Bayeses did she pass by to fix this paper crown on the busy official of the navy, who wrote with less regard to his readers than probably any other popular author! All the comic dramatists of the Restoration, as they are now styled, have gone, with their dry jests and elaborated humor, into the property-box of the English theater, and are shut up to be food for worms; their names fresh only in these pages and the footnote that explains the obscure reference. The real comedy, the one Fortune had fixed her favor on, was this one of the navy official, indited in prose, — no French influence to be observed in it, corrupting and enfeebling the old English stock, any more than in the Department he had in charge. But Fortune is wise, and out of her caprice has given us a good gift to make our advantage of, — the sincere history of one Englishman's life, selected, it would seem, almost at random from the intelligent men of his time, but one who remained at the bottom the mere human creature, and so by the weakness of our own nature creeps in to our hearts; and in our charity and remembrance and knowledge of ourselves he is as safely sheltered, perhaps, after all, as would have been the case had the shorthand volumes of manuscript never been disturbed.

THE COURTING OF DOROTHY OSBORNE

WHEN Macaulay made the fragments of the Osborne Papers which were accessible to him the text for his philippic against the dignity of history, and expressed so earnest a desire for more such letters, in preference even to state documents, as a means of obtaining that information for the sake of which alone it is useful to examine the past, he little thought what a treasure he had missed. In Dorothy Osborne's letters we obtain a sight of the way social life went on in England in the middle of the seventeenth century, quite the equal of that afforded in any other book, and much more interesting. It is the life of a young Englishwoman in a dull old country-house, but by no means secluded from the world. One sees how she thought and acted, what her principles were and how she applied them, the things she observed about her in human nature; in fact, she lives before our eyes, and, to crown all, she was in love. Sir William Temple is a grave figure in our literature. It is a singular freak of fortune that he should now be known to us in the ways he followed when he was young, and be more entertaining for his mistress's sake than for his own. The letters he wrote have perished; but something of their character may be inferred from the letters which he received in answer, and of these there is a good supply. He was only a youth of twenty when he first met Dorothy, herself but twenty-one. He fell in with her party while traveling, and a slight incident made them better acquainted. No one, however, would have been likely to prophesy a love-match from the encounter. It was the time of the civil wars, and their houses were hotly engaged on opposite sides of the great struggle. The balance had already declared for the fortunes of the Parliament. It was not long before Dorothy was living with her father at the family estate at Chicksands, taking care of him in his evil days, when the cause he fought for was lost, the master he had served ungrateful, and his peace made with the new order, which allowed him this quiet and lonely seat of his ancestors in Bedfordshire to end his broken life undisturbed. Meanwhile, William had been traveling and studying, perfecting his French and his Spanish, leading the life of a young man of expectations yet to be provided for out of the exchequer of state-offices. It is four years since the first meeting in the island of Guernsey when the correspondence begins, but in what way the two young people came to so sure a footing with each other is matter of conjecture. Dorothy ascribes Temple's attraction to his good-nature, which is not the first quality one thinks of in connection with him. She mentions the matter in one of her ingenuous passages upon human nature: "No, in earnest, nor I could not love any person that I thought had it not to a good degree. 'T was the first thing I liked in you, and without it I should never have liked anything. I know 't is counted simple, but I cannot imagine why. 'T is true some people have it that have not wit, but there are at least as many foolish people I have ever observed to be fullest of tricks, little ugly plots and designs, unnecessary disguises, and mean cunnings, which are the basest qualities in the world, and makes one the most contemptible, I think; when I once discover them, they lose their credit with me forever." It had been urged upon her that her own good-nature made her apt to be deceived, and from a worldly point of view was a questionable quality; but with all its faults, she avers, she "would not be without it." There was something more, however, than this mutual amiability to unite the lovers, and it would seem that the beginning of the courtship was not different from the usual course of true-love. "Can I remember," she writes, in a time of despondency, "how ignorantly and innocently I suffered it to steal upon me by degrees; how under a mask of friendship I cozened myself into that which, had it appeared to me at first in its true shape, I had feared and shunned?" So the coil of their long lovers'-troubles began; and in 1652 we come upon their history *in medias res.*

The difficulty arose from the worldly theory natural to the aristocracy, which insisted on the young of both sexes being "well married." Temple's father wished an heiress for his son, and Dorothy's kindred, and particularly the brother, who figures as the mischief-maker of the piece, desired that she should be mated with a fortune. It is the old story: the two lovers were poor. Their contests to prevent the alliance of their hands with wealth instead of with each other, and Dorothy's constant feminine survey of the matrimonial world about her, throw the strongest light on the marriage contract of the period in the great world, and illustrate one of the most unchanging characteristics of high society. Dorothy's task was incomparably harder than Temple's. He set aside at most one or two "good motions" of his father in his behalf. But Dorothy was a magnet; her very first letter confides to her un-

acknowledged "servant" the character and advances of
five suitors, and before the end the list of the refused
counts an incredible number. She writes very freely
of them, and gives them a short shrift in her letters.
A certain skill she had in striking off individual peculiarities, and especially foibles and ridiculous incidents, makes
the portraits in this gallery of rejected lovers very life-
like; and the exhibition of her own feelings is delight-
fully natural. Perhaps more than one would have been
discouraged, had he been able to read her description of
what she did not wish for in a husband. It is an inven-
tory of contemporary character.

"There are a great many ingredients must go to making
me happy in a husband. First, as my cousin Franklin
says, our humors must agree; and to do that, he must
have that kind of breeding that I have had, and used that
kind of company. Then he must not be so much a country gentleman as to understand nothing but hawks and
dogs, and be fonder of either than his wife; nor of the
next sort of them, whose aim reaches no further than to
be justice of the peace, and once in his life high sheriff;
who reads no books but statutes, and studies nothing
but how to make a speech interlarded with Latin, that
may amaze his disagreeing poor neighbors, and fright
them rather than persuade them into quietness. He
must not be a thing that began the world in a free school,
was sent from thence to the university, and is at his
furthest when he reaches the Inns of Court; has no acquaintance but those of his form in these places, speaks
the French he has picked out of old laws, and admires
nothing but the stories he has heard of the revels that
were kept there before his time. He must not be a
town gallant, neither, that lives in a tavern and an

ordinary, that cannot imagine how an hour should be
spent without company unless it be in sleeping, that
makes court to all the women he sees, thinks they believe
him, and laughs and is laughed at equally; nor a traveled
monsieur, whose head is all feather inside and outside,
that can talk of nothing but dances and duets, and has
courage enough to wear sashes when every one else dies
with cold to see him. He must not be a fool of no sort,
nor peevish, nor ill-natured, nor proud, nor covetous;
and to all this must be added that he must love me and
I him as much as we are capable of loving. Without
all this, his fortune, though never so great, would not
satisfy me; and with it, a very moderate one would keep
me from ever repenting my disposal."

When Temple replied to this that she seemed to know
better what she did not want than what she did, she
answered, readily enough, that she supposed he knew
that by his own exact pattern.

The suitors who presented themselves, in ignorance
alike of her tastes and of the fact that so far as her own
will and heart went she had already disposed of herself
privately, were of all sorts, from the country squire and
rich Londoner's son up almost to the highest in the land.
It was the time of Cromwell's height of power, and no less
a person than the Protector's son, Henry, "the debauched,
ungodly cavalier" of Mrs. Hutchinson, would have
wedded her. She did not suppress the reflection, later,
when Parliament was dissolved, how great she might have
been had she accepted him; but she also says that she
prizes a letter of Temple's more than all Henry Cromwell.
Another aspirant was her cousin, that Earl of Danby
who afterward figured in politics as a great minister of
the realm. The Londoner was the son of an alderman

who had bought a great estate. "Well, the best on 't is I have a squire now that is as good as a knight. He was coming as fast as a coach and six horses could carry him, but I desired him to stay till my ague was gone, and give me a little time to recover my good looks; for I protest, if he ever saw me now, he would never deign to see me again. Oh, me! I can but think how I shall sit like the lady of the lobster and give audience at Babram. You have been there, I am sure. Nobody that is at Cambridge 'scapes it." But the parvenu was not for her, either. There was a learned widower, Sir Justinian, who wrote Latin letters about her to his Oxford friends, and condescended to her own intellects. Thrice he made the attempt and was worsted, with a more laughing comment upon him each time in these private confidences; he is the butt among the lovers. There were numerous others, including one who had to have his letter thrown into the fire before his eyes, unread; and as they come and go they are successfully got rid of, though not without tribulation behind them. The brother, who was by and observing all, and taking a more or less active part, remembered them, and would bring them up in the quarrels with his sister, — all the lovers she had ever had, "like Richard the III.'s ghosts" to reproach her with. He was Temple's enemy in the fortress, and did not scruple to tell her once, in a heat, that her lover was without honor or religion, and would serve anywhere for advantage. But he had gone too far, and the brother and sister, who were esteemed as affectionate as any in England, did more than part with the "usual ceremony of a leg and a courtesy," which seems to have marked the worst of their disagreements; on this occasion he "renounced" her and she "defied" him. The reconciliation scene after this incident is a characteristic passage: "The next day, I, not being at dinner, saw him not till night; then he came into my chamber, where I supped, but he did not. Afterwards Mr. Gibson and he and I talked of indifferent things till all but we two went to bed. Then he sat half an hour and said not one word, nor I to him. At last, in a pitiful tone, 'Sister,' says he, 'I have heard you say that when anything troubles you, of all things you apprehend going to bed, because then it increases upon you, and you lie at the mercy of all your sad thought, which the silence and darkness of the night adds a horror to. I am at that pass now. I vow to God I would not endure another night like the last to gain a crown.' I, who resolved to take no notice what ailed him, said 't was a knowledge I had raised from my spleen only, and so fell into a discourse of melancholy and the causes, and from that (I know not how) into religion; and we talked so long of it and so devoutly that it laid all our anger; we grew to a calm and peace with all the world. Two hermits conversing in a cell they equally inhabit ne'er expressed more humble, charitable kindness one toward another than we. He asked my pardon and I his, and he has promised me never to speak of it to me while he lives, but to leave the event to God Almighty." It seems, however, that he still found room for his opposition to the match, notwithstanding this edifying scene.

Dorothy, in the midst of all this seeking in marriage, was still living quietly in the old house, so far out of the world that one would think of her as forgotten by it. She gives in one letter the history of her day, — and every day at Chicksands was the same: early rising;

the house and the garden; the "making me ready" about
ten; attending upon her father till dinner; the meal with
"cousin Molle" (a bachelor who spent his life in visit-
ing his relations) in a great room; reading or working
in the heat of the day; at six or seven the walk out on
to the "common that lies hard by the house, where a
great many wenches keep sheep and cows, and sit in the
shade singing of ballads"; some talk with them; then supper, — this is the course of each day's events; and at the
end, in the evening, comes this touch of sentiment, which
is too pretty and natural to be missed: "When I have
supped I go into the garden, and so to the side of a
small river that runs by it, where I sit down and wish
you with me (you had best say this is not kind, neither).
In earnest, 't is a pleasant place, and would be more so
to me if I had your company. I sit there sometimes till
I am lost with thinking; and were it not for some cruel
thoughts of the crossness of our fortunes that will not
let me sleep there, I should forget that there were such
a thing to be done as going to bed." It must have been
a rather lonely life; but there were neighbors, who called,
and occasionally Dorothy herself went to some near
country house for a dinner, at which she made shrewd
observations upon human nature and the whims of fortune. There were visitors at Chicksands occasionally,
but these were few. With such society and her books
— the French romances, Lady Newcastle's poems, "ten
times more extravagant than her dress," Pinto's travels, and the like — she passed her time; but writing
and receiving letters were evidently the most vital
matters. To give one more trifling scene, here is a lively
account of the coming of the mail in the days before
novels. The expected letter had not come, and with

this the extract begins: "The loss put me hugely out of
order, and you would have pitied and laughed at me if
you could have seen how woodenly I entertained the
widow, who came hither the day before, and surprised
me very much. Not being able to say anything, I got
her to cards, and then, with a great deal of patience,
lost my money to her, — or rather, I gave it as my
ransom. In the midst of our play, in comes my blessed boy
with your letter; and in earnest, I was not able to dis-
guise the joy it gave me, though one was by who is not
much your friend, and took notice of a blush that for my
life I could not keep back. I put up the letter in my
pocket, and made what haste I could to lose the money
I had left that I might take occasion to go fetch some
more," — in which purpose she succeeded, of course,
and made, she says, no haste back. These letters were
her life, and they show boldly and frankly her heart,
with the love that thinks not of concealment. Yet Temple seems to have been an exacting lover; or was it the
fashion of the day to complain of "unkindness," and turn
every trifle and torture phrases into lover's doubts?
This may pass with the remark that he was either very
jealous or very ardent. There came a period of real
trouble, however, when "in earnest," to use her pet
phrase, Dorothy was melancholy. Their trials had been
many, no doubt, and their union seemed as far distant
as ever. She was not one to let romance run away with
her, but would have their match seem prudent and made
with the consent of the families; and one Christmas-
tide, something, we know not what, occurred which
brought out all the difficulty of their situation, and
made the hopelessness of it bear more heavily upon her.
Temple seems to have been in some way to blame. At

all events, her courage breaks down, and she urges on him the worldly view of their position with all its force, and advises that they submit to circumstances; but in all this she seems to be pleading rather for his good than for herself. She makes the most devoted professions of her love and fidelity, but would not indulge a hope to the ruin of their lives. "Ah, if you love yourself or me, you must confess that I have reason to condemn this senseless passion, that wheresoe'er it comes destroys all that entertain it. Nothing of judgment or discretion can live with it, and it puts everything else out of order before it can find a place for itself. What has it brought my poor Lady Anne Blunt to? She is the talk of all the footmen and boys in the street, and will be company for them shortly, and yet is so blinded by her passion as not at all to perceive the misery she has brought herself to; and this fond love of hers has so rooted all sense of nature out of her heart that they say she is no more moved than a statue with the affliction of a father and mother that doted upon her, and had placed the comfort of their lives in her preferment." She reminds her lover that a thousand accidents might have taken her from him, and that then he would have done well, perhaps, to have placed his affections elsewhere. "There is a gentlewoman in this country that loved so passionately for six or seven years that her friends, who kept her from marrying, fearing her death, consented to it; and within half a year her husband died, which afflicted her so strongly nobody thought she would have lived. She saw no light but candles in three years, nor came abroad in five; and now that 't is some nine years past, she is passionately taken again with another." But these are old arguments of lovers' quarrels, and they had their

usual effect. The month passed away, and left the two
more securely bound.

This private matter, however, though it is the plot of
the story, does not monopolize it. These are by no means
conventional love-letters. Dorothy had a strong mind,
and took a lively interest in the affairs of society. She
complains, indeed, that since she came out of France she
had lost her gay spirits; she had the spleen, and occasionally drank the waters for it, and at home that infusion
of steel which was a bitter draught of the old medicine.
She refers many times to the criticism made upon her
by her friends that she was grave in demeanor, with a
certain stateliness of manner which was thought unamiable, but of the fault she says she is unconscious.
It plainly belonged to her strong nature, and the blending
of this strength with her frankness and good sense, together with the sprightliness of her pen, constitutes the
charm of the correspondence. She was well born, and
the gossip of society is frequently to be met with on the
page, but so presented as not to be tedious or frivolous.
There is a great deal of the comedy of manners and of
the pettiness of mankind in both sexes, of the humors
of country life and the folly of the fashionable world,
throughout the volume; this gives it great interest as
a picture of the life of the times. London, even, sometimes appears, with its Presbyterian dinners, its masks
at the gardens, the great duels, old Lilly the astrologist,
whom she interviewed and found a fool, and many little incidents which show how daily life went on. Stephen
Marshall, for example, was a great preacher; and this
is how she saw him: "God forgive me, I was so near
laughing yesterday when I should not. Would you
believe I had the grace to go hear a sermon upon a week-

day? In earnest, 't is true. A Mr. Marshall is the man
that preached, but never anybody was so defeated. He is
so famed that I expected rare things of him, and, seri-
ously, I listened to him as if he had been St. Paul; and
what do you think he told us? Why, that if there were
no queens, no lords, no ladies, nor gentlemen, nor gentle-
women, in the world, 't would be no loss to God Almighty
at all. This we had over some forty times, which made
me remember it, whether I would or not. The rest was
much at this rate, interlarded with the prettiest odd
phrases that I had the most ado to look soberly enough
for the place I was in that ever I had in my life. . . .
Yet I 'll say that for him, he stood stoutly for tithes."
An observation that ranges from the Presbyterian meet-
ing-house to Spring Gardens, from the maidens "singing
of ballads" to Lady Isabella Rich, from the foolish
squires, and booby husbands, and ridiculous widows of
the country to the Sidneys and Cromwells, affords wide
glimpses of seventeenth-century life; and to have all
this mirrored in the letters of a young lady of a strong
and vivacious mind, remarkable for womanly sense, and
herself one of the acknowledged ornaments of her
society, is great literary good-fortune. The charm, however, is nine tenths personal. Dorothy Osborne will be
the favorite of later times than her own. The soundness of the English nature was in her, and her letters
remind us how much of this survived through all the
eccentricities of the sects and the corruption of the courtiers, which together have monopolized the formal history
of the time, and given a warped impression of the nation.
It is a pleasure to find the story of her maiden life ending,
after all, in a marriage of the long-waiting lovers, even
the jealous brother joining in the business of the contract.

With the short notes preliminary to the wedding the correspondence ends. The life of the pair was happily and honorably lived, and in the single last letter, written late in life on a sad occasion, one finds the same qualities of mind and heart that have become familiar in the body of the volume.

A FRIEND OF GRAY

THE collection of the correspondence of the four friends (known at Eton as the "Quadruple Alliance"), Gray, Walpole, West, and Ashton, during their college days and the foreign tour of Gray and Walpole to the time of West's untimely death in 1742, at the age of twenty-six, is an interesting sidelight on Gray. Its object is really to set forth West's character and make a memorial of him. The material is drawn from Mitford's manuscript copies of the letters, and so much is added from previously published letters of West as will serve to make the correspondence continuous. West was highly valued by Gray, who meant to have collected his poems, but never did that pious labor. Mitford also seems to have intended to edit his remains. Mr. Tovey the editor has now accomplished this long deferred work, and, though the story is brief and slight, it has a literary as well as pathetic interest, and will be valued by those who care for Gray's circle of friends.

Of West's life no more is told than we knew before — that he was the son of Richard West, Chancellor of Ireland, and grandson of Bishop Burnet, attended Eton and Oxford, studied law without interest, and fell into consumption and died, after having the close of his life embittered by the knowledge that his mother, whom he loved, had been intrigued with by his father's secretary. Whether he was aware that his father's death was due to poison given by his mother is not certain;

but such a story is published by Mr. Gosse as coming through Dyce from Mitford. His letters, however, betray none of this tragic interest, except by the melancholy of their tone. They are made up of such pieces of college news, wishes for reunion, expressions of common literary interests, and other personal matters as one student at Oxford might send to his Eton friends at Cambridge, and they return the same in their answers. After college life was over there was little difference in the tenor of the correspondence as a whole, though the matter varies with the changed situation. The strain of personal affection is greater in West's letters to Gray, as his need was greater and his nature more tender; there is much restraint, however, in expression, and one finds in the entire collection of letters a certain refinement of personal behavior, a high breeding, which is very charming in effect. This is particularly true of West and Gray; Ashton was of coarser grain, and in Walpole one is more sensible of the man of the world's habit, or suspects its presence.

Whether or not West's few literary "Remains" detain one on their own account or for their relation to Gray, they serve to make West more substantial, to prove how much he had loved Milton and the more gentle Latin poets, to show a young poet's nourishing in that age as he followed his will among the classics, and the true and carefully wrought, if slight, performance of his learning hand; in his letters the nature of the man is more intimately and excellently shown, such as to win kind memory for him and not the least place among poets' friends. The balance of affection, one thinks, was more on his side than on Gray's, and the two saw little of each other after their boyish friendship at Eton.

The new material of Gray which follows, in the latter
half of the volume will be valued according to the
attachment of the reader to the poet. It has much of
curious interest, and one is thankful for this gathering of
the fragments that nothing be wasted. The journal of
the journey from Rome to Naples, in particular, is welcome. Most of the matter, however, is for the close
student of Gray, and need not be remarked upon in
detail. The editor corrects some errors in Mr. Gosse's
work, and restores some texts wrongly given by Mason.
His annotations are many, and seem thorough, though
he apologizes for not being more thorough. His estimate
of Gray's character is unusually good, by virtue of its
freshness, simplicity, and naturalness. He particularly
turns his face from the infelicitous conjectures of
Matthew Arnold, whose essay showed an activity of
imagination remarkable in the poet-critic. We are reminded, with regard to the text upon which Arnold
built, that it is not to be believed that "when good
Mr. Brown said of Gray that 'he never spoke out,' he
had anything in his mind but the fact that Gray did not
acknowledge to his friends how near he felt his end to
be"; and Mr. Tovey goes on to bring our minds back
to the obvious meaning of words, to the fact that his
melancholy was a kind of "leucocholy," that in "incidental treatment of public events he had about as
much 'high seriousness' as George Selwyn," that his
description of Pitt's eulogy on Wolfe (a cruel instance)
is in "the Walpolian not the Wordsworthian spirit,"
whence "to attribute *Weltschmerz* to him, or even any
uneasiness pointing that way, is the merest anachronism." He thinks that if Gray had been "born in the
same year with Milton," he would have been a "less

finished artist," but much the same man; and if "with Burns," then he would have written "less great poetry" and "perhaps more satirical verses and more prose."

In the way of literature, West sends his verses, Latin and English translation, and original, to Gray; and these, though not such as to foretell a real poet, show many good qualities of style framed under Latin influences, and though they have much of false taste derived from the age, exhibit talent and real taste, an occasional directness that might have become vigor, and sincerity of feeling. They are more interesting because they approach Gray, now a rather solitary figure, in their literary characteristics. They mirror, in a way, his early intellectual mood and immaturity. It may be fanciful if one seems to see here the classical influence leaving satire for ode in the development of English literature, the beginning of more personal feeling and a delight in nature, which were faint prophecies of a change in poetic style; but it would be natural to find such signs in Gray's environment. It may, perhaps, not be superfluous to refer, for the curiosity of the matter, to West's lines on the "Death of Queen Caroline," which Gray worked over into a famous stanza of the "Elegy":

"Ah me! what boots us all our boasted power,
    Our golden treasure and our purpled state?
    They cannot ward th' inevitable hour,
    Nor stay the fearful violence of Fate."

It is interesting to note, too, that a month before he died, West sent to Gray an "Ode to Spring" which was possibly the suggestion to him of his own ode, enclosed to West in a letter written just before learning of his sudden death.

The temper of Mr. Tovey's strictures upon the idealized figure of Arnold's inner consciousness is perfectly modest, and his remarks seem unusually sensible, and wholly untouched by that literary mood which impairs and often thoroughly vitiates judgments by literary men, of which Arnold's "Gray" is a conspicuous example.

A BIOGRAPHY OF CONGREVE

Mr. Gosse has the distinction of being the first biographer of Congreve. The trustworthy notices of his life are scanty, and especially wanting in the element of personal interest. Thackeray, it is true, built up a fine figure for us to have in our fancy when Congreve's name is on the lips, but he plainly outdid nature, and drew with the pen of the world's satirist, not of the literary investigator. Mr. Gosse holds this latter office. The range of his knowledge of the infinitely little is equaled only by the patience with which it has been acquired. He has a positive genius for the resurrection of dry bones, and, thanks to this, we have now a singularly excellent life of the wittiest English dramatist. It does not tell much about Congreve personally, because there is little to tell; but it corrects some misconceptions, fills up some blanks, reduces some dates to accuracy, and gives a just general conception of what Congreve was to his contemporaries; and, besides this, it sketches very completely the history of the stage during the poet's connection with it.

The most important modification made is that which destroys the notion that Congreve lived as a golden youth in a golden shower of sinecure offices. He had some patrimony and the income from his literary work, which was no doubt considerable, but his offices came slowly, after some tedious waiting; he complains that he has not enough "to have the few people that I love as near me as I want," speaks of the many "fair promises" that come to nothing, and invokes his philosophy to bear him out. A passage from Swift's poems points to anything but superfluous riches as his lot, and Swift thought it necessary to recommend him to the Lord Treasurer, when the change of parties came and Congreve was made anxious for fear he should be deprived of what little he had. Altogether, Mr. Gosse's view that Congreve is not to be considered rich until after he was forty, is so well supported that, in the absence of any positive facts to the contrary, it must be accepted.

But if he was not the favorite of fortune he has been depicted, he had his full share of favor. Whether his position, his friends, or his talents be regarded, he was at all points enviable. Dryden acknowledged him, with public praise as well as private kindness, as the heir-apparent to the literary throne; his youthful fame was immediate and great, and was grounded on such abilities as needed not to fear lest it should not be supported by mature genius; the town liked him, the literary circles were proud of him, and he had health, mind, and art in his own right. But he ended at thirty in the gout. Twenty-seven years more he lived, the victim of a broken constitution, in virtual retirement, with pain and partial blindness to afflict him, and intellectual tastes, friendships worth having, and at least £1,200 annually in sinecures to lighten his lot; but it was, after all, a failure. The best thing we know of him is that he kept his friends. There are many contemporary notices of his amiability, his good manners, his delightfulness socially; but without them we should know that the man in whose chambers Steele and Swift might have met, and Dennis and Pope might hope to be reconciled, was a liberal-minded gentleman, with tact and discretion enough to serve in any social emergency. The quarrels of the rest never disturbed the serene atmosphere of the rooms where they all liked to be. It is significant that he is called "unreproachful." He had kindness for all. When one remembers, moreover, that he was by common consent the wittiest man of his time in private talk, the wonder grows that he was so free from offence; for wit is as near akin to malice as pity is to love.

To complete the slight characterization, he was a good scholar and a man of pleasure. His genius was eminently intellectual. This comes out in his criticism, which shows studious cultivation and clear, keen thought. His remarks on the Pindaric ode belong to the best order of criticism, and were, moreover, serviceable: they mark the interregnum between Congreve and Gray, and prophesy the latter's verse-form. A surer sign of the intellectual base of his nature is that the one overmastering quality of his comedies is their style. Putting aside the wit and the life and the humanity (such as it is) that they contain, there remains still the exquisite charm of the words which fall upon the literary sense like honey from the honeycomb; nor would we hesitate to say that Congreve's style in the comedies has a quality as unique as Shakespeare's prose — a perfection of form seldom equaled and nowhere surpassed even by the great prose masters of his own age; not by Bolingbroke, nor by Swift, though their writings were on the grander scale. This is Congreve's distinction in our literature, that he has the most intellectual refinement of any of our comic dramatists and easily leads them; in fact, the purely intellectual element, both in the form and the interest, tends rather to the injury of his plays, which the theater found deficient in action. He was observer and satirist enough to be a dramatist, and he was, besides, a great writer so far as the mere art is concerned; he was, besides, something of a poet, and it is interesting to remark that he was really a student of verse-structure (as is proved by his criticism of the Pindarics), and derived from Milton, as Mr. Gosse thinks, some of his cadences in blank verse. This was while Milton's fame was in its nonage. It is more certain that his influence upon the blank verse which began with Thompson and expired in Wordsworth was considerable, and that Collins learned from him how to write odes, not scrupling even to imitate him with unmistakable directness. Nor is it without justification that a parallel has been made of Keats's famous lines —

> "Still, still to hear thy tender-taken breath,
> And so live ever, or else swoon to death" —

with Congreve's conclusion to the "Ode on Mrs. Arabella Hunt Singing":

> "Wishing forever in that state to lie,
> Forever to be dying so, yet never die."

Congreve's literary influence, although it must be acknowledged that the next age in poetry remembered him only to improve upon him, was far from insignificant, and he little deserved the contempt he has sometimes received. Nevertheless, the impression one has of him is of a genius which made only an imperfect expression of itself; of a man with more mind than his few comedies could hold, with tastes, culture, curiosity, a naturally fertile nature richly developed, but leaving no memorial of itself equal to its value. Ill health, in

connection with the laborious care with which he composed, is perhaps the secret of the matter; perhaps, too,
there was the indolence that goes with such superb
social gifts as Congreve delighted his companions with.
Or it may be that early fame had brought early ennui,
especially when the dramatist found his work was too
well done, too refined in quality to tickle the lungs of the
vulgar. He became sterile, and the activity of genius
gave way to the pleasures of taste. He was one of the
first to collect pictures in England.

In connection with the latter days of Congreve, one
should note the new turn which Mr. Gosse ingeniously
gives to the best known anecdote of the poet — that in
which Voltaire figures and replies to Congreve's hint
that he desired to be visited as a plain gentleman by
saying, "Had he been so unfortunate as to be a mere
gentleman, I should never have come to see him." Mr.
Gosse reminds us that Congreve had long been silent,
his literary ambition dead, and in its place, perhaps, an
old man's chagrin. If Congreve had really been a snob
of this sort, Mr. Gosse goes on, if he had "entertained
a mean idea of the literary profession, we should have
heard of it from Swift or Pope." That is certainly
very probable. Voltaire, in a word, mistook a modest
disclaimer of the compliments he had brought with him
for an insult to the literary profession. It is an interesting view of the conversation, and inasmuch as there is
no other evidence that Congreve preferred being "a plain
gentleman" to the fame which had flattered him when
Dryden handed down the laurel, one cannot but rejoice
to have so easy a defense. But no defense can serve
for our poet's abandonment of Mrs. Bracegirdle with
the paltry legacy and nothing can extenuate the mortal

comedy of his end as a *bon viveur* when the Duchess of Marlborough, whom he had made his heir, placed his waxen effigy at her table, so contrived as to nod when she spoke to it, wrapped its feet in cloths, and had a physician to attend upon it and render a daily diagnosis. With the seven thousand pounds remaining from the legacy, after this pleasant whim was satisfied, the young Duchess bought a diamond necklace. Mrs. Bracegirdle, the favorite of his early years, the woman for whom he had written the best of his characters and who shares his theatrical fame, was poor, but she shielded Congreve's memory by her silence, while the Duchess blazoned his infatuation by her diamonds. This was a death scene for a comic dramatist to observe.

ADDISON AND STEELE NEWLY
REVIEWED

Addison lies under more obligations to happy fortune than any other Englishman of high literary rank. Halifax saved him from the Church and the probable oblivion of a seat on the bench of bishops, and sent him to cultivate his genius by foreign travel. When, on his return, he seemed sinking into poverty, the same warm patron introduced him to Godolphin's notice and procured for him the inspiration of "The Campaign" in the shape of a promise of office. Throughout life, as thus in its opening, friends, admirers, employments, themes, and applause were found for him; and if in his death he had not the crowning favor of a good biographer, the defect was more than made up in later years by the luck of having Macaulay for his eulogist. It is not so long since those eloquent pages of the great essay declaimed of Addison's elevation and purity, his genius, his inestimable influence on English morals, and his superiority to Steele — "poor Dick," as Addison called him, well knowing his heart to be the warmest and most forgiving that beat with fidelity to his own. At the time, Macaulay's rhetoric, force, and fame bore down the feeble protests that strove here and there against the injustice and untruthfulness of the funeral oration he had pronounced over his predecessor in the Great-Mogulship of the middle classes. He had not, however, erased the name of "Atticus" — ah, if Addison had only escaped Pope's satire as nobly as Swift's jests! "Atticus" is a perpetual interrogation mark affixed to Addison's repute; it cannot be passed by; it tempts curiosity, it leads on to investigation, and the inquiry issues at last in a book like Mr. Courthope's study.

With all his sincere regard for his hero, and his regrets that there is nothing new to say, Mr. Courthope is a very candid biographer and frank critic. He strews the confessions of Addison's limitations along his pages instead of massing them, but they are all mentioned and defined. The early works, the translations, the "Account of the English Poets," the Latin verses are tenderly handled; the dust is hardly brushed off them. The opera, "Rosamond," is dismissed with the quotation from Dr. Burney that nothing more need be said of Addison's musical talent than that he was insensible to Handel and had a predilection for Clayton. The tragedy, "Cato" is bowed out on its merits, as owing its success solely to long-extinct party passions — a play in which "all the actors seem to be oppressed with an uneasy consciousness that they have a character to sustain, and are not confident of coming up to what is expected of them." The comedy, "The Drummer," is declared "a standing proof of Addison's deficiency in dramatic genius." Even as a poet, though a rally is made in favor of "The Campaign," Addison is suspected by Mr. Courthope of an "uneasy consciousness that he was really inferior to such men as John Phillips and Tickell." There is nothing left for Addison (of course he made no mark in Parliament or in his administrative offices) but to be found preëminent as an essayist; and yet Mr. Courthope, while acknowledging this necessity, can do plain justice to Steele:

"There is scarcely a department of essay-writing

developed in the 'Spectator' which does not trace its
origin to Steele. It is Steele who first ventures to raise
his voice against the prevailing dramatic taste of the age
on behalf of the superior morality and art of Shakespeare's plays. . . . Steele, too, it was who attacked,
with all the vigor of which he was capable, the fashionable vice of gambling. . . . The practice of duelling, also,
which had hitherto passed unreproved, was censured by
Steele. . . . The sketches of character studied from life,
and the letters from fictitious correspondents, . . .
appear roughly, but yet distinctly, drafted in the
'Tatler.' Even the papers of literary criticism, afterward so fully elaborated by Addison, are anticipated by
his friend, who may fairly claim the honor to have been
the first to speak with adequate respect of the genius of
Milton. In a word, whatever was perfected by Addison
was begun by Steele."

After Macaulay's studied depreciation of the origi-
nator and manager of the periodical form of the
eighteenth-century essayists, this is a very refreshing
passage, nor does it overstate Addison's debt to the fag
who idolized him from school-days. It is true that
Addison was master of a literary manner usually finer
than Steele's, though he had less heart, less earnestness,
less tenderness, less sympathetic humanity and practical
philanthropy. But the obligation to Steele should not be
understood to imply too much. Undoubtedly Addison
was far more effective in creating modern social public
opinion by teaching wit to be decent and virtue to be
amiable; by finding the true English mean between the
Court and the Puritans; by making good taste, good
sense, and good manners the characteristic ideal of the
commercial and professional middle class. When all is

said, that is the service he was really most instrumental
in accomplishing; but it is by its nature a passing one.
Sir Walter Scott did a very similar thing when he displaced the novels of the last age by his own; but the
value of this revolution is felt only by the historical
student. For posterity, Sir Walter's fame, like Addison's,
rests on the actual worth of his work to the new age as
it comes and goes. In Addison's case, while it is acknowledged that men ought not to cease to be mindful of the
humble beginnings by which they rise, nor forget to be
grateful to the pioneers of innocent literary amusement
and cultivated criticism, nevertheless it cannot be blinked
that the larger part of his work is at present essentially commonplace. A new Dr. Johnson might hesitate
to advise our youth to give their days and nights to
Addison; in fact, our youth do not read, nor perhaps
do they need to read, any of his sketches except the
"Roger de Coverley" papers and the "Tory Foxhunter."
The rest may be left, some to those who are still interested
in sedan chairs and link-boys, some to those who are curious about Boileau's standard and the properties, some to
those who do not yawn over homilies on cheerfulness.

What is the fascination that makes our men of letters
conceive a special liking for the things of Queen Anne's
reign? Thackeray is the embodiment of this partiality,
and he may have given a direction to Victorian taste;
but there is an original attraction in the age when
Bohemianism was classical, in the first of our literary
epochs to which we are admitted in undress, and especially in men so human that there is no presumption
in our thinking of the best of them oftentimes as of "the
friends who never could be ours." Austin Dobson is
under the spell; it has made him a seasoned *habitué* of

the haunts of Queen Anne's city. He knows his London
like an antiquary, and rebuilds it like a dramatist. The
strenuous exactness of modern biography, it is true, in-
terferes with the proper effects of theatrical art, the names
of the supernumeraries confuse the cast, the necessary
minutiæ of the action and episodes in corners crowd the
stage, and at the best it is only a chronicle play; but with
all this research and verification and detail of affairs
that cramp the literary hand at nearly every sentence,
Mr. Dobson's drawings have the lively truth of Steele's
own sketches of himself and the town. Something of this
vividness is due to taking many of the scenes *en bloc*
from Steele's confessions, — those autobiographic passages, so free from self-consciousness, which most endear
him, as they best paint him, to our thoughts. Such revelations, however, do not suffice for a biography, but must
be joined, and lighted up, and made to reflect upon one
another, and the other characters must be given their
right relation to the dialogue, and little anecdotes must
be told by the way; in all this there can be no aid from
Steele. By what felicity, for instance, shall the sem-
blance of a form be given to Mrs. Steele? Many a reader
must have shared our curiosity respecting her, and our
chagrin, also, at the ill-success of any efforts to get into
her good graces, if only so far as to obtain one fair view
of the domestic charmer to whom all those marital *billets-
doux* were sent. Who was she? — for that correspondence is like nothing so much as some torn romance, in
which one reads of only one lover. The biographer has
evoked her from the shades, unsubstantial, but at least
imaginable; he has even caught a glimpse of her, with
the mind's eye, still in "the indolent *sommeils du matin*
(dear to Millamant) of irresponsible maidenhood." He

first suggests her qualities: "As an unmarried woman she had been a beauty and a 'scornful lady,' to use the seventeenth-century synonym for a coquette, and she apparently continued to retain as a wife a good deal of that affected disdain and tenacity of worship which had characterized her as a spinster. She seems also to have been given to vapors, and variable beyond the license of her sex; and from her injunction to her husband, when choosing a house, to get one near a church, was probably something of a *dévoté*." Then, with literary tact, he concludes with a drawing quite in Thackeray's masculine manner: "The escape from impecuniosity is less easy for the woman than for the man. Steele, with his elastic vitality and his keen interest in human nature, could easily fling to the Cretan winds both Barbadoes and the bailiffs over a bottle with an opportune 'school-fellow from India.' But it must have been far otherwise for 'dearest Prue,' nursing the wreck of her expectations in tearful *tête-à-tête* with the sympathetic Mrs. Binns, or waiting nervously, in an atmosphere of Hungary water, for the long expected tidings that her husband's vaguely defined affairs were at last successfully composed." Such was "Prue," not without some traits of kindness for "good Dick," more than are indicated here.

As with the enigmatical and ever-retiring Lady Steele, so in a higher degree with the well-known persons and broadly flaunting fashions of the time, Mr. Dobson has the art of the literary limner. Addison and Swift, with the amiable gentlemen of the Guards, or the boards, or the public offices, Lord Cutts or Lord Finch, Estcourt or Mainwaring, or even her ladyship of various employments, Mrs. De la Rivière Manley, are continually gliding in and out; and the crowd of gamblers and duelists and

Mohawks of all kinds, the fops and gulls and boobies, the beaux and the fine madams, make up the busy background of the ever-frivolous town. It has sometimes seemed marvelous to us that such vitality resides in these old modes. Never was a literary work of high rank so burdened with mortality, one would think, as these "Tatlers" and "Spectators," and their sequent brood of ephemeral periodicals, interminably hatching, whose name truly was legion. If the comedy of manners is, as is said, necessarily short-lived, and satire does not survive its sting, and moralizing, however elegant, falls from the silver-lipped pulpit orator like lead to the ground, how is it that the fates have dealt so kindly with the Society-Circular that Steele edited, which is full of all such matter of decay? It lives, certainly, and still delights; and if the great reputation of Addison has made it classical, yet it is Steele's nature, as much as Addison's art, that keeps it whole and sound. Mr. Dobson continually reminds the reader of this, and rightly; for Addison's name has cast his loyal school-fellow's so much into the shade that it is with surprise that one comes upon such an encomium of Steele as is here quoted from Gay, in which the whole credit of the "Tatler," and the revolution of tastes and manners it began, is given with whole-souled vigor to the popular gazetteer. So welcome was Bickerstaff at tea-tables and assemblies, so "relished and caressed by the merchants on the Change," writes Gay, that "there is not a Lady at Court, nor a Banker in Lombard Street, who is not verily persuaded that Captain Steele is the greatest Scholar and best Casuist of any man in England." Steele deserved this praise, for he was not only the active and inventing principal in the venture, but to this day the humanity of his genius is as essential

to the immortality of the eighteenth-century essay as are
the contemplative benignity and the instinct for refining
the mind's creations which belonged to his more impos-
ing and more belauded associate. But let us not throw
stones at Addison, however unfairly the award of reputation may seem to have been made between the two
members of one of the most fortunate as well as famous,
literary partnerships; neither let us allow Steele to suffer too much by the humility of his affection, and the
readiness with which his own lips ran over with noble
compliments to his friend.

Criticism and biography, however, are very distinct
things; and Mr. Dobson invites and detains attention,
as he must that of any lover of literature who has felt
the glamour of that reign of Queen Anne's, not because
of his wise and kindly discrimination between the work
and genius of the two fraternal essayists, and his nice
allotments of place and fame to each; nor because of the
revival of the temporalities of the theater, the coffee-
house, the Parliament, the house in Bloomsbury Square,
and the box at Hampton-Wick, with all their belongings;
but because here is the life of a man who may properly
be inscribed as Mr. Dobson inscribes him, among English Worthies, who was, over and above all else, the
most humane, the most winning and cheerful heart in
the literary England of his time.

The discovery of Steele in the character of an English Worthy, instead of Man of Letters, has a touch of
the same humorous surprise in it that his comrades of
the mess must have felt at his original appearance in
literature as "The Christian Hero." In his own day he
found it a hard matter to deserve that reputation — to
be a wit of the coffee-house was the easy thing; now the

tables are turned, and the too humanly complying Captain of the Life-Guards, denied the boon companionship of Swift and Addison under the literary editing of our century, turns up among the worshipfuls. His heart would swell with the new title, could he be made to think it belonged to him. Mr. Dobson does his best to make the reader think so. He knows very well, however, that his is not the usual task of the biographer of a previous age, merely to evoke the spirit of a dead mortal: the historian and the novelist have been beforehand with him, and when the literary imagination has seized upon a character of the past, truth has as little chance against its illusions as against a popular hero. Macaulay's sinister dislike and Thackeray's warm affection have created a Steele for us; and different as their judgments are, the divergence springs rather from their temperaments than from their conceptions of the culprit's career. Mr. Dobson suggests that Steele, in this character of the culprit, whether graceless or humbly apologetic, is not a justifiable representation of the whole man, and that the flings of the one and the condonements of the other of the great literary portrait painters are too much in one tone of color. For himself, he has tried, though against tremendous rhetorical odds, to give us only a natural picture.

Had it not been for some intricacies in his career, and the entanglement of his fame in consequence of that famous foreign alliance by which he called Addison to his aid, Steele's character would never have seemed anything but simple. It is not even rare, except for the excess of its attractiveness and the subtle power which the literary gift seems to blend with the other elements of human nature. Indeed, Thackeray was able to idealize it so plausibly because it approaches so near to a general type. Mr. Dobson analyzes it briefly into a weak will and an honest purpose; and this conjunction, as in the case of other people, frequently brought Steele into trouble. Furthermore, his own lips and the lips of his enemies, and fortune in the shape of hundreds of his familiar letters, made his affairs the open gossip of Queen Anne's tavern and our own libraries. It was perhaps a disadvantage to him that he always "owned up" and ate humble pie. His reputation affords a striking instance of the damaging effects of self-depreciation, not only in his life, but in literature. Of the trio, Swift had more mind, Addison more cultivation — vastly more; and Steele was as destitute of the contemplative serenity of the one as of the intellectual fury of the other. But he was distinguished from both as being the man of heart, the lovable one, the one "like unto ourselves." Mr. Dobson has indicated this primary quality in Steele while discussing Addison's superiority as a "classical" writer; "but," he says, "for words which the heart finds when the head is seeking; for phrases glowing with the white heat of a generous emotion; for sentences which throb and tingle with manly pity or courageous indignation, we must turn to the essays of Steele." Style, of this sort, is one of the great virtues of a writer.

Nor did Steele lack a second great virtue, invention. If one were disposed to cavil, he might smile at this, and remind us of the search Steele made in the beginning of his career for the philosopher's stone, and of the fish-pool patent he took out at the end of it; and truly he had his share of the follies that attend projectors, among whom he is placed by his fertility and the restless practical energy that belonged to his mercurial tem-

perament. But the eighteenth-century essay was a pro-
ject of another sort, and Steele did originate and conduct
it — one of the distinct historic forms of English literature; and, moreover, this involved the invention of light
social satire, domestic genre-painting, and all the other
forms in which he was the adventurer before Addison
came to occupy the land. Though the country perpet-
uated the name of Americus, let us remember who discovered it. And Steele, in doing this, was not only the
forerunner of Addison, to whom at his best he is superior in feeling as at his worst he is inferior in finish; he
wrote what Goldsmith read, and ushered in the novelists.
But one should not push too far the advantage a man
holds by virtue of his historical position in the tendency
of a literary age, nor, on the other hand too readily fall
into the strain of those writers whose papers on
Steele are made up of apologies and claims. It
is so natural to love Steele, and to feel that in
the world's hurly-burly for justice he is irretrievably the under-dog, that one's pen pleads for
him before the head is aware, and, like Lord Finch,
"could fight for this man."

Mr. Dobson masks his batteries, but they are there,
and they play silent havoc on all those who have undervalued Steele's part in the Queen Anne time, whether in
the hen-pecking manner of Macaulay or with the patronizing charity of our much-beloved Thackeray. It be-
hooves the reader to be wary, or he may suddenly be
believing that possibly Steele was a better man than he
thought himself; that the political fervor which made him
a partisan, and drew the rancor of faction on his name,
was patriotic duty; that the moral sense which made him
denounce gamblers and duelling, his indignation at wrong,

his pity for the suffering, and the quick alliance of his sympathy with the weak, which made him in no sentimental sense the friend of humanity, — and especially that his loyalty to an ideal yet human virtue, which made him such a censor of the town that he pleased them with the wholesome truth about themselves — the reader may begin to know that these are in fact the traits of an English Worthy, and not of the traditional Culprit, the Steele of fiction. He may even find himself admiring him; and if at the end, when all is done, and the pretty Welsh scene near the death, and the dance afterpiece which Mr. Dobson provides are both over, he coolly remembers the Captain of Life-Guards and the Lover-Gazetteer and the Sir Knight at Edinburgh, and cannot quite make up his mind that Steele was a hero, after all, yet he will surely think of him more truthfully, and recognize in him more manhood. That one prefers to think of him as a man of letters, with the failings and brilliancies and the human charm that belong to that quality, is no diminution of praise.

This is the first true life of him, written fully and with sympathy and judgment at once. Steele himself is its subject; and he is found to be as much a man of affairs as of letters. He was, of course, born with the "gift"; but he seems to have employed it usually in the service of life, and on some occasion more pressing than the ordinary call of pure literature to the young man to sit down and write. He was always busy, almost continuously a place-holder, and generally entangled besides with private embarrassments, growing out of his unrealizable fortunes. He had leisure to observe the world, nevertheless, and he was filled from his earliest literary days, at any rate, with a missionary fervor to reform

first his own morals and then those of his fellows and
of the town. He had a quick eye, and an impulsive pen
was a good second to an impressible heart. The comedies, the essays, and the tracts tell the rest of the story,
so far as literature is interested. In politics and in all
the relations of private life, he acted, at the critical
points, with courage, feeling, and honor, whether toward
Swift, or Oxford, or Addison. He has written his own
domestic and social character where all the world can
read it. He suffered from an irresistible temptation to
make a clean breast of all his transgressions, on the slight-
est provocation; and this quality together with the flings
of faction at his private name, have laid his weaknesses
bare. These Mr. Dobson does not conceal; he does not
probe them with respectable morality, nor cover them with
patronizing solicitude, but toward the close of his account
of a most manly life, so far as purpose, conscience, and
honest effort go, he writes down explicitly the obvious
truth that there "have been wiser, stronger, greater men";
but he adds the graceful words, — "Many a strong man
would have been stronger for a touch of Steele's indul-
gent sympathy; many a great man has wanted his genuine largeness of heart; many a wise man might learn
something from his deep and wide humanity. His virtues redeemed his frailties. He was thoroughly amiable,
kindly, and generous. *Faute d'archanges il faut aimer
des créatures imparfaites.*"

CULTURE OF THE OLD SCHOOL

THE "Gentleman's Magazine," — both the name and the thing belong to a bygone time. A hundred and more years ago the magazine was the property of cultivated persons, just as later on it was the reviewers', and now is the people's. *Quanto mutatus*, one involuntarily falls into saying not with regret, but because in consequence of this change there is in the opening volumes of the series that is to preserve the salvage of the wealthiest periodical in English a peculiar quality, not perhaps to be called classical, but analogous thereto, — a unique mark, the seal and the brand that suggest age and arouse whatever instincts of literary epicurism linger among us. The best, the characteristic, portions of this serial are nearer the Queen Anne than the Victorian style, both in literature and in social traits. In many a passage one feels that Addison is not far off, and that Macaulay, who was the first true heir of his high and mighty seat on the throne of the British middle class, is as yet unthought of. Something of the variety that is essential to a complete impression of the tastes of our reading great-grandsires is lost by the method of grouping the extracts by topics; the virtuoso's collection thus provided misses the charm of being random and helter-skelter, as in the crowded rooms of Walpole's wonderful treasury of bric-a-brac at Strawberry Hill, but the modern editor of a scientific age must classify his specimens and sort each to its own case, just as he adds an index to the end. These

volumes are less books of reference than sources of amusement and information, not about things as they are, but
about the light in which the old masters of the liberal
arts once saw them; if one can only get a fair look
into their wainscoted studies, that will be enough for one
day.

The old *magistri liberalium artium,* indeed, they were;
though, as standards now run, they were an unscholarly
lot. Yet with what an air they wore their patches of
Roman learning! With what a natural ease and the
amiable vanity of an antiquary, as they looked on at the
rural sports and traditionary customs of the yeomanry,
would they warm their memories with reminiscences of
the festal days and rites they had read of in Ovid!
The mythology of antiquity was their "open sesame" to
the curiosities of May-day and weddings and harvest
homes. The modern investigator smiles at their apt
quotations from the classics, and from the Welsh or
Scottish scene described his thoughts fly farther and
wider to the old Erse laws, the hill-country of primitive
India, and the raids of Australian aborigines in the
obscure region of the lowest savagery. Learning with
us is a pursuit instead of a pastime; the men of the last
century were nearer the facts (for the ancient English
customs are now fallen into disuse, and shun our eyes),
but we are much nearer the theories, and so the student
will fancy that he now attends only to what the old
scholars observed, and may skip what they thought.
There is truly a mine of observations in these books
with regard to country manners that were then to be seen
as periodically as the seasons themselves. Many of the
contributors seem to have lived in the country, — clergymen, one thinks, for the most part; and they had an eye

for the old and the picturesque in the people's life, and were as much interested in such finds as some of us are in unearthing Indian relics. No inconsiderable part of the charm of these pages lies in their passing but vivid disclosure of some old English sight. One passage, in particular, is so fine a bit in the old manner, as given in the familiar yet well-bred style of the letters of that period, that we cannot forbear quoting it at length. *Tempus; Anno Domini* 1793.

"Passing along that beautiful range of valleys between Bradford in Yorkshire to Kendal, we saw a number of country people rush out of a church founded upon a pleasant hill, and immediately the bells chimed most merrily. We desired the coachman to stop in the village underneath, till the group approached, following a new-married couple: — the whole bedizened with ribbons, — the bride most glaringly so, — large true-blue bows were across the full of her breast, lessening till they reached the waist; white, red, and every other color were conspicuous about her gown and hat, except forsaken green, which I was glad to perceive was not worn by one of the throng. It would have gladdened any heart to have seen them striking down the hill, — such kissing, and such romping, and such laughter, I never heard or saw before. Rustic happiness was afloat; the girl's faces were tinged beyond their native bloom, and the maidens' blush enlivened the lilies around them. The men's legs and arms were as busy as if they had hung on wires. In an instant half a dozen youths pulled off their shoes and stockings, when I noticed their legs had been previously girt with party-colored ribbons. On being started by the bride, they spanked off as hard as they could, amidst the whoops of the young and old. This I understand is a

race of kisses: and he who first reaches the bride's house
is rewarded with a kiss and a ribbon. If they were to
have been rewarded with a bag of gold, they could not
have looked more eager; they took different roads (without heeding the rough stones they had to encounter),
and which we were told were previously agreed upon,
in proportion to the known swiftness of the candidates.
We regretted that we could not stay to see the result of
this Hymenean race; and left them in the midst of their
mirth, after a donation which would not take from it,
but which was only received, on condition of mutually
drinking healths, and our accepting a ribbon apiece. I
got upon the top of the coach to look at them as long as
I could. Marrowbones and cleavers could not express
half the hilarity which we witnessed; and when the coach
set off they gave us *breastsfull* of huzzas. We answered
them with such sincerity, I shall have a twist in my hat
as long as it lasts; and for some time after we left them,
we heard bursts of noise.   A RAMBLER."

Dick Steele would have welcomed such a correspondent, and given the scene the immortality of a page of
the "Tatler," at least, and that was the most he could
confer.

This spirit of geniality, together with the landscape
that makes so fit a background for the antiquarian lore,
gives one constantly the sense of being in pleasant company, with a touch of oddity in the people. One would
like to meet a man who found an absorbing interest in
the history of signboards, and took pains to catalogue all
that were in his neighborhood or had been swinging there
within the memory of men; and even a modern Shakespearean scholar, although he stands aghast at the etymol-
ogies of his fathers, must experience some fellow-feeling

with the correspondent who tried to crack that nut of "leading apes in hell" with which Beatrice still puzzles the commentators. The frequency of references to Shakespeare, too, by these Englishmen before Schlegel is very gratifying, with its ample proof of the enormity of that pretentious falsehood which declares that the Germans discovered Shakespeare for us. Our ancestors knew a good play as well as good ale, and that they were seldom deceived is tolerably clear to those of us who have worried through the reprints of the comedies and tragedies they damned. Shakespeare had a place in their minds with Lucan and Virgil, because they were educated to seek for worth, and what they gathered passed into their lives and became related to things about them; now, knowledge is the cry, and a large part of what is recovered seems meant only to pass into libraries, and be stood up there as the Egyptians embalmed the dead. Thus, considered generally, these volumes bring home to the mind very sharply the change in the temper of our scholarly class. A literary instead of a scientific spirit informs them; cultivation as contradistinguished from exact knowledge is the trait that especially belongs to the writers in them; in other words, they are a fine illustration of the culture of the old school.

The peculiar propriety of the old word for the branches of a liberal education, "the humanities," is thus one of the striking impressions made by the perusal of most of the work. The interest of the author in his subject is generally not due to any cultivation of the historical sense, which makes time long past an object of curiosity as ardent as is felt in contemporary affairs; some fact of experience instead of one of book-learning is the source of his little essay, or note, or query, as the case may be,

and his limited stock of information is drawn upon only
to illustrate and elucidate the matter in hand. Possibly
one is now and then reminded of our old and delightful
friend the Antiquary himself, and how he found the lines
of the Roman *castra* and quoted his polysyllabic author-
ities apropos thereof, when the beggarly Ochiltree could
have told him in good broad Scotch the facts about his
mare's nest, and so spared him his Latin; but the exhibit
of learning is occasioned in the same way by something
seen or heard, and comes as naturally in place as gen-
ealogies to the lips of country gossips when an old man
dies. These parish clergymen, who read with interest
the forms and ceremonies of the Biddings to Welsh
marriages, might have felt a less lively curiosity about
the kingdom of the Hittites that Professor Sayce has
rescued from the maw of oblivion; and they, we dare
say, would try much harder to intrepret that curious
letter in the Shetland dialect, or to get the exact sense
of the "Exmoor Courtship," than to translate cuneiform
inscriptions or enjoy the love-songs of the Egyptians
before Moses, as we have them now in that very valuable
collection of the leaflets of antiquity published as "Records of the Past." Not that there was no true learning in
those easy-going days, nor any lack of an enlightened interest in it; but men who were merely cultivated had
a narrower range, and did not trouble themselves much
with what did not in some way come with warmth to
their hearts and have a personal value to them;
and even the men of widest acquisitions wore their
learning, as Milton did, like a panoply in which
to endure themselves when the controversial giant
should appear on the other side. Now we go
light-armed, and if any fray arises, take an index

and write our rejoiner by its aid. Beside those great battles that used to be waged, our modern contests seem mere fencing-bouts. We do not carry what we know about with us any more, whether it be much or little, but put it into a dictionary for reference. In other words, knowledge has been becoming more and more impersonal, just as scholarship has gradually taken on a professional character. One smiles at the very suggestion of an Englishman of the old school taking a "disinterested" view in any matter; and disinterestedness, as we are told, is the essence of the modern scholarly ideal. A student nowadays is much like a lawyer or docter: he makes an investigation and writes a book as they examine and conduct a case, and when he is through with his task the volume is put on the shelves, and he goes on to a new work as they to a fresh client or patient. Nor does the frame of mind in which he goes through the routine of research differ much from that of his brethren at the bar; for his pursuit is to him a business, and is as disconnected with his own affairs as is the case with the others. Scholarship is in fact already one of the professions, and its votaries, who were once nearer the literary, are now nearer the scientific class. As a consequence, learning, which was once truly, like poetry, a part of culture, is passing over to that division where it becomes, like the study of the law or of medicine, merely an item of civilization; it ceases to be a thing that can be incorporated into the body and substance of our lives, and now constitutes a part of those possessions of society in common with which the individual is concerned not continuously nor for his own sake alone, but incidentally and as a social being. An obscure perception of this change underlies the opposition to classical studies, which in becoming largely the apparatus of a profession have lost their character of being modes of culture. Even the undergraduate does not need a very thorough acquaintance with the books and conversations of the gentlemen of the old school in order to conclude quite certainly that if he knows more Latin they knew vastly more Horace. In our academies and colleges the language is taught as never before, but the old boys of Eton and Harvard learned what the language was used for, and that was their great gain. The whole literature of the eighteenth century proves how truly the classics were appropriated then by those who read them; and when an elegant writer of compliments now and then pleasantly mentions "our own Waller," the accent of the phrase discloses a state of education, of literary standards and modes of comparison, very different from any that now obtain either here or in England. It is not that the humanities have lost their humanizing power, but that they are inculcated as sciences. Culture must always be literary, but the classics, in consequence of the change in the ideal of scholarship, have become philology, antiquities, and cognate branches of research. This subject, however, is too broad and too old a one, and is in a fair way to be settled, willy-nilly, by the logic of social needs. It is glanced at here, because the older contributors to the "Gentleman's Magazine," and by inference the far larger number of its readers, exhibit admirably the strength and weakness of that old culture, so living, personal, familiar, so uninterruptedly entering into daily interests, so at ease with itself, and, with all the limitations that made it parish-like, so essentially humane. What is to be in the place of it, what a gentleman may be assumed to know and how he shall bear his knowledge, belongs to the future, since at present the intellectual furniture of a well-bred man, beyond a conversational acquaintance with the talk of the hour, is a matter almost of haphazard, an unlimited curiosity being perhaps his most useful trait; but let the education of the next age be what it will, it can hardly make men more agreeable, refined, and truly enlightened than were the gentlemen bred under the old régime, nor leave a pleasanter tradition behind it than flavors the pages of their monthly.

From what has been said it will be thought quite rightly that these are volumes to be read in by a winter fire, and not studied. The seeker after facts will take the books of latest authority, which the editor has been careful to list in his prefaces as furnishing the necessary corrections to the vagaries of the old-fashioned text, and find in them the knowledge he desires; but when study grows wearisome, he can scarcely have better diversion, nor one more consonant with his tastes, than in the rambling and gossipy antiquarianism of the body of the volumes. On the whole, one cannot more easily characterize their contents than as the literature that old men are especially fond of; for the instinct of the antiquary can hardly consist with the sense of utility so engrossing in young minds. In fact, too, one must have some spice of the old culture in order to enjoy the magazine that flourished under its influence; he cannot otherwise be placed *en rapport* with it. The list of the London pageants, for example, will be dry unless one is already attached to the memory of those parades, and can imagine from a hint the moving *tableaux vivants* of the trades; and no inconsiderable part of the attraction there is in discussion of proverbial sayings, village customs, and disused games lies in the familiarity they have acquired by being mentioned in our old dramatic literature, or memoirs, diaries, and letters. The local coloring that was unconsciously put upon their works by the writers of a former day, before it became a recognized element in the novelist's art, is brightened, and the blurred and faded spots are restored by the reminiscences and survivals of ancient customs and the descriptions of forgotten things that are gathered here as in a final repository. Next to the very valuable record of traditional usages in the life of the country people, the dialect pieces seem of most interest and best worth reprinting, from the view of modern scholarship, though they add little to the collections of the Dialect Society. When it is remembered that Gibbon first proposed the scheme that is now, almost a century later, being carried out, the vitality of the interest the series has seems beyond question; and, after all, he will be a dull reader who does not find in it, however much he may smile at its unscientific character, something more than the most complete and varied expression of the spirit that breathed in the now discredited education that bred Gray and Joseph Spence and John Evelyn.

NOTES ON THE
SEVENTEENTH CENTURY POETS: A
COLLEGE SYLLABUS

THE Fletchers, Phineas (1582-164?) and Giles (1588?-1622), stand in literary development between Spenser and Milton. Elizabethan verse is distinguished by a certain clarity of tone in sound and melody; it takes on nobleness when the subject is noble and becomes sweet when the subject is sweet. In Spenser these two strains perpetually interchange and blend, and constitute his peculiar charm of vocal expression. In the Fletchers this Spenserian blend still persists, and in Milton's youthful verse it survives. In other poets there is a separate two-fold development. In the intellectual poets the noble strain remained, but lost fullness of melody and rang hard; in the amatory or cavalier poets the sweet strain lost charm and its naïveté, and became affected and gallant, acquiring more and more the accent of society. This gradual fading out of the music of poetry in the seventeenth century until lyric verse was hardly more than a theatrical air in the Restoration days, is a most noticeable incident.

The Fletchers are distinctively religious poets, as their manner of handling the theme is pre-Elizabethan. The drama developed rapidly out of allegorical and abstract into entirely human forms, and in Shakespeare this humanization is complete. The same movement in religious poetry took place more slowly. Spenser like Sack-

ville works by impersonation of moral qualities viewed
abstractly; the Fletchers employ the same method, which
gives a remote and often fantastic character to their
work; nor was the moral and religious narrative truly
humanized until Milton carried it to its proper art-
culmination in his epic. Religious poetry, in the earlier
period of the Fletchers, sought imperfect humanization
in two ways: first, by laying stress on incidents in the
Life of our Lord, such as the Nativity, the Resurrection,
either in narrative or meditative expression, — and of
this sort are the youthful poems of Milton on these
subjects, which he treated in common with many other
Christian poets; secondly, by ecstasy, rendered through
sensuous imagery of the ardor and beauty of passion
under the types of Bride and Bridegroom. The Song of
Solomon is the model of the latter; its mood is Oriental,
and it arises especially in southern races and in emotional
Catholicism everywhere, of which a modern instance is
the late Coventry Patmore. To us, generally, the effect
is that of a singular and foreign trait, and is distasteful;
but the kind can be easily understood by comparing the
conclusion of the "Purple Island" with Spenser's "Epi-
thalamion," or by reading the description of Christ in
the "Triumph." Milton shows no trace of this method of
rendering religious emotion more concrete. In reading
the Fletchers, these points should be borne in mind; and
their relation to Spenser in versification, in sensuousness,
in moral feeling and method, in pastoral taste, and their
relation to Milton in what they suggested to him in
imagery and phrase, and their influence on him in less
defined ways should be carefully followed out.

Drummond of Hawthornden (1585-1649), a Scotch
gentleman of cosmopolitan literary culture, which isolated

and distinguished him among his countrymen, was in the line of English tradition the descendant of Sidney. In external interests, his letters recording his visit to London, 1605, show Sidneian traits. The love poems, especially his sonnets, which record a real passion, show direct modeling on the "Astrophel and Stella" series; they also show, in structure, the influence of Petrarch. Italian literature was formative in him in other ways, and much of his work is directly imitative of, or translated from, Marini and Guarini. In his love poems he is thus regarded as a Sidneian modified by later immediate Italian models in addition to the common Petrarchism of the sonnet everywhere. The fantastic, that is, the excessive emphasis of the artificial element in form, is a trait of the time that takes on many shapes. It is to be readily illustrated by the formal taste in gardening. It also appears curiously in the shapes of love-knots, temples, altars, and the like, shown on the printed page by arranging the types in these emblematic forms, as in Browne and Herbert. It is made manifest intellectually by the addiction of the poets to conceits, so-called, a fashion most marked in Italy and thence affecting the literary world. This should be noted in Drummond, but in him it seems a transplanted and conventional style, and cannot be said to be naturalized, as it is in Herbert and Donne.

There was a strong infusion of Platonism, intellectual mysticism, in the reflective poetry of the entire period. It is illustrated in Drummond by the prose piece, "The Cypress Grove."

There is also in the poetry of the entire period a certain domain which is occupied by coarseness different from the Elizabethan coarseness. It appears to me to be derived from or modeled on the Latin classics and the writers of the Italian Renaissance. It is not native English, but academic and learned; the Latin classics, as in controversy they encouraged vituperation and grossness, seem to have induced in verse foully worded expression of physically brutal ideas and imaginations; and the literature of Italian humanism aided and abetted this rude taste. Scholars and gentlemen appear to have felt no shame in writing stanzas that had a precedent in Latin. Such passages and poems are in Drummond, as well as in Herrick and Donne. The taste in these poets seems to me literary, a product of culture in depraved books, and not indigenous to English soil.

In Drummond there are apparently irreconcilable elements — refined Sidneian eloquence and passion, sensual thought and wit which Sidney cannot be believed to have tolerated, religious feeling, and Platonic speculation, showing the heterogeneity of his culture; he is to be remembered as a courtier and scholar, tolerant among the fanatic Scotch sects, a friend of the King and writer of political pamphlets, singularly unlike all his neighbors, and, in literary ways, as the friend of Alexander and Drayton, and the host of Ben Jonson, whose conversations with Drummond are recorded and should be read.

William Browne (1591?-1645). The poet of "Brittania's Pastorals" continues the pastoral tradition of Sidney (he was a protégé of the Herberts) and of Spenser, in a fluent literary way without the accent of distinction of the one or that of supreme beauty of the other. He was precocious, and the friend of poets and scholars, well thought of and well beloved; he illustrates the charm and hopefulness of the fertile abundance of extremely youthful talent; he has stylistic sweetness and frequent

felicity in line effects; in holding the thread of an endless maze of pleasantly monotonous narrative (but with
next to no human interest) he recalls William Morris;
in fatuity of rustic illustration, without the sense of what
is either trivial, paltry or humorous, he recalls Wordsworth at his inexplicable worst; and yet, though there is
nothing that he wrote which it is necessary for mortal
man to read, he pleases in a kind of "bodiless creation"
of "Acadia," with occasional passages of natural description and joy in the country and scenes from Devonshire
days that are human.

Donne (1573-1631) was the chief of the metaphysical school, so-called. It has for some years been an intellectual affectation to admire him. He wrote some
satires, which are rude, probably intentionally, as thereby resembling Roman exemplars; these, re-wrought by
Pope, kept his name alive at one time. In his poems,
much the best and most characteristic of his work, he is
noticeable for the eccentricity, extravagance and tor-
tured ingenuity of his conceits. These conceits, in his
case, have a real intellectual or imaginative meaning.
All his poems yield illustrations. He was a profligate in
youth and in later years a clergyman. He was a writer
of religious verse also, more philosophical than theological or pious; he united, without blending, the sensual
and intellectual, the mystical and matter-of-fact. He
may be analyzed as a fine intellect united to a coarse
physique, and the fruit of the union is, artistically and
morally, hybrid. Such beauty as he has is partial and in
spots, and neighbors too nearly his defects, like soft eyes
in some loathly or unbeautiful creature. Tastelessness,
however, in diction, abnormality in image and recon-
diteness in thought, a pervading unevenness as of some

ill-made elaborately curious construction, characterize all the school; but to some minds this singularity is attractive. This view is an extreme one, and other views will be found in essays that see only the substance of thought and imagination and do not appear to be affected by any disgust in their concrete rendering or any displeasure in their artistic dryness and involution.

Herbert (1593-1633) was a poet of the English Church and is so remembered; his "Temple," like Keble's "Christian Year," is a Church poem. His career and personality are interesting for human qualities, independently of his being a poet. He was well born, bred by his mother, and brought up an Oxford man, made orator to the University and had hopes of advancement through court friends high in power. He neighbors the cavalier type of gentleman, with fine address and manners, a liking for good clothes, with enough of the world in him to have been the making of a worldly prelate under unfavorable circumstances of temptation. His hopes perished with the accession of Charles I., and he was turned into a more humble career as a simple clergyman, almost saintly in the end of his life, and dying a pure Christian. In his poems the characteristics of the age in poetry are marked: the conceits, the tastelessness in diction, the intellectual, fantastic and uneven traits are all there; but the humility, the self-abasement, the real conflict in the religious sphere of experience are there, too, and especially a spirituality of unusual purity, simplicity, sincerity, depth, lacking intensity and passion, perhaps, but with the mark of suffering and the healing touch of comfort. The faults of his work are contemporary and external; one must pass into his spirit by

the keys of experience. In minor matters one notices
how slight his hold is on the things of nature; though
there is country feeling, there is no landscape or nature-
atmosphere in him, only a delight in the most obvious
details of natural life, like the bird's song and the Sab-
bath weather; one notices, too, strength and justness of
thought, a real intellectual element, though eccentric and
ingenious in its operation, — which is expressed by saying that the quaintness characteristic of him is one of
thought as well as of image and phrase; but all these
things are fused, and find their artistic wholeness in his
spirituality.

Vaughan (1621-1695) was in the line of descent
poetically from Herbert, and, though less known, is but
little inferior in the best traits. He was in early life an
amorous poet, but his fame lies in his religious verse.
He was, in style, related to the prevailing school of conceits but less extravagant on the whole; he has the
common faults of over-wrought ingenuity in thought and
image, of uneven imaginative force, of tasteless diction;
but he has a singular majesty in world-imagery and in
rendering our apprehension of the divine, singular pathos
in his nature-sympathy with birds and trees and the
detail of living things of the earth, and singular grace
and tenderness in dealing with human grief, whether of
bereavement or of repentance, and its consolations. He
was, too, a Platonist (all of this Platonism should be connected with that of Spenser in his "Hymns"). The place
that the stars and constellations fill in his verse is noticeable; scarce any other English poet is so "starry." To
me he has for many years been a solace and refuge; in
poetic beauty of detail, in freshness and sincerity of
phrase, in his mood of submission mixed with aspiration,

in his atmosphere of peace—the clearness of his heavenly horizon—in the spontaneity of his spiritual fountains, he exercises charm over me, but in this there may be something personal; he is less literary, in a way, than Herbert, less bookish and cloistral, and in style and matter criticism would place him lower, but he makes the personal appeal in a more intimate way.   There is none of these religious poets that it would give me more pleasure to know that students liked.

Crashaw (1612-1650) was a royalist, a friend of Cowley and in the exiled Queen's Court, who finally became a Roman Catholic and died a canon of San Loretto at Rome.   Crashaw was also like Vaughan of kin to Herbert, and like all the school has the faults noted of thought, image, and diction.   He had more of the enthusiam of the poetical genius than any of these poets. He was especially sympathetic with music, and in his secular poetry one should read "Music's Duel," and also "Wishes: to his supposed mistress."   His characteristic or peculiar poetry is religious; and he exemplifies that use of the language of love-passion to interpret religious emotion, noted above, in a form which might, if any can, reconcile the colder and more disembodied religious emotion of the northern clime to this mode of interpretation. The language is that of love-passion but directed to supersensual objects of desire.   This is the graceful and pure form of that which in Donne seems harsh and impure; and to appreciate it is a lesson in innocence. The poem "Prayer" is an illustration.   The "Nativity" should be compared with Milton's "Hymn."   One should notice in all the verse the spring, the abundance, the unceasing and voluble melody, together with the heat, the suffusion of warmth of passion, the color and clear tone of color throughout, showing the temperament of his genius — all qualities of richness, fluency, beauty, the sensuous side of life subdued to an expression of the ardors of religious emotion and expressing joyousness (in opposition to Puritan and reformers' modes of religious emotion generally). He seems to me more the born poet than any of the others, and you will readily see is nearer to the Fletchers and to Milton than they are. In considering all these religious poets it is useful to remember that though they had, in some cases, Puritan tendencies in temperament as did Spenser and Sidney, they are Church of England poets, — and thus one corrects our usual traditionary notion that the Puritans had all the true piety and religious conviction on their side. These men were, in a sense, the Falklands of the Church party; but they show how much of true English religion was, like much of English manliness, in the Cavalier party which was the Church party too.

Wither (1588-1667) is to be connected with Browne in conjunction with whom he at one time wrote, and recollected as a master of octosyllabic verse of which "Shall I, wasting in despair" is the type. This has the quality of the cavalier lyric. His originally varied and literary poetic gift was practically lost in the development of his religious and political interests as a Puritan in the civil wars. His "Juvenilia" and "Hallelujah" are sufficiently illustrative of him.

Quarles (15-16-) should be briefly glanced at as affording an instance of emblem literature.

Herrick (1594-1674) holds the most important place in English literature as a writer of short poems after the manner of the Greek Anthology. He is by poetical descent on the English side, the continuer of Ben Jonson, whose "Forrest" was the seed-plot of much of the minor verse of the age. Herrick has always been popular with the "little masters" of the muse, the amateurs, and those whose main business is the elaboration of a pretty idea or fancy in small space and with perfect technique. The kind is indigenous in every cultivated literary age, but it tends toward artifice, formality, intellectual and moral trifling and light wit. Herrick's range is varied, and Swinburne's description of his verses as a diet of alternating sweetmeats and emetics is an excellent characterization. He was a clergyman, but his religion was of very slight consequence; he was, in many poems or epigrams, as coarse as it is possible for thought or language to be; even in those verses which are merely gallant, prettily complimentary, "dainty" as the kind is often called, there is constant offense; and in general, it is not unjust to say that the subject of his amatory poetry is not love, but sex, and its mood is of the senses without the heart. This is the plain meaning of the words when he is styled pagan, Arcadian, hedonist, and the like. His versification is remarkable for its successful rhyming; but to my ear the verse, as compared with the Elizabethans, has a hard ring. In dealing with nature, especially with flowers, he is often charming. His poetic gift was great, and he developed it fully; but he was interested in detail usually, and his subject-matter, in itself not of high value, is treated in a way, which when it ceases to be unreal often becomes vulgar. It is as if life were a ballet and he its musician. In saying this I am thinking of his work as a whole; he gains by selection, and volumes of such selections have been made in which his fancy, liveliness of rhyme, felicity of phrase,

condensation, and elaboration of graceful detail combine
to make a charming book. Here, as in the case of Donne,
criticism generally dwells on his better qualities and
ignores the remainder. He seems to me to owe his
merits largely to literary culture, to Ben Jonson and the
ancients, and not to personal qualities; from these latter
proceed his defects; but an unusual number of the young
scholars of modern verse have maintained his cause.
One has only to open the Greek anthology to see how
narrow is his vein and its clear inferiority in style, matter
and tone.

Carew (1589-1639) was a licentious courtier whose
work belongs to the song literature of the cavalier period.
He stands between the verse of Jonson and that of the
Restoration, and in him is easily seen the decadence of
love into gallantry, of sentiment into compliment, of
imagination into sensuality.

Cowley (1618-1667), once a great name but now little
known except as a tradition, was a precocious poet, a royalist closely connected with the exiled Queen, and is regarded, with Donne, as a chief of the metaphysical
school. Johnson in his "Lives of the Poets," under
"Cowley," gives an excellent account of this school. I
have sometimes thought that this whole "metaphysical"
movement should be regarded not merely as an Italian
importation from Marini and his like, extending its development on narrow lines of conceits, ingenuities, remote
allusions, from Drummond to Dryden, but as a minor
current in the development of the sententious quality of
Seneca in the Elizabethan time through the drama and
these poets to Pope who perfected this sententious quality
and in whom the movement ended; on the side of imagery
it doubtless owes most to Italian sources, directly or in-

directly, but on the side of thought it seems to me sympathetic with Chapman, for example.

Suckling (1608–1642). "Natural easy Suckling," one of the cavaliers and only incidentally a poet, is the forerunner even more distinctly than Carew of such later writers as Sedley and Rochester. The movement is the same noted above, but his work is more careless and flowing and shows the invasion of "good sense," as it came to be known, into love poetry. Read the "Ballad upon a Wedding" (in the original text) and look at the "Session of the Poets," a subject often attempted by later writers.

Lovelace (1618-1658), always united in fame with Suckling as a cavalier, should be known by his two famous songs.

CHARLES LAMB; OR ELIA

CHARLES LAMB really came into this world under the name of Elia; as a "son of memory," so he was christened, and by it he is known, for it is his name, not of his creature-life, but of his better part. His personality finds expression in it, freed from the sad or mean accidents of his mortal career; and it recalls only what in him was touched with the light and shadow of an inconstant genius or penetrated with the simplicity of the heart, and yet leaves room for that eccentricity, that strangeness heightened to the point of quaintness, which is an element in the attractiveness of character not less than, as Bacon declared, in beautiful things. Elia is a name of the imagination; but it was borne by an old acquaintance, an Italian who was a fellow-clerk at the South-Sea House when Lamb was a boy there, thirty years before he sat down to write these Essays; and, as a piece of pleasantry, he borrowed his friend's true face to mask his own. He went, he tells us, to see the Elia of flesh and blood, and laugh over the liberty he had taken, but found the Italian dead; and the incident — the playfulness of the odd plagiarism ending unexpectedly in a solemn moment, a pathetic close — is so in character with the moods of these pages, that even their maker could not have invented better what life gave into his hands. The name had devolved upon him now, he said; he had, as it were, unknowingly adopted a shade, and it was to go about with him thenceforth, and watch

at his grave after he too should depart. For two years
he used the ruse of this ghost of a name, but the un-
canniness of it was his own secret; to the reader of the
"London Magazine," in which he published, Elia was —
what it is to us — a name of the eternal humorist in
life's various crowd.

The form which Lamb chose for himself, the familiar
essay as it had been developed in England, was as well
fitted to him as his natural voice. He had begun as a
poet, but lacked the condensation, the directness and
singleness of intellectual aim, the power of control, which
are essential to the poet; he was an observer of the world
without, a rambler in all things, and tended inevitably
to that dissipation of the eye among the multitude of men
and things, which ends in prose; even as a humorist he
loses himself in his impressions, and becomes reportorial.
But he had an eye for oddities, and with it went the sav-
ing grace that he loved the absurd in man. The spirit
of caricature was not in him. He lived in a nation
marked by freedom of caprice, and in its chief city;
but it is seldom that he chooses his subject from among
those whose eccentricity is self-assertive; the absurdities
that amuse him are those of nature's making, — "the
fool" whom he loves; and the peculiarities that arrest
him are oftenest those which result from the misfortunes,
the rubs and the dents, all the rude buffeting of life
leaving its marks on the form and mind of those who are
submitted to its rule. How frequently his characters are
the broken "hulks" of the voyage! in what author is
old age so dreary, or the boon companion so shabby! for
Lamb's humor seldom ends in the laughable, but is a
plea for toleration, sympathy, forgiveness, — the old
phrase of the prayer-book, "miserable sinners are we all,"

but, principally, small sinners in small things. I cannot free myself from the feeling that, as a humorist,
Lamb is the father-confessor of venial offences, tender
to waifs and cripples, the refuge of the victims of mean
misery. It is as if the Good Samaritan should turn
humorist. Yet he leaves an impression that is ill-rendered
by such a description, because he blends so many strands
of human nature with this main thread.

The charm of these Essays is personal, and it is made
a mastering one by the autobiography they contain.
Lamb was not less an egotist than a humorist, and in
the familiar essay egotism has unimpeded way. He discloses his tastes and habits, and disguises not those things
in which he differs from conventional man; he is proud
of them, and goes his own pace. There is infinite amusement in a certain kind of self-gossip, seen to its perfection
in Pepys; and though Lamb's likings in meat and drink
are not to be confounded with things of the Pepysian
order, yet the tone is sometimes not to be discriminated
from such "pure idleness." The sinister reflection of
how much social hypocrisy saves from, of what conces-
sions of individual preference or even conviction are made
to the company, reacts in us and heightens the enjoyment
when an egotist stands to his egotism and is unabashed
though pilloried in men's minds. Frankness is always
engaging, and Lamb wins us by his confidingness. He
gives more than this sense of intimacy; he does really
surrender himself, and all his relatives besides, into our
hands. At the time he had the grace to conceal, by
appearances, the characters he drew; but the veil was
thin, and nothing is now left of it. His strong domestic
feeling, his love for the things of home, enhance the
humanity of the portrayal, and each picture is seen

beyond the contrasting foreground of "the lonely hearth" where he sits writing; "the old familiar faces" are illumined there, in the later years, with as tender a melancholy as in the poem of his youth. Scenes from his own life make up no small part of the book; and the humor is always softened by the atmosphere of mingled affection and sentiment in which it works. His confessions of childhood are especially touching. No one has revealed the poignancy of children's sufferings, their helplessness, their solitariness, their hopelessness, the physical nearness of all grief at that age, with a pen so crying out shame. But, as in his description of middle and elderly life there is a predominant strain of misery and triviality, a never-absent pathos, so in what he draws from childhood, where are the cheerfulness, the innocence, the gayety, the wild and thoughtless happiness? They are not in his life. Even his child-angel is a sorrowful conception. When he was "at Christ's" — was it such a child's hell? and was that all he knew of childhood? One cannot help such reflections; and they underlie, in truth, the melancholy that attended him and the sentiment that sprang up in him, both of which preserve these Essays equally with their humor.

Sentiment stood for him, perhaps, in the place of love in his life. The romance, which is now the memory of "Alice W——," certainly was cherished, in the sphere of sentiment, by him life-long; and in his musings in imagination upon what might have been, there is much of that mournful fancy, that affection for things unrealized, which betray heart-hunger; even in his attachment to old places and accustomed ways, and to what he called "antiquity" (of which in his own mind he and his belongings were part and parcel), there is something of the wandering of the else-unsupported vine. His is the sentiment of a melancholy, a suppressed, down-borne, and retarded nature, cabined, cribbed, confined. It was almost his sole good fortune that literature offered him a resource from the deprivations of his life, and gave him freedom of thought and feeling in the ideal world; there he found objects worth his constancy, and being gifted with sensibility and discernment, he became a discoverer in "the realms of gold," an antiquarian whose prizes were lyrics and sonnets and snatches of song,

"And beauty making beautiful old rhyme";

and he forsook the modern days to delight himself with the curious felicity of the "Arcadia" and Sir Thomas Browne, with single great scenes of the Elizabethans, and with the breath of Marvell's garden. He escaped into the golden age, into "antiquity," — for he meant by that favorite phrase little that was older than Sackville.

It is easy to overestimate the service of Lamb and his friends in the revival of the older English literature. It was not begun by them. Throughout the eighteenth century the rill of Parnassus had been flowing, and now the stream had become broad. Lamb's group was borne on a deeper common current. But he, with Coleridge, Hazlitt, Hunt, and others of the time were agents in the diffusion of the new taste, and their critical appreciation and authority gave them a place as supporters of the innovation, sufficient to define a historical moment. Lamb is not to be regarded as the author of the revival of which he was rather a part. He felt it more than he directed it. Leadership was not in his bundle of qualities. He responded, however, to the influences of the re-discovered literature with marvelously perfect sympathy.

The more recondite and esoteric portions of it were most to his taste. The humorist in him answered the most exigent demands of the occasion; and oddities of language and thought, conceits, quaintnesses, even conscious affectations, attracted him, just as the same qualities in living human nature called forth his motley-seeking wits. His originality, or native eccentricity, felt something kindred to itself in the old writers; their queernesses, worn like nature, kept his own in countenance; their affectations were a model on which his innate whimsicality could frame itself. And, possibly, more than all (yet excepting the pure charm of poetry), their sentiment, lingering on from days of chivalry and the allegorical in literature, fed a fundamental need of the emotional nature in such a life as Lamb's, perforce, was. He became an imitator of antiquated style, a mannerist after his favorites, given to artifice and fantasy as a literary method, and yet he remained himself. The disease of language does not penetrate to the thought.

Thus there were mingled in Lamb literary artifice with truth to nature, egotism with humanity, humor with sentiment, — both dashed by something melancholy; and one spark of genius, fusing this blend, has made the book of Elia a treasure to many. It is not a great book, but it is uncommonly interesting. It is human from cover to cover. The subjects may be trivial, the company "low," the incidents farcical; but of such is the kingdom of this world, — as least it was so in London then. Lamb was a good observer; and, as in the sketches of the earlier essayists of Queen Anne literary historians point out the beginnings of the social novel of the next generation in that century, may not one find a foregleam of Dickens in these pages, of the lot of children, and the look of

lives grown threadbare, and the virtues hidden in commonplace people?   There is, no doubt, the trace of
Smollett; but in addition is there not the spirit of humanity which took possession of our fiction and subdued it
to democracy?   The exaggeration, both of humor and
of sentiment, in Dickens, the master of the craft, Lamb
was free from; but the curious tracer of literary moods
in the century would hardly hesitate to include Lamb
in the succession.   On other sides Lamb faced the past;
but here was his one window on the times he lived in,
or else he must be set down as one of those "sports" of
the intellect which have no relation to their generation.
In description and in character-drawing he was, of course,
as simply personal as in his criticism.   He might have
smiled or scoffed at the idea that he was a forerunner in
fiction as that he was a leader in the romantic movement.
He cared nought for such things, as little as for science
or music.   He worked as an individual only, and told his
recollections or described his friends and acquaintances
just as he read his folios, because he pleased himself in
doing it.   But it is hard for a writer, however idiosyncratic, not to be a link between the days.   The taste
that classes him, in his work as a humorist, is his love of
Hogarth, whom he appreciated more intelligently and
fully, perhaps, than any one between Fielding and Thackeray.   When it is objected that the quality of ordinary
life as he presents it is "seaminess," we should recall in
what company he exhibits it; and if his humor does not
always hide the deformity and avoid the pain of the
spectacle, our generation is probably more acutely aware
of these things.

The human interest in the Essays, however, is not
confined to what Lamb saw of the absurd and grotesque,

the cruel and pathetic, in other lives. He is himself his best character, and best drawn. He was extraordinarily self-conscious, and the pages yield little that he did not mean to be told. One must go to the silent part of his biography to obtain that sobering correction of his whimsies and failings, that knowledge of his manliness in meeting the necessities of his situation, that sense of honesty, industry, and generosity, which he kept out of his books. The side that most men turn to the world he concealed, and he showed that which is commonly kept secret. He had been a poet in youth, and he never lost the habit of wearing his heart upon his sleeve. He was never as a poet to get beyond sentiment, which in a romantic age is but a little way; and in degenerating into prose (as he thought it) he gave no other sign of poetic endowment than this of sentiment that he could not surrender; but to what length he carried it without exceeding the bounds of true feeling! Sentiment, like humor, needs a delicate craft; but he, though not so penetrating, was as sure of hand as Burns. Even under the temptation of an antique style, he does not err: with affectation commanding every turn and cadence, his feeling goes true; and the heart answers to it through all the gamut, playful, regretful, melancholy, wailing. The word is not too strong; turn to "The Dream-Children," — it is the tragedy of sentiment. Other moods too he revealed, and especially the melancholy ground of his nature. He disclaimed the fierce earnestness, the bitter experience, the hopeless despondency of "The Confessions of a Drunkard," nor should one charge him with the burden of so dark a tale; but that there are elements of autobiography in it, of things foreseen if not experienced, — a vision of the road to its end, — is, unhappily, too

plain a matter. I refer to it, not to reproach or extenuate, but as one sign of several which indicate that, like
all natures lacking in the principle of reason and control, Lamb was subject to spells of penitence, of bewildered appeal, which were at the roots of that insistent melancholy, and help to explain why, when it
comes upon the page, it is never imaginative, but always
real.

Yet Lamb, though always, I think, a pathetic figure
in men's memories, does not in these Essays give such
an impression except at moments, just as he affects us
only at intervals with the dreariness of the human life
he describes. One reason is that his personality is diffused in varying essays, and besides, his reputation as
a wit, and what we know of his suppers, and the whole
social side of the man, blend with the mode of address,
the familiarity, the discursive manner, the frequent whim,
the anecdotage, the multifarious interest of the whole.
The Essays are pleasant to read, and winning; the predominant, and at first almost engrossing impression is
of the companionableness of the writer, — he is excellent company. The style, too, is fitted to secure its
effects. We know that he wrote them with great care,
and sometimes with difficulty; and if the heart of Lamb
is always close at hand in the page, his mind is there too.
In some of the critical parts especially, there is that kind
of reflection which gives substance to a book otherwise
meant simply for entertainment. The dramatic sketches
also lighten the whole effect by their apparent impersonality. It is only when the more famous papers are
thought of by themselves, and those most autobiograph-
ical in matter, that Lamb's humor and sentiment, his
egotism and humanity, his literary artifice in all, and

the narrow limits within which these had their field, become so prominent as to seem to constitute the book as well as the man. These qualities have established the Essays in literature, and their author, Elia, in the affections of kind hearts.

AUBREY DE VERE, POET AND CRITIC

I. THE POET

THE qualities of Aubrey de Vere's poetry are not far
to seek. Lyrical in verse, strong in style, mainly historical in theme, heroic or spiritual in substance, above all
placid, it stirs and tranquilizes the soul in the presence
of lovely scenes, high actions, and those

> "Great ideas that man was born to learn";

and its outlook is upon the field of the soul regenerate,
where suffering is remembered only through its purification, blessed in issues of sweetness, dignity, and peace.
It takes wide range, but is predominantly either Bardic
or Christian. The sympathy of the poet with the ancient
Irish spirit must have been fed with patriotic fervor,
akin to renewed inspiration, to permit him to render the
old lays of his country with such fidelity to their native
genius. Cuchullain once more becomes credible to fancy,
— the imagination of a childhood world; and the songs
of Oiseen and Ethell strike with a music as of anvils.
The versions of the three monuments of old Irish story
— the "Sorrows of Song" — are our best. The English
lines have the definiteness and precision that belong to
primitive narrative; and yet each tale is involved in that
atmosphere of "the shore of old romance," of the marvelous, the picturesque, the childlike, which appeals to
our eyes like the distances of spring — the haze of time

lying along the early world. In each of the three mythic poems there are pictures of novel and strange beauty: the boy, Cuchullain, riding laughing home in his car after the deeds of his knighting-day, with the leashed wide-winged birds flying over him, the six leashed stags following the chariot captive, the bandits' heads upon its front; or, the lovers, Naisi and Deirdré, hand in hand on the foot-bridge pouring forth the lay that hemmed them with the clansmen of Usnach; or King Lir, "with under-sliding arms," by the bed of the gold-woven bridal veil, lifting the children from its dawn-touched glittering tissue to "the first light from the sky." These are such pictures as Burne-Jones is too often thought to have invented.

Of all, Cuchullain is the noblest figure in this old Irish verse; and the poem which relates his deeds — with its episodic tales of his youth, the background of his island-boyhood with the friend he was doomed to slay, and the long duel between them which closes in his lament over the dead man he loved and his retirement to the forest — is so inwrought with bravery, pathos, and emotional beauty as to give it the first place, while the hero's Achillean return to the host places it among true epics. The second of the three Sorrows — "The Sons of Usnach" — is characterized by a strange proces-sional beauty, as of a pageant pilgriming, and by a clear spirit of joyfulness in the midst of the mov-ing cloud of fate, like "the tempest's heart of calm." But the last — "The Children of Lir" — touches the heart most deeply. The idea of the poem — the first human effort to extend the bounds of Divine Mercy, to reach through the "dark backward and abysm" of the thousand pagan years, and gather to its fold these children

to be the first-fruits of Christ in their land — is very
noble; but great as is the idea, it is subdued into a simple
idyl of childhood.   The poem is, indeed, unique, and the
handling (Tennyson treated it less admirably) is exquisite.   The children in their home are dear, and in
their transformation into swans there is no discord.
The swan-nature, already half-human in poetic tradition, blends of itself with the ideal image of childhood; and the nearness of the little exiles to humanity, after their change, is sustained by their mystical
night-long singing overheard by men, and by the tale
told their poet listening solitary by the sea in the sixth
century of their woe.   In their life with nature, too, a new
aspect sympathetic with childhood emerges; and lastly,
though lost, they still live in a world of their own, as
children do.   This beautiful tradition of the Irish race
must become a part of the child-literature of our
language.

The Christian element in this last story prepares the
way for the poet's more voluminous and distinctly religious work — and it is with poets of religion that he
is to be classed — in which he selects his themes from
the saintly legends of the Church, and shows the abundance and power of that life, idealized in holy tradition,
which converted the nations and revivified the world.
The Reformation was a great source of great mortality
in literature; and the loss which Protestantism sustained
in surrendering the Catholic centuries, with their long
record of this ideal life among mankind, was spiritual de-
privation to the northern imagination, which the noble
lives of three later centuries have not yet made good.
So complete is the gap now, that the times of which
these poems reflect the imaginative beauty have the re-

moteness of a golden age, and in reading the verse a
sense of dreaminess invades the mind.   This portion of
the poet's work makes its mass; and its interest, though
various, is so even that one could as easily divide the
summer landscape as choose and pick amid its beauty.
The subjects are, in the main, from Irish, English, or
Roman traditions of the early Church.   The tales of St.
Patrick, which illustrate the conversion of Ireland, are
roughened by the old Bardic strength overcome by the
new gospel, and masculine vigor is thus infused into
it, while a poetic continuity with the primitive lays is
preserved.   "Aengus" is a representative instance of these
legends of the Christian dawn, but milder than the most.
The tales of Saxon times, which illustrate the conversion of England, are almost pastoral in tone; and again,
"St. Cuthbert's Pentecost" is, like Aengus, only a solitary
example.   Others of this series are shown with fine
imaginative effects, like that of the lonely Julian Tower
casting the shadow of Rome on the consecration of Westminster Abbey: —

> "On Saxon feasts she fixed a cold gray gaze;
> 'Mid Christian hymns heard but the old acclaim —
> 'Consul Romanus' ";

or, with eloquent lines, like those on the Primates of
Canterbury: —

> "From their fronts,
> Stubborned with marble from St. Peter's Rock,
> The sunrise of far centuries forth shall flame";

or, with passages of brief pathos, like Bede's words: —

> "Poor youth! that love which walks in narrow ways
> Is tragic love, be sure."

The poem, devoted to Cædmon, is especially rich in such felicities both of image and phrase.

So these Christian poems succeed one another, as the poet's memory wanders back to the legends of the Empire on the first establishment of the faith in Roman lands and along Asian shores, or moves through medieval times with Joan of Arc and episodes of the Cid that recall Culchullain in their light-hearted performance of natural deeds, now under the Cross. The beauty of these separate stories is equable and full of a softened charm; but in them, too, as in the Bardic myths, there abides that distance of time, which makes them remote, as if they were not of our own. They are highly pictorial; and in reading them, each secluded in that silent, old-world air that encompasses it, one feels that here is a modern poet, like those early painters of pious heart who spent their lives in picturing scenes from the life of Christ; and one recalls, perhaps, some Convent of San Marco where each monastic cell bears on its quiet walls such scenes from the shining hand of the Florentine on whose face fell heaven's mildest light. These poems of Aubrey de Vere — to characterize them largely — are scenes from the life of Christ in Man; and there is something in them — in their gladness, their luminousness, their peace — which suggests Fra Angelico, the halo of Christian art.

Yet one reads to little purpose, if he does not discern also an intellectual element, constant in the poet's work, which gives it mental as well as spiritual character. It is not so much thought, as comprehension, which his poetry most evinces: that comprehension which is the genius of the historian and grasps the governing principles, follows the essential ideas, watches the doubtful issues of the inward world of conviction and illusion, of which alone the fate is significant. This philosophic interest in history is most directly expressed in his two dramas, "Alexander the Great" and "St. Thomas of Canterbury," where social movements, so irresistible as to be rightly called providential principles, were centred in great personalities. In these, his eye sees, not the men merely, but ideas greater than they, of which they were servants; this is true, also of such single portraits as those of Odin, Constantine, and Hildebrand. His prefaces disclose a similar distinctly historical aim in his tales, but their character as particular narrative renders it less obvious; the poetical element in them absorbs and conceals the didactic purpose. He has also occasionally inwoven in his verse more abstract and purely logical argument, of which "The Death of Copernicus" is an example. His sonnets and odes show, in addition, occupation with political and other modern questions. In his single contemporary Irish tale, "The Sisters" — a tale which makes one regret so complete an absorption of his narrative powers in other lines — the criticism upon Ireland's history has both edge and weight, and its conversational temper is charming. Together with the gaunt reality of "The Year of Sorrow," this story of the actual reveals the heart of a patriot, near to his living land. Indeed, in whatever division of his verse he approaches the subject of Ireland, his style gathers fire, and often, as must be the case, deepens into melancholy passion. This is shown most characteristically in the ideal conception of Ireland, which he sometimes suggests, as a Sacrificial Nation, whose lot is to show forth spiritual virtues under perpetual earthly misfortune, and it is natural to such a mind; but there is difficulty even in

its poetical acceptance, so heavy is the weight of a nation's burden. It is a great conception, but it is not a
political idea. It is young Richard's refuge — "that
sweet way I was in to despair." But throughout the
entire range of national and religious themes which in a
long life-time the poet has touched, one recognizes a
conscientious and keen thoughtfulness as well as the other
qualities of warmth, imagination, and delight in natural
and moral beauty which are more upon the surface of the
verse; and to miss this reflective temperament would
be to lose sight of much of the inward significance of these
longer poems.

Of shorter pieces he has written few in comparison
with the body of his work. For one who belongs to the
generation of Tennyson and who was the youthful friend
of Wordsworth, the impersonality of his verse is marked.
He paid the tribute to Love, which is required of the
gentle heart, in a few musical lyrics, usually with the
sad cadence; he paid also his tribute to human liberty
and the general hope of man in some fervid sonnets that
spoke from the breast; and, lastly, he paid his tribute to
his friends — for he was rich in friendships — laying his
loyal laurel upon each remembered grave. Finally — to
compress much miscellaneous verse into small space — in
Antar and Zara he treated a difficult theme of love with a
delicacy and truth of feeling and a melodic power that
justified its inscription to Tennyson; in many odes and
sonnets he exhibited the love of nature, the sentiment for
landscape and its living creatures, and the sense of the
moral power of the external world, which became a true
disciple of Wordsworth and continuer of his tradition;
and in "The Search after Proserpine," and elsewhere, he
is a neighbor to Shelley. In all this portion of his work,

which is more nearly related to his own country, except at rare moments he remains impersonal, and deals with ideas through images, in accordance with the great tradition of poetry from the first, for their own and not for the poet's sake.

Such, in general, is the poet's work. But it possesses some qualities which so highly distinguish it in modern verse and gives it peculiar character beyond what has been indicated, that a word more must be said. One constant element is its praise of the life of the lowly, in the old Christian sense, as the soil of many virtues, and those the noblest and most endearing. The affinities of his subject-matter, both on the national and the religious side, make this natural; but its source is rather in a true sympathy with lowly lives and knowledge of them, whether among the poor by fate or those who have renounced by choice the things of fortune; and the ground of this praise — and this is the significant matter — is one that was old when Rousseau was born. So Truth comes into her own again. A second distinguishing element in the verse, as a whole, is its praise of devotion, that loyal surrender to a man or a cause which is one of the ideal passions of Love, and the vital triumph of the soul. To realize what is denoted by this characteristic, and how sharply it severs old and new, needs only a thought of the quite different way in which — to take the main instance — Tennyson presents this virtue, in his greatest poem of man's life — how maimed and impotent in Arthur, Guinevere, and Lancelot, how doomed to tragic failure in the lesser persons, for Galahad's career is magical, not human; and the fact that this enfeebling of the principle of devotion is not a trait that, in Tennyson, most strikes a modern reader, measures the distance between the moral ideals that are and those that were. In this, also, Aubrey de Vere returns to the ancient fountains. A third such element in the verse is its purity, which is due, in part, to the fact that the poet is fond of youth, and fills his poems with many fair figures, fresh and ardent and beautiful, and touches with especial delicacy the tenderness of childhood and the grace of boyhood, so that there is a morning air in his world; but something is also due to his own limpid sincerity and the clarifying power of that spirit which can but represent virtue, however suffering, as joyful. His heroes are always glad. And lastly, to bring these remarks to an end, faith is an element in this verse, not to be passed over in silence. It is faith of the sort not to be rivaled among our poets by any other than Shelley, — faith in the power of truth to subdue mankind to goodness. What to Shelley was dream and vision is here that golden age of the triumph of Christ over the heathen world, when whole nations heard and were baptized. That this is not fanciful paradox a single passage will show, and it affords a striking and useful literary parallel: —

"They sleep not, on the loud-resounding shore
In glory roaming. Many a feud that night
Perished; and vengeful vows, now mockery made,
Lay quenched in their own shame. Far shone the fires
Crowning dark hills with gladness; soared the song;
And heralds sped from coast to coast to tell
How He the Lord of all, no Power Unknown,
But like a man rejoicing in his house,
Ruled the glad earth. . . .
                            With earliest red of dawn
Northward once more the wingèd war-ships rushed,
Swift as of old to that long hated shore —
Not now with ax and torch. His Name they bare
Who linked in one the nations."

This is the feast, the chant, the flame of Laon and Cythna. In this faith, again, there is the fundamental Christian quality, that older spirit, of which the other elements that have just been mentioned are also branches. Thus, in all this poetry, however its phases be successively turned to the eye, or itself be inwardly searched, there is one light and one breath — the light of the Spirit and the breath thereof. It cannot but have a peculiar, though in its own century almost an exotic, charm. Joy and peace, the first Christian message, spread abroad with its music; and, heard or unheard, the song of the poet speeds that old evangel.

II. THE CRITIC

It is rare good fortune to find criticism in which the ideas are more excellent than the manner, and the spirit finer than the ideas; in which it is not the keener sympathy of the poet that speaks, or the sure sense of the trained artist for expression, or any single faculty, but the whole nature of the man; in which the judgment rendered does not proceed from any particular part of his mind — the scholarly or moral or esthetic element by itself — but is felt to be grounded upon his total convictions. Aubrey de Vere's essays, therefore, are worth more than ordinary attention. He writes principally of Spenser and Wordsworth, and also of Milton, Shelley, and Keats. He considers mainly the doctrine of this poetry. He values it chiefly for its highest office as a teacher of moral wisdom, and a quickener of the spiritual part of our nature. He justly decides that its real subject is man's life; this is the center of interest in all great thought, and the rest is but ornament and episode. He is a Christian idealist, and he refuses to regard poetry except in the light of those great ideas which belong to the spirit, and, being nobly and beautifully interpreted, are the substance of the poets who live by their wisdom as well as by their charm. The ethical, the philosophical element in a large sense, is to him the engrossing thing; and criticism of this sort, so incited and so aimed, has a reality that does not fall far short of the worth of direct reflection upon the things of the mind, though it deals with them through the medium of literature instead of in life itself.

With Spenser, naturally, he has many affinities. The medievalism, the sentiment of chivalry, the allegorizing spirit, and not less the Puritan elevation of the first of the Elizabethan poets, exercise a special fascination over a Catholic mind for whom the Ages of Faith, as he likes to call them, have in a peculiar degree the ideality that clothes the past. One no longer looks for original criticism of the father of English verse, who, more than Chaucer, may claim the paternity of great poets in later days; but to remind us of his excellence has become, in the lapse of time and the decline of poetic taste, almost as desirable an office as it once was to unfold its secret. Spenser is a poet who requires no common critic to speak justly of him. His position was a unique one, and by some infelicity of his stars he failed to rise to the greatness which seems to have been possible to him. Aubrey de Vere remarks that the great romantic poem of the Middle Ages, one that should sum them up on the human as Dante did upon the divine side, was never written; and, looking back, it appears to us that Spenser was the choice spirit that missed this destiny. His pure poetic quality, that sensibility to beauty and delight in it as in his element, was perfect to such a degree that Milton and Keats, who possessed it in something of the same measure, seem almost to have derived it from him, whose poems nourished it in them. The sweetness and noble ease of his expression reveal the presence of a marvelous literary faculty. His responsiveness to the historical and legendary elements in the past, his power of abstracting and idealizing them for poetic use, and his profound interest in human life, were great endowments, and he possessed in a high degree and a pure form that moral reason which is the attribute of genius. But by defects as striking as this gift he made his poem less than we fondly think it might have been. The Elizabethan prolixity, the obscure perception of the nature of form in literary work, the artificiality incident to the allegorizing temperament, account for much of what he lost; but, for all that, his poems are marvels of the creative intellect, and it is this intellect that Aubrey de Vere dwells on. Any one can point out Spenser's loveliness, but the great spirit that brooded over his verse is not so easily realized. His aim was "to strengthen man by his own mind," and it is this effort which the critic analyzes, and by so doing tries to show how well he deserved the epithet "grave" as well as "gentle Spenser."

His work, with its intricate allegory, its machinery of faëryland and chivalry, its ideal landscape, is regarded as remote from life; but just as the creations of art, which also have this unreality, are yet the expression, oftentimes, of the most real human feeling and the most substantial thought of the mind, so the figures of his embroidered poem compose a procession of true life. They

are conceived and used in accordance with a comprehensive doctrine of the nature of humanity, which Spenser
undoubtedly meant to enforce through the medium of the
imagination; this doctrine, in fact, is the stuff they are
made of.

It is not an easy thing to resolve into its moral elements
the creations of a poet who blends many strains of truth.
His method is not the consecutive process of logical reflection and explication, but the simultaneous embodiment
of what, however arrived at, he presents as intuitive,
needing only to be seen, to be acknowledged. In the
analysis, the distinctive poetic quality is too apt to be
dissipated, and the poet is forgotten in the philosopher.
Certain broad aspects may be easily made out. Chivalry,
with its crowd of faëry knights, certainly rests, in
Spenser's great work, upon the old conception of the
Christian life as one militant against the enemies of the
soul in the world; and quite as clearly he also represents
this entire life as being, within the breast, ideal peace.
Peace within and war without: these are two root-ideas
out of which the poem flowers on its great double
branches. He teaches specifically how to attain self-
control, and how to meet attacks from without; or rather
how to seek those many forms of error which do mischief in the world, and to overcome them for the world's
welfare. This is a bald statement, but it indicates well
enough in what way Spenser employed the knightly
ideal of succor on one hand, and the Christian ideal of
moral perfection on the other, in order to make a poem
which should instruct as well as delight the world. He
himself asserts that his aim was so lofty, and to a man
such as he was a lower aim, a merely artistic purpose,
would have been impossible. It is fortunate that he

was not less endowed with the sense of loveliness than with a serious mind; for he thus illustrates not only the possible union of the two principal aims of poetry in all times, but also the truth that to a man whose perception of beauty is most perfect the beauty of holiness is the more impressive and authoritative in its commands. Aubrey de Vere devotes himself especially to the declaration and the proof that Spenser's poetic character was essentially that of a man deeply interested in human life, and he tries to prevent the poet's severely ideal, and sometimes fantastic, method from obscuring, as for many minds it does, the real nature of that allegory, so marvelous for invention, eloquence, and perpetual charm of style, which is seldom thought to be more than an intricate and lovely legend of the imagination. The critic is not blind to the great defects of the work, — and no poem of equal rank has more, — nor does he neglect the excellences that are obvious to the least thoughtful reader; but he succeeds in placing before us its intellectual and moral substance.

In doing this he reveals his own theory of poetry, and it is one that derives its philosophy from the great historic works of our literature, and is grounded on the practice of the English masters whose fame is secure. Its cardinal principle is that man is the only object of interest to man, all else being subordinate, and valuable only for its relations to this main theme; and more particularly this subject is the spiritual life, not the material manifestations of his energies in deeds apart from their meaning. The Italian masters of Spenser too often lost themselves in incident, in romance, in story for its own sake; they were destitute of that ethical spirit which insists on planting in the deeds their significance, and regarding this as an integral, and indeed the only immortal, part of the action. The laws of life, not the chances of individuals, were Spenser's subject, and in this he differs from Ariosto, and leaves his company. Spenser's genius was thus abstract and contemplative, and Platonic in the sense that he used images always with some reference to the general truths that transcend imagination, and are directly apprehended only intellectually. Allegory was therefore his necessary method. Spenser never succeeded in harmonizing the disparate elements of the material to which he fell heir by literary tradition; and besides the inconsistencies and incoherences of the Renaissance culture, which never reached any unity in its own time, there were also special disturbances in his intellectual life because of the political and religious conflicts in England itself, from entanglement with which he was not free; and, moreover, he does not seem to have subdued the philosophical and poetic impulses of his own nature to any true accord. His poem, therefore, did not take on that perfection, that identity of purpose and execution, which would have placed it in the first rank, and he remains below the supreme poets of the world. The study of his work, as an illustration of the conditions and art of poetry, is most instructive. Its defects teach more than its excellence, but they do not disturb the theory which Aubrey de Vere sets forth; and he would be but a blind critic who should easily argue that Spenser succeeded when he obeyed the pure artistic impulse, and failed because of the interference of his graver genius with the poetical mind, his thought with his sensibility.

Aubrey de Vere's contemplative mind, his strong hold on the abstract rather than on the concrete, help him over the poetically dry places in Spenser, and serve him even better in the case of Wordsworth. This is choosing the better of two alternatives; for, if the landscape of Arcady is incomplete for him unless there is some "swan-flight of Platonic ideas" over it, such as he says is always in Spenser's sky, he has an appreciation for beauty as steadfastly as for the higher truths of life, and it is better to suffer with deficiencies in poetic art for the sake of the matter than to be content with art alone.

The great difference between Wordsworth and Spenser is, that Spenser was concerned with the moral virtues and man's acquirement of them, while Wordsworth was more narrowly limited to the influence of nature in forming the soul. Both looked to the same end, — spiritual life; but Wordsworth had a different starting-point. His mind was more individual, and he assumed that his own history was typical; he was less rich in the stores of antiquity, and he had less sensibility to beauty in its ideal forms; but he knew the place that nature held in his own development, and he became specifically the poet of nature, not only as beauty visible to the eye, but also, and mainly, as an invisible influence in the lives of men. Much of his verse was a pastoral form of philosophy; meditation counted for more than beauty in it; but the scene was the English country, and the characters were rustics. There was, too, something of imaginative untruth in it, no doubt, similar to that inherent in all pastoral poetry. These common men, however, were not individual, but stood for man, and Wordsworth, in delineating their histories, was writing a parable as well as a story. In other portions of his verse he used a more abstract method. As a moralist he was much given to maxims; and in all that concerns the social and political life of man, as well as his personal relations to virtue,

Wordsworth was, as the critic affirms with much emphasis, filled with a certain ardor, which may be called passion if one likes. The lack of passion in the ordinary sense — and it cannot be made out that Wordsworth possessed this quality — only renders more plain the moral endowment of the poet, his absorbing interest in the manly virtues, and the supreme value which he placed on the spiritual life and its ideal relations. He considered these relations most directly as existing toward nature, and having their operation in the emotion which nature excites. He did not altogether escape from the pantheism incident to such a constant preoccupation of the mind with the works and course of nature, and consequently he is less distinctively Christian than Spenser; but Aubrey de Vere easily makes it out that Wordsworth's philosophy, much as it differed from Spenser's, is concerned with the same topics of moral and spiritual life, and is the substance of his poetry.

It is not surprising that a writer of Aubrey de Vere's temperament is annoyed by the charge that Wordsworth is destitute of "passion." He has much to say on this point. Wordsworth himself gave as the reason why he did not write love-poems the fear that they would be too passionate. Aubrey de Vere makes what defense he can by pointing out the half-dozen idealizations of woman in the shorter lyrics; but his real apology consists in the counter-assertion that Wordsworth is especially distinguished for "passion." He uses the word, however, with a difference, and means by it the poetic glow, the exaltation of feeling, the lyrical possession, which attends the moment of creation and passes into verse. Of this sort of passion every form of poetry is as capable as is the amorous: the *sæva indignatio* of satire would come

under this head as properly as the moral enthusiasm or
the patriotic fervor shown in the "Ode to Duty" or the
"Sonnets." Wordsworth truly possessed this capability,
and it gives to his poems their masculine strength.
Whether equal success is to be credited to the critic's
glosses upon the more commonplace subjects of Wordsworth's muse, is doubtful; it seems rather that he makes
the mistake which Coleridge attributed to Wordsworth
himself, of giving a value to the idea which it has in his
own mind, but which it does not have in the bare words
addressed to the reader. When the idea and the expression are not identical, every poet suffers from this
cause; in his mind the idea, coming first, dignifies the
words, but to the reader the words coming first, too
often mutilate the idea. It is a good result of Aubrey
de Vere's Wordsworthianism that it gives him courage
to force into the front of his essay the "Orphic Odes,"
which are among the least known of the poet's work, and
contain some of the noblest of his lines.

To Milton he seems somewhat unjust. The earlier
poems receive his warm appreciation, but of the later
ones he is hardly so tolerant, and nowhere does he give
him his due. This is the passage: —

"It is not, however, its deficient popularity so much as
its subject and its form which proves that Milton's great
work is not a national poem, high as it ranks among
our national triumphs. Some will affirm that he illustrated in his work his age if not his country. His age,
however, gave him an impulse rather than materials.
Puritanism became transmuted, as it passed through his
capacious and ardent mind, into a faith Hebraic in its
austere spirit — a faith that sympathized indeed with
the Iconoclastic zeal which distinguished the anti-Catholic

and anti-patristic theology of the age, but held little consort with any of the complex definitions at that time insisted on as the symbols of Protestant orthodoxy. Had
the Puritan spirit been as genuine a thing as the spirit
of liberty which accompanied it; had it been such as
their reverence for Milton makes many suppose it to have
been, the mood would not so soon have yielded to the
licentiousness that followed the Restoration. . . . To him
the classic model supplied, not the adornment of his
poem, but its structure and form. The soul that wielded
that mould was, if not exactly the spirit of Christianity,
at least a religious spirit — profound, zealous, and self-
reverent — as analogous, perhaps, in its temper to the
warlike religion of the Eastern Prophet as to the traditional faith of the Second Dispensation. Such was the
mighty fabric which, aloof and in his native land an exile,
Milton raised; not perfect, not homogeneous, not in any
sense a national work, but the greatest of all those works
which prove that a noble poem may be produced with little
aid from local sympathies, and none from national traditions."

Some expressions in this passage, and many others
scattered through these volumes, indicate where
the current of sympathy was broken by default
of which the critic understands Milton imperfectly.
Ideal he was, but there is no poet who is more
bone and flesh of the English nation in the substance
of his genius, or in whom it developed a spirituality more
noble; nor are his defects, in his conception of womanhood for example, such as cannot be easily paralleled
from the other poets of highest genius in the line from
Spenser. But, on the other hand, the critic is more than
just to Keats, and towards Shelley he exhibits a respect,

a penetration of the elements of his thoughtful temperament, and a comprehension of the remarkable and intimate changes of his incessant growth, that are almost unexampled in authors writing from Aubrey de Vere's standpoint. In writing of the others he has opportunity for still further illustration of the theory of poetry he holds, and he shows that these later poets have their best success the closer they keep to the subject of man, and the more they treat it with a pure, spiritual method; while on the other hand, they are defective in proportion as they fail in this.

It would be impossible for a critic with such standards as these to pass in review the work of the moderns, and not to notice the general decline in the moral weight and the spirituality of late poetic literature. Materialism, both as respects the objects of man's pursuit and the character of his speculation in philosophy, has been so important and growing a factor of the times, that, if there is any validity in this theory of poetry, it must follow that our poetic work has lost elevation, meaning, and utility. Religion itself, so far as the general thought of nineteenth-century civilization is concerned, has suffered a diminution of its authority, and consequently the spiritual life of man has filled a less prominent part in the eyes of these generations.

In connection with this, room should be made for some original remarks of the writer upon the Pagan element in our modern poetry. He is very well affected towards Platonism, and recognizes it historically as "the chief secondary cause of the diffusion of Christianity, doing for it more than the favor of Constantine could ever have done." He thus affirms for Greek religion and Greek philosophy "an element of greatness and truth."

Our poets, in returning to its life and thought, seem to him to be making a return to the spiritual element which in the revolutionary ages has been obscured and too often lost. He speaks in this as a Catholic, but he is more Christian than Catholic, if it may be permitted to say so; and all religious writers admit and lament the inroad of skepticism and consequent materialism. The turn he gives to these facts is a striking one: —

"The arts of the Middle Ages soared above Paganism: the imaginative mind of modern times stands for the most part aloof from it; but it often stands aloof from Christianity also. Secularity is its prevailing character, while even in Paganism there is a spiritual element. We may not, without a risk of insincerity and presumption, indulge in either an exultation or a regret higher than corresponds with our low position. Can we with truth say that the portion of our modern literature which reverts to ancient mythology is less religious than the rest? Is it not, in the case of some authors, the only portion which has any relations, even through type or symbol, with religious ideas? Would Dante, would even Milton, have found more to sympathize with in the average of modern literature than in Homer or in Sophocles, in Wordsworth's 'Laodamia' or Keats's 'Hymn to Pan?' What portion of our late poetry is Christian either in spirit or in subject — nay, in traditions and associations? Admirable as much of it is, it is not for its spiritual tendencies that it can be commended. Commonly it shares the material character of our age, and smells of the earth; at other times, recoiling from the sordid, it flies into the fantastic. . . . It is our life which is to be blamed; our poetry has been but the reflection of that life."

This is valuable, not only for its suggestion, but because it sums up and speaks out plainly the protest which is implicit in all this criticism. The esthetic lover of beauty, the artist who is satisfied with feats of poetic craft, will not find anything to his liking in Aubrey de Vere's essays. They are presided over by a severe Platonism intellectually, by an exacting and all-including Christianity when the subject touches upon man's life, and they will prove somewhat difficult reading, perhaps, because the thought continually reverts to great ideas, to that doctrine of life which the author seeks for in the poets, and prizes as the substance of their works. But it is well, in poetic days like these, to be brought back to the more serious muses which inspired the great ideal works of our literature, and to converse with them under the guidance of such a spirit as fills these essays with a sense of the continual presence in great literature of the higher interests of man, his life on earth, and his spiritual relations to the universe. These essays contain the fruits of habitual familiarity with poetry, the convictions of a lifetime with regard to those things which are still important subjects of thought to thoughtful men; and there is, mingled with the style, the sweet persuasiveness of a refined and liberal nature, which is only too well aware that it must plead its cause, and pleads with strength and charm.

THREE MEN OF PIETY

BUNYAN

THE word genius is often used to conceal a puzzle which the critic, through defects of analytic power or sympathetic insight, is unable to solve; but perhaps this short and easy method was never more feebly resorted to than when a writer, with a strong prejudice in favor of sweetness and light, described Bunyan as a "Philistine of genius." In this designation there is much darkness and some acerbity. The wonderful thing about this man was not so much his gifts as the strange combination of them. There must be, of course, something extraordinary in any common man who becomes a leader in the higher life of the race. The history of the Church, however, is starred with the names of the ignorant and the humble who, since the fishermen were called from their nets by Galilee, have been chosen to be shepherds of the flock and evangelists of the faith. Bunyan was visited with the experience of Protestant Christendom, of which the successive terms are an outraged conscience, an offended God, and a miraculous pardon, and when he came to his peace he spread the glad news, acceptably to the pious, and convincingly to the impenitent; but tens of thousands in Christian lands have passed through that same strait gate, and hundreds of them have discovered that they possessed the gift of tongues. Had Bunyan done no more his sermons would have turned to yellow dust long ago, and his memory would be treasured only by a sect, for, eloquent as he was, he was not one of the missionaries who are world-famous. He wrote a book; and it turned out that this book of an uneducated man was a great literary classic. Had he written an epic it would have seemed less marvelous, because there is a popular superstition that nature makes poets, but in prose does not enter into competition with the common school. Bunyan wrote verses, it is true, and the man who set the delectable mountains on the rim of earth had the magical sight; but just as surely his doggerel shows that he had not the singing voice. He was a master of prose, and wrote a book that neighbors the Bible in our religious homes.

Two things are, of course, indispensable to a boy of genius, — imagination and the gift of expression. Now Bunyan was fond of expressing himself as very wicked in youth; and so he was, from his own point of view. The worst he can say for himself is, that he lied and swore, without malice or injury to others, but because he had a talent for tales and oaths. It is not trifling to remark that his powers of invention and forcible Saxon speech appear to have found their first channel in this sort of mental activity. The possible openings for the development of genius in the tinker's cottage at Bedford were few. It is plain that the mind of the young man was one of intense life, and, in the lack of guidance and knowledge, wandered at random or turned to feed upon itself. The only intellectual or moral ideas that came to him were conveyed from the Bible, mostly through the medium of the parish church in the years of the Puritan ascendency. The commonplace that the Bible affords a good education, especially on the imaginative and moral sides, is true, and the theology that attaches to it has developed strong intellects; it was, in the end, the total book-culture of Bunyan, — all that he knew of that vast and various world. But in the primary classes it is not a simple text-book of life, especially for a boy of genius who is all sense, all spirit. Bunyan in after years did not regret his first lessons; he preached that children should be taught the terrors of the law. Certainly his own mind laid hold of the easily apprehended images of threatened vengeance, and was filled with vague alarm and driven to a torturing scrutiny of his own spirit. The experience of conversion repeats in the individual the religious history of the race in the same order in which it is developed in the evolution of Biblical thought itself, and Bunyan's case was not substantially different from that of others, Puritan or Catholic, to whom there is no Calvary without a Sinai. The peculiarity lay in the soil into which this fiery seed was sown. His imagination ceased its childish fabling and became visionary; he saw, as the eye sometimes will, his mind-pictures, and this the more readily because his uneducated mind was accustomed to move through concrete ideas, and hence would be characterized by a high visualizing power. That this was a marked trait of his mental habit is shown by the fact that all his stories about himself are localized in a distinctly remembered place.

At this stage his mind approached the danger-line of religious madness: his descriptions of his moods, of his despairs, and of his struggles with fancies, whose importance to his intellectual life arose from the fewness of his ideas and the limited field of their play, show that he had no power over his thoughts, that he had not learned to use his will in thinking. This objectivity of his religious experience and his powerlessness before it, which have been recorded of other intense lives likewise, gave him a strong sense of the reality of spiritual things; and when he at last had laid his doubts and come into the calm, he kept this conviction to such a degree that earthly matters, even when religion was largely interested in politics, seemed of no consequence: this world was a dream, and the account of this conversion seems to indicate a lack of sanity, a spirit touched with the fever that ends in fanaticism; but we may be sure that to his hearers there was nothing incredible in it, nothing that could not be paralleled out of what they had known in themselves or heard from their neighbors. So, early in life, the plot of his career was brought to its crisis. In this faith in the reality of eternal things his mind reached its growth, and afterward knew no change.

But with this sure hold on the spirit and its high concerns there went a perfect realism. Bunyan was the opposite of a mystic. His common sense in his sermons of advice is extraordinarily close-packed and hard, and exhibits acute observation of the ways of human nature in practical life. He wrote once what was almost a novel, a history of one Mr. Badman, which is probably truer to contemporary life than the adventures of Jonathan Wild in the next century. If he did not weaken his eyesight over books, he sharpened it on men and women. All his volumes abound with anecdotes and incidents which he had evidently seen in the town streets or by the roadside, and with phrases and proverbial sayings close to the soil. Not the least agreeable of the signs of this realism, this sight for the bare fact in sense alone, are those descriptions of the country, of the birds, and flowers, and fields, and the simple cheerfulness of them to the country-born boy, which strew his pages from cover to cover. So, when he came to write his great book, he united in a perfectly natural way, and without forethought, the reality of a journey on earth with that of the search for heaven. The success with which, in a literary work, truth is fused with fact, is a measure of genius. It is, perhaps, more striking in this case because the work is an allegory, which is usually so drearily pale a kind of composition. The characters and action of the "Pilgrim's Progress," on the contrary, are a transcript of life, so vivid that it cannot wear out. It is not more realistic, however, than other portions of Bunyan's voluminous writings, in which one may get an idea of English provincial character of high historical value and human interest. How close, how truthful to his surroundings he was as a literary workman, is brought home with great force, though perhaps unconsciously, by the view which his biography gives of Bedford things and people.

From it one may reconstruct the religious state of the poor people of the Lincoln diocese in Bunyan's time, and bring very near the look of the lowly life which was the original soil of English dissent and the field of the tinker-preacher's labors. In reading terse extracts from the old documents — "short and simple annals of the poor," truly — of prayers in the barn and fines in the court-house, of levies on workmen's tools and old women's chattels, of these families of "the meanest sort," as the Bishop's schedule calls them, whose petty share of poverty was confiscated for the security of a Stuart throne and the Anglican prayer-book, — in reading of these things, a chapter of the history of the English people comes out which has been too closely written over with the wit and frolic of Charles's court; and the query as to what became of the Commonwealth when Cromwell died does not seem so wholly unanswerable as the silence of standard history on the point would indicate.

After all, one is almost inclined to say that no man ever owed more than Bunyan to his limitations. Within his bounds, he used all his spiritual and earthly experience, and, aided by a native gift of imagination and of fluency in the people's speech, blended them, and poured the full fountain of his life through his books. Had his youth included other powerful elements of emotion and knowledge besides his conversion, had theology or learning, or wider duties removed him somewhat more from the life of his neighbors and friends and the folk of the diocese, of which he was jestingly called the "bishop," he might have found so complete self-expression a mere difficult task. As it was, he told all he had to tell, — told the highest truth in the commonest words and made it current. It is curious to observe that he exhibits no consciousness that he is writing a great work; he speaks of a rush of thought and fancy, and an attractiveness in the subject, but he does not seem to think that he is doing more than adding another to the two-score publications he has already sent out. It is noticeable, too, that he did not meditate upon it for years beforehand, nor spend more than a few months in its composition. Some passages were added at a later time, but as a whole it was a spontaneous and rapid composition. The reason is that he was ripe for it. Without knowing it, he had been working up to this crowning book, both in thought, treatment, and style, through many years of sincere and straightforward, face-to-face conversation with men and women whom he was endeavoring to guide in the way which he had traveled. "Pilgrim's Progress" has been

called the last book that was written without the fear
of the reviewer; it is of more consequence that it is one
of the few works that have been composed without
ambition.

Bunyan's memory is singularly agreeable. Personally
he was free from the defects of assumption, dogmatism,
and spiritual pride, which entered largely into the religious character of his epoch, and his sensitive conscience
seems to have kept him humble after he had won a name.
The two great elements of his work — the homely
quality and the Christian quality — were deep-seated in
his nature, and give him charm. In an age of sectaries
he was not a narrow bigot, and did not stickle for meaningless things; and in a time of political strife, growing
out of religious differences, and though himself a sufferer by twelve years' imprisonment in early manhood,
he did not confuse heaven with any fantastic monarchy or
commonwealth of Christ in London, nor show any rancor
or revengeful spirit as a subject. It is worth remembering that out of Puritanism, which is regarded as a
narrow creed and life, came the only book since the
Reformation which has been acceptable to the whole of
Christendom, and is still regarded as the substantial
truth of the Christian life in all the churches that preach
it under any creed of orthodoxy. The life of the man
who could evolve such a story must have been very
simply typical of the Christian life itself. "A Philistine
of genius" — is there no light nor sweetness in this?

COWPER

The career of Cowper, as all the world knows, was one
to fill the pessimist with perennial gladness; and, in

fact, if it were possible to look at the natural order of things only as Cowper was affected thereby, it might seem that nothing short of malignity in the overruling powers could account for the fiat that gave up so pure, simple and cordial a nature to be the prey of the seven devils, and rendered so many delightful traits of character futile to achieve the happiness of their unfortunate possessor. In his letters, flowing on in the old, sweet, fresh English, one perceives the rare literary faculty, the shy humor, the discrimination, the sound sense, all the many graces of style and many virtues of intrinsic worth, that have long been familiar to scholars; and, more than that, one gladly recognizes again the companionable, softhearted, pathetic man whose pastimes, whether in gardening, or poetry, or caring for his pets, were a refuge from the most poignant anguish; who played only to escape his terror, and at last failed even in that. The piety of Cowper's life, however, although it contributes to his poetic attractiveness, is only a small part of what must be dealt with by the observer of that life as it appears in his letters. These, as a body, it is needless to say, hold a place from which they are not likely to be dislodged. Nevertheless, letters at the best are not a high form of literature; even when, as in the present case, their workmanship entitles them to rank as classics, their interest must finally reside in their being unconscious autobiography rather than in their artistic perfection. Hence, instead of regarding this correspondence as an object of literary *virtu*, it may be well for once to consider it with a more direct reference to the sober facts it chronicles and the spirit it reveals.

Few persons experienced in the world would be likely to hold up the routine of Cowper's days as worthy of

imitation. So far as earthly matters were involved, it
was a life of very small things; its mundane interests were
few and trivial, and sprang for the most part out of pursuits that belong usually either to the domain of childhood or invalidism. This is not said disparagingly, but
with due regard to the fact that for the larger part of
his career Cowper's condition was such that this attention
had to be distracted and his mind amused, as is the case
with children or invalids. In his later years the composition of verses became one mode of such diversion,
and was undertaken practically as a sanitary measure;
and thus his larger interests, involving conceptions of
the eternal world and sympathy with his fellow-men,
were extended to his hours of recreation. These larger
interests, as they must be called, were from the first
peculiar. When he was not attending to his hares or his
vegetables, or versifying, or taking rural walks, he
was engaged in devotional exercises of one kind
or another. In 1766, for example, every day the
time from breakfast until eleven o'clock was spent in
reading the Bible or sermons, or in religious conversation; the hour from eleven to twelve was passed in church
at service; in the course of the afternoon there was a
second period of religious conversation or hymn-singing;
at night there was commonly another sermon and more
psalms, and after that family prayers. In other words,
it appears that Cowper's life, at that time at least (and
it is a fair sample of the whole), consisted of an almost
monastic religious routine, relieved by the diversion of
country pursuits on a small scale, and, later, of literary
pursuits in addition. At present, as has been said, few
qualified judges would consider this a life of high order,
either in the way of wisdom or utility; but in Cowper's

case, the peculiarity of his mental condition and the
charm of his nature, revealed at its happy moments in
pleasant letters, blind the reader to the monotony and
vapidity of this existence, for such were its characteristics, except in so far as the healing influences of natural
scenes, to which Cowper was very sensitive, and the kindness of his household friends, gave it variety and substance.

Now, it is a very striking fact that while Cowper spent
the larger part of his time in religious reading and conversation, and besides meditated in private on the same
themes, his letters do not show in any degree that insight
into spiritual things which would naturally be looked
for from real genius occupied with such subjects. Spirituality should have been his trait if religion was his life,
but, in fact, these letters are in this regard barren. The
anomalous nature of his poetic life — the fact that he
used his powers, not to express his deepest emotions,
but to escape from them — may be pleaded in extenuation of what seems at first a surprising defect; but
a more likely explanation lies in another direction. It
was sermons that he read, theology that he talked about,
a theory of grace and salvation that he meditated upon
in secret; his religion occupied his thoughts rather than
his acts, touched his future rather than his present,
— in a word, it was a system rather than a life, the source
of doubt instead of inspiration. To put it in the simplest
form, he derived his light, not from his own inner experience, but from the creed. In his case the light was
the darkness of insanity; but his own conviction in the
matter is shown in his characterization of Beattie, —
"a man whose faculties have now and then a glimpse from
Heaven upon them, a man not indeed in possession of

much evangelical light, but faithful to what he has, and
never neglecting an opportunity to use it." A poet who
identifies "evangelical light" with "the vision and the
faculty divine" may write "The Castaway," but one is not
likely to find in his works those intimate revelations
of truth that flash in convincing beauty from the lines
of the true spiritualists, such as Wordsworth, Shelley,
or Emerson. Cowper's misfortune, both as a man and
a poet, was this substitution of dogma for instinct, which,
operating in so sensitive and feeble a nature, made religion, which was his vital interest, not a life but a disease,
and gave to the activities of his higher powers the character of mania. It is misleading, therefore, to think of these
letters as the fruit of a deeply religious mind; they are
the record of the efforts of a creed-believing mind to get
rid of itself, and their virtues — their amiability, their
delight in small adventures, their interest in literature
and humanity — exist not in consequence of but in spite
of the religious bent of their author.

Cowper was deficient, too, esthetically as well as
spiritually, and the character of his limitations was much
the same in both respects. His sense of beauty was
practically confined to landscape and small animals. The
cramping influences amid which he lived are well indicated by his remarks upon a clergyman who, it should
be said, richly deserved censure: —

"He seems, together with others of our acquaintance,
to have suffered considerably in his spiritual character
by his attachment to music. The lawfulness of it, when
used with moderation, and in its proper place, is unques-
tionable; but I believe that wine itself, though a man be
guilty of habitual intoxication, does not more debauch
and befool the natural understanding than music — al-

ways music, music in season and out of season — weakens
and destroys the spiritual discernment. If it is not used
with an unfeigned reference to the worship of God, and
with a design to assist the soul in the performance of it,
which cannot be the case when it is the only occupation,
it degenerates into a sensual delight, and becomes a
most powerful advocate for the admission of other pleasures, grosser, perhaps, in degree, but in their kind the
same."

Whatever truth there may be in this estimate of the
influence of music, the limitation of its use to church
choirs and organs is an expression of Puritan iconoclasm
which acquaints the reader at once with Cowper's provincialism. The passage is English to the core, and not
only does it suggest the esthetic deficiencies of the poet
and his life, but it also brings up once more the characteristic English picture of the family singing psalms and
reading sermons, year in, year out, with which the letters
begin. This correspondence has made that group of interest to the world; but in answer to the question, What
was its life and its spirit, can one help feeling that trivial,
not to say belittling, occupations, and a narrowing
theology, were principal elements? Cowper's work, in
the main, has only the sluggish vitality of this life; in
his letters more than in his verses, speaking generally,
there is literary grace and a personal charm; but in both
they seem a sort of salvage. A vision of quiet green
fields, inhabited by respectable gentlefolk who led an
existence of humble routine in a neighborly way, made
up Cowper's world; he lived in it overshadowed by the
ever present fear of damnation, and at last, sunk in
despair, he died in it. Out of such a world no great
poet either of the soul or of nature could come.

CHANNING

Channing was the chief ornament of the American pulpit in his day. Like nearly all men illustrious in the religious life, he has won a kindlier and wider regard by his character than by his opinions, because the moods of devotion are simple and are universal in human nature, while opinion in theology is more variable and eccentric, and in some degree more accidental, than in any other branch of speculation. The deepest interest of his life lies not so much in the fruit of his genius as in the light of his spirit. Indeed, this acknowledgment is wrapped up in the indiscriminate eulogy by which his admirers have injured his fame, for they have presented him as a saint rather than as a thinker, as an example of ideal living rather than as a finder of truth. To put a man in the catalogue of saints is merely to write his epitaph; his life is the main thing, and Channing, although his biography records no great deeds in the world and no great crises of inner experience is not alone in being far more interesting in his humanity than in his canonization. A refined and sensitive childhood, shadowed in some partially explained way, so that he never remembered it as a period of joyfulness, was followed by a spirited and dreaming youth, caught by the fervors of French revolutionary ideas and exalted by its own noble motives. In those early years, as well as in his late maturity, he experienced, on the beach at Newport and under the willows at Cambridge, moments of insight and impulse which stood out ever after in his memory as new births of the spirit prophetic of the future. His career was especially determined, however, by the twenty-one months which he passed at Richmond as a private tutor, immediately after leaving college. There, in loneliness and poverty, in stoical disregard of health and courting privation, in Christian conscientiousness of motive, led on by glowing reveries in which visionary objects seemed realities within reach, he devoted himself in written words to the service of mankind by the instrumentalities of religion. It is painful to read the narrative of this intense personal life in the years most susceptible to enthusiasm for remote and ideal ends; there can be no wonder that after such experience he returned home with the seal of the religious life set upon his soul, and with a body inexorably condemned to life-long disease. He entered upon his ministry in the field where he could best do good and find peace in doing it; morally the child of the New England religious spirit, and intellectually the disciple of those ideas of the nature of humanity and the right course of its development which the French Revolution had disseminated. Throughout his life he was governed mainly by a deep sense of the dignity of manhood, under whatever form, and by an abiding conviction of the aid which Christianity gives to the imagination and heart in obeying the rule of love and obtaining permanent peace of mind.

The most acute criticism ever passed upon Channing's character was by that unnamed critic who said, "He was kept from the highest goodness by his love of rectitude." The love of rectitude was his predominant trait; he was enslaved by it. He exacted more of himself, however, than of others. Right he must be, at all hazards, in motive, in opinion, and action. It is melancholy to read page after page of his self-examination, so minute, intricate, and painful, so frequent and long continued.

It almost awakens a doubt of the value of noble character to find it so unsure of itself, to see its possessor so
absorbed in hunting his own shadow within the inner-
most retreats of thought and feeling. Channing seems to
have preached more sermons to himself than to the world.
His love of rectitude led him to this excessive conscientiousness, but brought him great good in other directions.
It gave him a respect for the opinions of other men as
catholic as it was humble. He did not practice toleration
toward them, for that expression implied to his mind a
misplaced self-confidence; but he practiced charity, as
toward men who felt equally with himself the binding
force of the obligation to be right, and who had an equal
chance of finding truth. His conviction of the universal-
ity of this obligation and his perception that it necessi-
tates the independent exercise of individual powers encouraged in him a remarkable admiration for individuality, for the unhampered exercise of thought and unquestioned obedience to motive in which the richness
of individual life consists.

His second great quality, as pervasive and controlling
as his desire to be right, was sensibility. It was revealed
in the sympathies and affections of private life, which
are known to the world only by the report of friends;
but it may be seen with equal clearness in the intensity
of his delight in nature, and the ardent feeling by
which he realized ideal ends and gave them a living
presence in his own life as objects of continuous effort.
His sensitiveness to natural beauty was so keen that in
moments of physical weakness it caused pain. "There
are times," he wrote, "when I have been so feeble that
a glance at the natural landscape, or even the sight of
a beautiful flower, gave me bodily pain from which I

shrank." As life drew on to its end, the indestructible loveliness of nature became to him a source of joy and peace ever more prized. "The world grows younger with age!" he exclaimed more than once. In emotional susceptibility to ideas he resembled Shelley, and probably it was this likeness of feeling which led him to call Shelley, in ministerial language, but with extraordinary charity for that age, "a seraph gone astray." He retained through life the intellectual sympathies of his youth, and in his last days still had an inclination toward community of property as the solution of the social problem; like Wordsworth and Southey he recoiled from the excesses of the French, but he never gave up the tricolor for the white cockade. In his generation nearly all men were hopeful of the accomplishment of beneficent reforms; but Channing was filled with an enthusiasm of hope which was almost the fervor of conviction. He was without that practical enthusiasm which is aroused by the presence of great deeds immediately to be done; the objects for which he worked were far in the distance, scarcely discernible except from the mount of vision; but he was possessed by the enthusiasm which is kindled by the heat of thought and is wrapped in its solitary flames, and he lived under the bright zenith of that mood of which Carlyle has shown the dark nadir and Teufelsdröch standing in its shadow gazing out over the sleeping city. These three principles — rectitude, sensibility, enthusiasm — were elemental in Channing's nature; and because they are moral, and not intellectual, he lived a spiritual rather than a mental life; he gained in depth rather than in breadth, and worked out his development by contemplation and prayer rather than by thought and act.

It appears strange, at first, that a man with these endowments should have been so conservative in opinion, and so little inclined to force upon the world what advanced opinions he did hold. A lover of truth unwilling to make proselytes, an enthusiast unwilling to act, seems an anomaly; but such was Channing's position. One cause of his aversion to pushing Unitarianism to its conclusion is found in the history of his own conversion and in the character of his attachment to the new faith; he was a revolter of the heart; he was liberalized by his feelings. "My inquiries," he said, "grew out of the shock given to my moral nature by the popular system of faith." He was moved by sentiment in his rejection of Calvinism, and he was kept by sentiment from giving up the theory of the mysterious character and mission of Christ. The strength of his feelings operated to render him conservative, and the low estimate he apparently placed upon logical processes contributed to the same end. "It is a good plan," he wrote, "ever and anon to make a clean sweep of that to which we have arrived by logical thought, and take a new view; for the mind needs the baptism of wonder and hope to keep it vigorous and healthy for intuition." Either this distrust of the understanding working by logical processes, or else a native ineptitude for theological reasoning, prevented him from following out his principles to their conclusion. If he had framed a system, he would have held his views with greater certainty; as it was, he not only allowed the greatest liberty to individual opinion, but he distrusted himself. "You young thinkers," he said, "have the advantage of us in coming without superstitious preoccupation to the words of Scripture, and are more likely to get the obvious meaning. We shall walk in shadows to our graves." The strength of inbred sentiment could not be overpowered by such feeble intellectual conviction. He was a moral, not an intellectual, reformer; his work was not the destruction of a theology, but the spread of charity. He felt more than he reasoned, and hence his rationalism was bounded, not by the unknown, but by the mystical. He was satisfied with this, and does not seem to have wished to make a definite statement of his beliefs. The whole matter is summed up by Miss Peabody when she says, "The Christianity which Dr. Channing believed . . . was a spirit, not a form of thought." A spirit of devotion toward the divine, a spirit of love toward the human Channing preached to the world and illustrated by his life; but a new form of thought which shows the intellectual advance that alone is fatal to conservatism — this was not part of his gift to men.

In the antislavery cause his conservatism appears in a less pleasing light. Here he exhibited the scholar's reluctance to initiate reform, the scholar's perplexity before the practical barriers in the way of action. He was displeased by the rude voices about him, and frightened by the violence of determination which the reformers displayed. He looked to find the peace of the pulpit in the arena, and was bewildered by the alarms of the active strife. He did not choose his side until the last moment, and even then he delayed until he called down the just rebuke of May and the just defense that reformer made for his comrades: "The children of Abraham held their peace until at last the very stones have cried out, and you must expect them to cry out like the stones." Then, indeed, Channing showed that he was a Falkland on Cromwell's side, not acting without a doubt, but taking his place, nevertheless,

openly and manfully beside the friend whom he had
left alone too long. Yet he never lost, even in that
stirring cause, the timidity of culture. He was of the
generation of those cultivated men who earned for Boston the reputation for intellectual preëminence; but the
political future of the country did not belong to him nor
to his companions; it belonged to Garrison and Lincoln.
Here it is that Father Taylor's keen criticism strikes
home: "What a beautiful being Dr. Channing is! If
he only had had any education!" Channing's education had been of the lamp, and not of the sword; it
seemed to Father Taylor pitifully narrow and palsy-
stricken beside his own experience of the world's misery.
Channing's life affords one more illustration of the difficulty the cultivated man finds in understanding and for-
warding reform in its beginning; but he deserves, the
credit of having rid himself of the prejudices and influences that marked the society in which he moved, to a
greater degree, perhaps, than any other of his circle.

The value of Channing's work in religion and in
reform will be differently rated by men, for his service
was of a kind which is too apt to be forgotten. The
intrinsic worth of his writings remains to be tested by
time; but their historic worth, as a means of liberaliz-
ing the New England of his day, was great and memorable. He gave his right hand to Emerson and his left
hand to Parker; and, although he could not accompany
them on the way, he bade them Godspeed. It was, perhaps, mainly through his influence that they found the
field prepared for them and the harvest ready, although
he would not put his sickle in. It was largely due to
him, also, that Boston became the philanthropic center
of the country. During his lifetime he won a remark-

able respect and admiration. An exaggerated estimate of his eloquence, powers, and influence will continue to be held so long as any remain alive who heard his voice and remember its accents; in later times a truer judgment may be reached. Personally he was amiable, kindly, and courteous, notwithstanding the distance at which he seems to have kept all men. Dr. Walker said that conversation was always constrained in his study. In his nephew's narrative, it is said that the interview with him was "solemn as the visit to the shrine of an oracle." He himself told Miss Peabody after their friendship had lasted several years, that she had "the awe of the preacher" upon her. Finally, we read that no man ever freely laid his hand upon Channing's shoulder; and we wonder whether he ever remembered that St. John had "handled the Word made flesh." This self-seclusion, this isolation of sanctity, as it were, did not proceed from any value he set upon himself above his fellows; it was that natural failing of a man who lived much within himself, and who always meditated the loftiest of unworldly themes. He was a faithful and well-beloved friend; and if in this, as in other directions, he "failed of the highest goodness," there are few in the same walk of life who attain to equal sincerity, charity, and purity, or equal serviceableness to the world.

JOHN GREENLEAF WHITTIER

THE time has come to pay tribute of farewell upon the occasion of the death of Whittier. The popular instinct which long ago adopted him as the poet of New England is one of those sure arbiters, superior to all academic judgments upon the literary works of a man, which confer a rightful fame in life, and justify the expectation of a long remembrance. Whittier was distinctly a local poet, a New Englander; but to acknowledge this does not diminish his honor, nor is he thereby set in a secondary place. His locality, if one may use the expression, was a country by itself; its inhabitants were a peculiar people, with a strongly marked social and moral character, with a landscape and an atmosphere, with historical traditions, legends often romantic, and with strong vitalizing ideas. There was something more than a literary fancy in the naturalness with which Whittier sought a kind of fellowship with Burns; there was a true resemblance in their situation as the poets of their own kin and soil, in their reliance upon the strength of the people of whom they were born, and in their cherished attachment to the places and scenes where they grew up. New England, moreover, had this advantage, that it was destined to set the stamp of its character upon the larger nation in which it was an element; so that if Whittier be regarded, as he sometimes is, as a representative American poet, it is not without justice. He is really national so far as the spirit of New England has passed into the nation at large; and that vast body of Western settlers who bore New England to the frontier, and yet look back to the old homestead, find in him the sentiment of their past. There can be little question, too, that he is representative of a far larger portion of the American people than any other of the elder poets. His lack of the culture of the schools has here been in his favor, and has brought him closer to the common life; he is more democratic than he otherwise might have been; and the people, recognizing in him their own strain, have accepted him with a judgment as valid as that with which cultivated critics accept the work of the man of genius who is also an artist. One calls him a local poet rather to define his qualities than to characterize his range.

The New England which Whittier represents has now become historical. The length of his life carried him beyond his times. It is plainer now than it was at an earlier day that his poems are one of the living records of a past which will be of perennial interest and ever held in honor. That his early poetic career fell in with the anti-slavery movement was not a misfortune for his Muse; the man fed upon it, and drew therefrom an iron strength for the moral nature which was the better half of his endowment. He was, too, one who was destined to develop, to reach his powers, more by exercising than by cultivating his poetic gift; and in the events of the agitation for the abolition of slavery he had subjects that drew out his moral emotions with most eloquent heat, and exalted his spirit to its utmost of sympathy, indignation, and heroic trust. The anti-slavery movement was his education — in a true sense, the gymnastic of his genius; but in the whole body of his work it was no more than an incident, although the most stirring and most noble, in his literary career, just as it was no more in the career of New England.

The great events with which a man deals, and part of which he is, obscure the other portions of his life; but it should not be forgotten that Whittier began as a poet, and not as a reformer, and it may be added that the poet in him was, in the long run, more than the reformer. He did not resort to verse as an expedient in propagandism; rather, wearing the laurel — to use the good old phrase — he descended into the field just as he was. He had begun with those old Indian legends in lines which still echoed with Byron's tales, and he had with them much the same success that attended other aboriginal poetry. It seems, as one reads the hundred weary epics, from which Whittier's are hardly to be distinguished, that the curse of extinction resting on the doomed race clung also to the Muse that so vainly attempted to recompense it with immortality in the white man's verse. These were Whittier's juvenile trials. He came early, nevertheless, to his mature form in the ballad and the occasional piece; his versification was fixed, his manner determined, and thenceforth there was no radical change.

This is less remarkable inasmuch as it is a commonplace to say that he owed nothing to art; the strength of his native genius was all his secret, and when he had freed a way for its expression the task of his novitiate was done. He had now a mold in which to run his metal, and it satisfied him because he was not exacting of perfect form or high-finish; probably he had no sense for them. This indifference to the artistic workmanship, which a later day prizes so much as to require it, allowed him to indulge his natural facility, and the very simplicity of his meters was in itself a temptation to diffuseness. The consequence was that he wrote much, and not always well, unevenness being usually characteristic of poets who rely on the energy of their genius for the excellence of their work. To the artist his art serves often as a conscience, and forces him to a standard below which he is not content to fall. Whittier, however, experienced the compensations which are everywhere to be found in life, and gained in fullness, perhaps, more than he lost in other ways. The free flow of his thought, the simplicity of his structure, the willingness not to select with too nice a sense, but to tell the whole, all helped to that frankness of the man which is the great charm of his works, taken together, and assisted him in making his expression of old New England life complete. No man could have written "Snow-Bound" who remembered Theocritus. In Whittier, Nature reminds us, as she is wont to do from time to time, that the die which she casts exceeds the diploma of the school. Art may lift an inferior talent to higher estimation, but genius makes a very little art go a long way. This was Whittier's case. The poetic spark was inborn in him, living in his life; and when academic criticism has said its last word, he remains a poet, removed by a broad and not doubtful line from all stringers of couplets and filers of verses.

Whittier had, in addition to this clear native genius, character; his subject, too, New England, had character; and the worth of the man blending with the worth of the life he portrayed, independent of all considerations of art, has won for him the admiration and affection of the common people, who know the substance of virtue, and always see it shining with its own light. They felt that

Whittier wrote as they would have written, had they been gifted with the miraculous tongues; and this feeling is a true criterion to discover whether a poet has expressed the people rather than himself. They might choose to write like the great artist of letters; they know they never could do so; but Whittier is one of themselves.

The secret of his vogue with the plain people is his own plainness. He appeals directly to the heart, as much in his lesser poems as in those which touch the sense of right and wrong in men with stinging keenness, or in those which warm faith to its ardor. He has the popular love of a story, and tells it more nearly in the way of the old ballad-makers. He does not require a tragedy, or a plot, or any unusual action. An incident, if it only have some glamour of fancy, or a touch of pathos, or the likeness of old romance, is enough for him; he will take it and sing it merely as something that happened. He was familiar with the legendary lore and historical anecdote of his own county of Essex, and he enjoyed these traditions less as history than as poetry; he came to them on their picturesque and human side, and cared for them because of the emotions they could still awake. It is to be acknowledged, too, that the material for these romances was just such as delights the popular imagination. The tales of the witches, notwithstanding the melancholy of the delusion, have something of the eeriness that is inseparable from the thought of the supernatural, and stir the dormant sense of some evil fascination; and the legends of spectral shapes that haunted every seacoast in old times, and of which New England had its share, have a similar quality. Whether they are told by credulous Mather or the make-believing poet, they have the same power to cast a spell. When to this sort of interest

Whittier adds, as he often does, the sights of religious persecution, or some Lochinvar love-making, or the expression of his faith in heaven, his success as a story-teller is assured. In reality, he has managed the ballad form with more skill than other measures; but it is because he loves a story and tells it for its own sake, with the ease of one who sits by the fireside, and with a childish confidence that it will interest, that he succeeds so well in pleasing. In his sea-stories, and generally in what he writes about the ocean, it is observable that he shows himself to be an inland-dweller, whose acquaintance with the waves is by distant glimpses and vacation days. He is not a poet of the sea, but this does not invalidate the human truth of his tales of voyaging, which is the element he cared for. Perhaps the poetic quality of his genius is most clear in these ballads; there is a freer fancy; there are often verses about woman's eyes and hair and cheeks, all with similes from sky and gold and roses, in the old fashion, but not with less naturalness on that account; there is a more absorbing appeal to the imagination both in the characters and the incidents. If these cannot be called his most vigorous work, they are at least most attractive to the purely poetic taste.

In the ballads, nevertheless, one feels the strong undertow of the moral sense dragging the mind back to serious realities. It is probably true of all the English stock, as it certainly is of New England people, that they do not object to a moral, in a poem or anywhere else. Whittier's moral hold upon his readers is doubtless greater than his poetic hold. He appeals habitually to that capacity for moral feeling which is the genius of New England in its public life, and the explanation of its extraordinary influence. No one ever appeals to it in vain; and with such a cause as Whittier took up to champion, he could ring out a challenge that was sure to rank the conscience of his people upon his side. His Quaker blood, of which he was proud, pleaded strongly in his own veins. He was the inheritor of suffering for conscience' sake; he was bred in the faith of equality, of the right of every man to private judgment, and the duty of every man to follow it in public action; and he was well grounded in the doctrines of political liberty which are the foundation of the commonwealth. It is more likely, however, that his enthusiasm for the slave did not proceed from that love of freedom which is the breath of New England. It arose from his humanity, in the broad sense; from his belief, sincerely held and practiced, in the brotherhood of men; from the strong conviction that slavery was wrong. It was a matter of conscience more than of reason, of compassion and sympathy more than of theoretical ideas. These were the sources of his moral feeling; his attitude was the same whether he was dealing with Quaker outrages in the past or with negro wrongs in the present. In expressing himself upon the great topic of his time, he was thus able to make the same direct appeal to the heart that was natural to his temperament. The people either felt as he did, or were so circumstanced that they would respond from the same springs which had been touched in him, if a way could be found to them. Outside of the reserves of political expediency, the movement for abolition was harmonious with the moral nature of New England. Yet Whittier's occasional verses upon this theme made him only the poet of his party. In themselves they have great vigor of feeling, and fre-

quently force of language; they have necessarily the
defects, judged from the artistic standpoint, of poems
upon a painful subject, in which it was desirable not
to soften, but to bring out the tragedy most harshly.
The pain, however, is entirely in the facts presented; the
poetry lies in the indignation, the eloquence, the fine
appeal.   These verses, indeed, are nearer to a prose level
than the rest of his work, in the sense of partaking of
the character of eloquence rather than of poetry.   Their
method is less through the imagination than by rhetoric.
They are declamatory.   But rhetoric of the balanced and
concise kind natural to short metrical stanzas is especially well adapted to arrest popular attention and to hold
it.   Just as he told a story in the ballad with a true
popular feeling, so he pleaded the cause of the abolition-
ists in a rhetoric most effective with the popular taste.
In the war time, he rose, under the stress of the great
struggle, to finer poetic work; the softer feelings of pity,
together with a solemn religious trust, made the verses
of those battle-summers different in quality from those
of the literary conflict of the earlier years.   He never
surpassed, on the lower level of rhetoric, the lines which
bade farewell to Webster's greatness, nor did he ever
equal in intensity those rallying cries of defiance to the
South, in which the free spirit of the North seemed to
speak before its time.   In these he is urging on to the
conflict — a moral and peaceful one, he thought, but
not less real and hard; in the war pieces, he seems
rather to be waiting for the decision of Providence, while
the fight has rolled on far in the van of where he stands.
The power of all these poems, their reality to those times,
is undeniable.   Their fitness for declamation perhaps
spread his reputation.   Longfellow is distinctly the chil-

dren's poet; but Whittier had a part of their suffrages, and it was by such stirring occasional verses that he gained them. In those years of patriotism he was to many of them, as he was to me, the first poet whom they knew. At that time his reputation in ways like these became established. If he had not then done his best work, he had at times reached the highest level he was to attain, and he had already given full expression to his nature. His place as the poet of the anti-slavery movement was fixed. It is observable that he did not champion other causes after that of abolition was won, and in this he differed from most of his companions. The only other cause that roused him to the point of poetic expression was that of the Italian patriots. Some of his most indignant and sharpest invective was directed against Pope Pius IX, who stood to Whittier as the very type of that Christian obstructiveness to the work of Christ which in a lesser degree he had seen in his own country, and had seen always only to express the heart-felt scorn which descended to him with his Quaker birthright.

It would be unfitting to leave this part of the subject without reference to the numerous personal tributes, often full of grace, of tender feeling, and of true honor paid to the humble, which he was accustomed to lay as his votive wreath on the graves of his companions. One is struck once more by the reflection how large a part those who are now forgotten had in advancing the cause, how many modest but earnest lives entered into the work, and what a feeling of comradery there was among those engaged in philanthropic service in all lands. The verses to Garrison and Sumner naturally stand first in fervor and range as well as in interest, but

nearly all these mementos of the dead have some touch
of nobility.

The victory of the Northern ideas left to Whittier a
freer field for the later exercise of his talent. It was
natural that he should have been among the first to
speak words of conciliation to the defeated South, and
to offer to forget. He was a man of peace, of pardons,
of all kinds of catholic inclusions; and in this temperament with regard to the future of the whole country,
fortunately, the people agreed with him. With the coming of the years of reconciliation his reputation steadily
gained. His representative quality as a New Englander
was recognized. It was seen that from the beginning
the real spirit of New England had been truly with him,
and, the cause being now won and the past a great one,
his countrymen were proud of him for having been a
part of it. At this happy moment he produced a work
free from any entanglement with things disputed, remarkable for its truth to life, and exemplifying the character
of New England at its fireside in the way which comes
home to all men. It is not without perfect justice that
"Snow-Bound" takes rank with "The Cotter's Saturday
Night" and "The Deserted Village"; it belongs in this
group as a faithful picture of humble life. It is perfect
in its conception and complete in its execution; it is the
New England home, entire, with its characteristic scene,
its incidents of household life, its Christian virtues.
Perhaps many of us look back to it as Horace did to
the Sabine farm; but there are more who can still remember it as a reality, and to them this winter idyl
is the poetry of their own lives. It is, in a peculiar
sense, the one poem of New England — so completely
indigenous that the soil has fairly created it, so genuine

as to be better than history. It is by virtue of this poem that Whittier must be most highly rated, because he is here most impersonal, and has succeeded in expressing the common life with most directness. All his affection for the soil on which he was born went into it; and no one ever felt more deeply that attachment to the region of his birth which is the great spring of patriotism. In his other poems he had told the legends of the country, and winnowed its history for what was most heroic or romantic; he had often dwelt, with a reiteration which emphasized his fondness, upon its scenery in every season, by all its mountains and capes and lakes and rivers, as if fearful lest he should offend by omission some local divinity of the field or flood; he had shared in the great moral passion of his people in peace and war, and had become its voice and been adopted as one of its memorable leaders; but here he came to the heart of the matter, and by describing the homestead, which was the unit and center of New England life, he set the seal upon his work, and entered into all New England homes as a perpetual guest.

There remains one part of his work, and that, in some respects, the loftiest, which is in no sense local. The Christian faith which he expressed is not to be limited as distinctly characteristic of New England. No one would make the claim. It was descended from the Quaker faith only as Emerson's was derived from that of the Puritan. Whittier belongs with those few who arise in all parts of the Christian world and out of the bosom of all sects, who are lovers of the spirit. They illustrate the purest teachings of Christ, they express the simplest aspirations of man; and this is their religious life. They do not trouble themselves except to do good, to be sincere, to walk in the sight of the higher powers with humbleness, and if not without doubt, yet with undiminished trust. The optimism of Whittier is one with theirs. It is indissolubly connected with his humanity to men. In his religious as in his moral nature there was the same simplicity, the same entire coherency. His expression of the religious feeling is always noble and impressive. He is one of the very few whose poems, under the fervor of religious emotion, have taken a higher range and become true hymns. Several of these are already adopted into the books of praise. But independently of these few most complete expressions of trust and worship, wherever Whittier touches upon the problems of the spiritual life he evinces the qualities of a great and liberal nature; indeed, the traits which are most deeply impressed upon us, in his character, are those which are seen most clearly in his religious verse. It is impossible to think of him and forget that he is a Christian. It is not rash to say that it is probable that his religious poems have reached many more hearts than his anti-slavery pieces, and have had a profounder influence to quiet, to console, and to refine. Yet he was not distinctly a poet of religion, as Herbert was. He was a man in whom religion was vital, just as affection for his home and indignation at wrongdoing were vital. He gave expression to his manhood, and consequently to the religious life he led. There are in these revelations of his nature the same frankness and the same reality as in his most heated polemics with the oppressors of the weak; one cannot avoid feeling that it is less the poet than the man who is speaking, and that in his words he is giving himself to his fellow-men. This sense that Whittier belongs to that class of writers in whom the man is larger than his

work is a just one.   Over and above his natural genius
was his character.   At every step of the analysis, it is
not with art, but with matter, not with the literature of
taste, but with that of life, not with a poet's skill, but
with a man's soul, that we find ourselves dealing; in a
word, it is with character almost solely: and it is this
which has made him the poet of his people, as the highest art might have failed to do, because he has put his
New England birth and breeding, the common inheritance of her freedom-loving, humane, and religious people
which he shared, into plain living, yet on such a level
of distinction that his virtues have honored the land.

The simplicity and dignity of Whittier's later years, and
his fine modesty in respect to his literary work, have
fitly closed his career.   He has received in the fullest
measure from the younger generation the rewards of
honor which belong to such a life.   In his retirement
these unsought tributes of an almost affectionate veneration have followed him; and in the struggle about us for
other prizes than those he aimed at, in the crush for
wealth and notoriety, men have been pleased to remember him, the plain citizen, uncheapened by riches and
unsolicitous for fame, ending his life with the same habits
with which he began it, in the same spirit in which he
led it, without any compromise with the world.   The
Quaker aloofness which has always seemed to characterize him, his difference from other men, has never been
sufficient to break the bonds which unite him with the
people, but it has helped to secure for him the feeling
with which the poet is always regarded as a man apart;
the religious element in his nature has had the same
effect to win for him a peculiar regard akin to that
which was felt in old times for the sacred office; to the

imagination he has been, especially in the years of his age, a man of peace and of God. No one of his contemporaries has been more silently beloved and more sincerely honored. If it be true that in him the man was more than the poet, it is happily not true, as in such cases it too often is, that the life was less than it should have been. The life of Whittier affects us rather as singularly fortunate in the completeness with which he was able to do his whole duty, to possess his soul, and to keep himself unspotted from the world. He was fortunate in his humble birth and the virtues which were about his cradle; he was fortunate in the great cause for which he suffered and labored in his prime, exactly fitted as it was to develop his nature to its highest moral reach, and lift him to real greatness of soul; he was fortunate in his old age, in the mellowness of his humanity, the repose of his faith, the fame which, more truly than can usually be said, was "love disguised." Lovers of New England will cherish his memory as that of a man in whom the virtues of this soil, both for public and for private life, shine most purely. On the roll of American poets we know not how he may be ranked hereafter, but among the honored names of the New England past his place is secure.

JAMES RUSSELL LOWELL

MR. LOWELL has written into his works his many titles
to public remembrance with singular completeness. One
need not go outside of the ten volumes in which the
fruits of a long literary and public life are gathered to
know what he has been and has done. The sign-manual
of the poet, critic, and scholar is set upon the various
page; moods of the fields and the homestead, the permanent attraction of human nature, patriotism profoundly
felt are equally found in essay and poem; and in the
admirable addresses there is stored up a lasting memory
of the years of his distinguished service abroad. The
fullness of this expression of a many-sided career is remarkable; but even more striking is the harmony of
all these phases of life, one with another. There is no
dividing line which sets off one part of his activity from
its neighbor part; in his poetry there is politics, in his
learning there is the vivifying touch of humor, in his
reflection there is emotion, in the levels of his most
familiar prose there is, at inconstant intervals, the sudden
lift of a noble thought; and hence his works are at once
too diverse and too similar — diverse in their matter and
similar in the personality through which they are given
out — to be easily summed or described by the methods
of criticism. If there is a clew that may be used, it is
to be sought in his individuality, in the fact that his ten
talents have somehow been melted and fused into one,
and that the greatest — the talent of being a man first

and everything else afterward. It goes with this that
one looks in vain for any separation of his work into
marked periods, such as may be observed in those writers
who are absorbed by successive moods of the age or by
new foreign influences in thought or literary forms, or
generally are determined in their character by external
forces. Mr. Lowell, with all his free curiosity, alertness of attention, and openness to the world of the
present and of the past, has exercised a power of reaction equal to that of his receptivity, and illustrates the
slow native growth of a self-assured mind. From the
first to the last of his pages the unity of mind is such
that, unhelped by the context, one could rarely say with
certainty whether a particular passage was from earlier
or later years. Neither the style nor the way of thinking materially changes; the same person speaks with the
same voice throughout. This singleness of Mr. Lowell's
personality, by virtue of which he has held the same
course from youth to age, as it is most obvious, is a
cardinal matter. It were impossible to condense into
the brief critical sketch for which only there is now
occasion, all that criticism must find to say upon his
writings throughout their reach; but in the absence of
such a complete and careful survey, something may be
arrived at, possibly, by attending to this stamp of individuality which gives likeness to all his works and imparts
to them that quality of the living voice which most interests and best holds men, and is besides the invariable
accompaniment of an original mind in literature.

It is commonly a disadvantage to a poet to be reputed
a scholar. Belief in the spontaneity of genius is deeply
implanted in men's mind, and culture is set over against
the simple primitive powers of feeling and thought as

something by nature opposite. In this popular opinion there is a share of truth. Instinct is the method of genius, but culture, until it has been absorbed into character and temperament, works by afterthought. The conflict which is indicated by this widely diffused impression of the incompatibility of learning and inspiration is often felt by a poet himself in his own experience. Mr. Lowell, who more than any other writer of his time expresses the moods of that borderland which lies between instinct and reflection, speaks more than once of the intrusion of thought upon the natural way of living, and shows the old annoyance, that poetical regret for a simpler habit of life, which underlies the dream of the golden age and is the source of the charm of all pastoral. In a considerable portion of his nature-verse he accepts the Wordsworthian doctrine and goes to the fields as an escape from books, lays thought down like a burden and plays it is holiday with him, and in coming back to the study seems to make an unwelcome return to himself. Yet he is not slow to acknowledge that the true poet has a pedigree that goes far into the past of men as well as a kinship of the day and hour with sky and birds and trees, the soft air and the warm landscape. If he seeks impulses in nature, he must find art in books; and from his earlier poems it is plain to see what sources in literature he most haunted. Imitativeness in youthful verse is a measure of susceptibility, and is rather a sign of strength than of weakness. The test of originality, or of the native force of the poetical endowment, lies in the quickness with which one type shifts with another. It is noticeable that Mr. Lowell reproduced kinds of poetry rather than particular authors, style rather than moods, the cast of the words, not ideas; and the sign of culture in these beginnings is shown in the number of types which attracted him. So a similar literary scholarship, an acquaintance with what the poets of many lands had written, gave to Longfellow in his mature life, as well as at the outset, models of style which he made his own rather by graceful use of them than by informing them with original genius. In Mr. Lowell's case, perhaps, the single peculiarity is the taste he early showed for certain of the English poets of the seventeenth century whose defects of oddity and unevenness could not destroy the largeness of their phrase and the purity and elevation of their continuous style at its best. One need not read Mr. Lowell's criticism to discover what value he placed upon Donne and Vaughan, for example, and those who neighbor them in the "well-languaged" manner. Culture of this sort, delight in poetry, has been the possession of many of those poets who are most thought inspired, and genius has thrived upon it; but usually the greatest of them have felt the gap between such poetry of the past and the nature they stood in presence of, and each in turn has reconciled his genius with his own age in some original way.

Mr. Lowell soon developed several styles in which he wrote poems of many kinds, and gave literary expression to sentiment, thought, and emotion; but he was later preëminently distinguished by three forms of verse. The most popular of these, apparently, and certainly the most original, is that in which he employed the native Yankee speech. It was fairly by accident, he says, that he discovered the power of this New England lingo to express the character of the breed of men who used it and its fitness for the purpose in dealing with the subjects to which he applied it. Nevertheless, chance has

as little place in literature as in other affairs of life.
One finds only those things to which his faith has led
him.   There are reasons in plenty why Mr. Lowell, and
not any of his contemporaries in letters, made the happy
discovery of the Yankee idyl.   His own roots go deep
into the native soil; he loves that from which he sprang,
and the past was realized to his apprehension most
directly through the old time, which still lingered about
the Cambridge of his growing years, and through its concrete characters of diverse types from clerical to rural
which interested his human sympathy, struck his humorous sense, and embodied for him the long tradition of
a dying age showing its results in man.   This strong
attachment to the paternal acres because of old associations is a trait common to New England; but none of the
poets of the land have given more frequent and free
expression to the feeling or shown its power in an individual more constantly.   The old New England character
appealed to him in the same way that the Scotch type
drew Sir Walter Scott's heart out; each found in the
ancient habit of life of "sixty years since" a literary
opportunity, but not by thought prepense; in both the
old ways, crystallized in human nature, were loved for
their own sake with a kind of natural affection, and were
besides dignified by a true respect for their moral quality
felt through all their humorous peculiarities.   Scotland
had more of history, of romance, and picturesqueness to
mingle with the human element of common lives; in
New England there was less of circumstance, but there
was a core of character equally sound, a way of thinking and a freshness of expression, marked and peculiar,
characterizing a people.   The attractiveness of such
survivals from the old days as Mr. Lowell either knew in

the beginning of life or met with from time to time in the still uninvaded country districts was enhanced further by the fact that they stood for that simpler mode of existence, already referred to, which the poet is fain to think of as the better way of living, could he make the impossible escape from his own bonds; and it was entirely natural that the two moods should blend and the keen air of New England suffer the pastoral change with the least artifice in the world. In the poem in which he describes his day under the willows Mr. Lowell reveals in most phases the feeling habitual to his mind, of the sense of nature as a refuge, of the strength of associations with a familiar landscape, of the welcome he would give to the rude molds of man, and, in a word, shows the attitude of the poet, who is also a man of thought, toward nature and human nature met face to face; and in this reflective reverie, full of personal expression, the elements are the same as in pastoral verse though seen under a different aspect. When he came to imaginative expression through the medium of old New England, he escaped at once from the literary atmosphere, finding both a subject and a language wholly unworn by use in books; and what he was to express was just that type of character in which human nature was most fresh, sincere, and genuine to his senses and could be entered into most completely by virtue of native sympathies long active in his blood, while the medium of speech was the tongue of the country people as they themselves had fashioned it for their own uses. Not since Theocritus wrote the Sicilian idyls has the pastoral come so near to real life or been not merely so free from artificiality but so slightly transformed in the change from life into art. Mr. Lowell did not

attempt the useless task of saying what the average
up-country man would have said if left to himself; but,
in expressing the true genius of the New England character with a precision and range impossible except to a man
of his own faculty, he succeeded in keeping both thought
and language within the limit of the character through
which he spoke. He permitted himself to use elevation
or pathos or the beauty of natural scenes, which both
true art and the impulse of his own awakened powers
required; but he has managed all with so sure a hand,
such discernment and sensitiveness in his feeling for the
form used, that all is as definitely objective as drama
or novel, and the sense of reality is heightened, and the
expression of the old spirit made more complete, by the
curious prose of the pulpit in which the poems are set.
It remains only to add that in taking public affairs for
the main body of the matter of the verse Mr. Lowell
chose the subject that fitted the mind of New England
as perfectly as the country language fitted its lips.

The second form of verse in which Mr. Lowell has
most excelled is next of kin to the Yankee poems. He
was not only the son of New England, but he was born
also to the wider inheritance of his fellow-countrymen
everywhere, and could lay aside the provincialism of his
eastern accent and phrase for the ampler English of
the nation's speech. Love of home is the seed-plant of
patriotism, and it was inevitable that faith to New England should grow to the larger compass of faith in America; and if in attachment to the native soil itself, such
as Mr. Lowell expresses, there may be a certain closeness
and peculiar warmth of the hearthstone, in his love of
country there is more of what is purely ideal. When he
first collected his political papers, there was some sur-

prise at the amount and value of his writings upon the
public topics of the time; but though this work in prose
had been forgotten, it would still have been plain enough
from his poems that he was ever in a true sense the
citizen. In thinking of his patriotic verse attention is
commonly too exclusively given to the group of odes
which were rather the last and crowning work of a life-
long labor than isolated productions. In the very start
he gave his country the ringing stanzas of "The Present
Crisis," with the one indelible line, and that sonnet to
Phillips which still stirs the blood; and, as time went
on, in the first series of "The Biglow Papers" he dealt
with a great political question of the period, and coming
to the strong passions and immeasurable issues of the
civil war he could scarce write of anything else. It was
only after the peace, and in the assured triumph of the
centennial anniversaries of the united country, that he
closed the extensive series of poems, inspired by public
spirit in the widest meaning of that phrase, with the
long odes which by their solemn movement, their gravity,
and the loftiness of their finer passages have that stateliness which makes them seem to dwarf his less impressive poems in this kind. He had been the true citizen-
poet for almost a lifetime before he was called to this
ceremonial laureateship, and had used the lighter instrumentalities of humor, satire, and wit, the edge of epigram
and poignancy of pathos, as occasion arose; so that one
may fairly say that first and last he employed well-nigh
all the resources of his mind in the service of his country. To think of the odes mainly as Mr. Lowell's patriotic verse would be a grave injustice both to the man and
the poet, for passages may be found in the earlier verse
equal, at least, to anything except the best in this last

group. The distinction of the odes, and one reason why they have affected the public disproportionately in comparison with the best of the other poems, is their style. It is a style which Mr. Lowell has developed for himself, and is to be met with here and there in detached passages of his earlier poetry, but nowhere else is it so even and continuous as in the odes. It is characterized by a breadth and undulation of tone and a purity hard to describe, but these traits are not of consequence in comparison with the certainty with which, no matter how finally resonant the wave of sound may be, the thought absorbs it and becomes itself vocal and musical. The diction itself and the cast of phrase metrically seem to derive from that period of English subsequent to the Elizabethan ferment, when the language retained freedom and spirit and a certain amplitude from the past age, but had not yet subsided into the formalism, however excellent in itself, of the great age of prose; but if Mr. Lowell found the elements of this grave and full style in that period, he has so recombined them in his own manner that to trace out the source is at most only to hazard a guess. It is, however, this felicitous and well-commanded style which is the noticeable literary quality of the odes, and of the finer stanzas of other poems, such as "The Washing of the Shroud," to name one of the first; to have elaborated it is, possibly, the highest distinction of Mr. Lowell as a writer, in the strict sense, on the purely original side of his literary craftsmanship.

It is, however, almost a diversion to direct attention to the literary quality of these poems. What is most to be remarked in them, aside from their earnest intention and the emotion that is sometimes the welling-up of a

deep passion, is the purity of the democratic feeling in
them, the soundness of their Americanism. Mr. Lowell
in one of his earlier volumes laid his wreath on the grave
of Hood, and there are a few of his poems that express
the sympathy of philanthropy with the poor and outcast;
but this is a comparatively crude form of the democratic
idea and hardly exceeds charity. It is easy to pity
suffering in any shape and to believe in the virtues that
poverty is commonly thought to favor; it is a harder
matter to put faith in man. But that rooted interest in
human nature, which has already been spoken of as cardinal in Mr. Lowell's habit of mind, as it helped him to
reconcile poetry with the life of rural New England,
aided also in the generation of his democratic faith, for
when a man is once interested in his fellows he is already
halfway to being friends with them and thus coming to
know how human they are. To accustom one's self to
disregard the accidents of manner and station sufficiently to see the man as he is, to have a clear sight
for genuine character under any of the disguises of un-
familiarity and prejudice, to know how simple and how
common are the elements that go to the making of
manhood, are the paths to belief in democracy; and to
do this, it is enough to live out of doors. Culture that
lives in the library may easily miss its way. "The
Biglow Papers" by themselves would be sufficient proof
of such democracy as goes to make a town-meeting; but
the American idea is a larger thing. The better proof
which Mr. Lowell gave of his quality was in the recognition he gave to Lincoln. He was the first of our
writers to see what name led all the rest, and the truth
which he intimated in "Blondel," and spoke more plainly
in prose, he made at last shine out in the most famous

passage of his greatest ode. One could not be so early to perceive this unsuspected fame before it filled the world and while it was yet in the clouds through which it broke, unless faith in man came natural to him. It was so in this case, and Mr. Lowell understood the "new birth of our new soil" not only in the fact that another name was given to immortal memory, but also in the profounder truth that the soil which had borne such a son was the heir of a new age. With all the faith he had in his own people of the past, the poet looked forward to the new race which is yet forming in the womb; and nowhere in our literature is there more direct expression of the national faith in mere manhood than in a few great lines of these patriotic poems, or more soberly and explicitly in the essay upon Democracy. It may seem little that a man should believe in what his country believes in; but it may fairly be thought that Mr. Lowell, from his place in conservative thought, is as much beforehand in his recognition of democracy in the larger sense as he was earlier than others in his recognition of Lincoln.

Besides the New England and the national poems, Mr. Lowell has written a third sort that stand in a class apart and have a distinction, if not so unshared as these, shared certainly by no other poet of this country. They are what would ordinarily be called poems of culture, the verse of a man deeply imbued with the literature of the past. This definition rests on their form rather than their subject-matter. They are run in the molds that have been handed down in the tradition of literature and belong to the guild. Mr. Lowell, who has shown a disposition to experiment in verse and try many kinds, has used a variety of these set measures, but in two sorts he has shown a hand of unrivaled mastery. In the verses "Credidimus Jovem Regnare" there is, perhaps, the best example of one sort, in which the intellect finds crystalline expression; modern as it is in substance and strongly personal in quality, this poem is at once recognized as being composed in a classic style which is neither a revival nor archaic, but, though written yesterday, has the look of century-old verse still fresh. Another instance is the poem upon the goldfishes, one of the best from his pen. The second sort in which this perfection of style is equally found is illustrated by the letter to Curtis as aptly as by any single piece; the terseness, ease, and finish of these lines, in which compliment blends with the wisdom of life and the whole is subdued within the range of personal talk from friend to friend, are qualities unique in our poetry and recall the habits and modes of utterance of a more polished lettered age, when intellect and manners held their own beside emotion, and the literary life was more complete in manly powers. In both these sorts of pedestrian poetry, if the devotees of inspiration will insist on the distinction, it is rather the man of cultivation conversing with others than the man of genius expressing his soul whom we find; but the classic literature of the world owes much to the poets who have put into just such verse the mind and morals of their time undisturbed by the strong emotion which has latterly ruled so supreme. Mr. Lowell has certainly strengthened his work by varying it with this element of the prose of verse both in the octosyllabic and the pentameter forms. It was necessary, too, for the complete expression of himself that he should give out his literary culture in art, and also find fit channels for that power of pure thinking which divides with the poetic impulse his allegiance to literature. For, when the end is reached and one looks back over the range of Mr. Lowell's poetical works entire, the one thing that binds them all together and runs through them, besides that unresting interest in man which is their blood, is the equally single and widely diffused presence of thought, which is their spirit. In no other poet of our land, at least, is there to be found so large a number of single thoughts, to apply but one test, as in these poems; and there is so little need to say that in none other is there continuous reflection to the same degree, that Mr. Lowell is reputed rather for an excess of thought. To examine the matter further, to consider such a poem as "The Cathedral," for instance, would force this sketch beyond its limits; but the poems of pure reflection should be at least referred to. So, too, the type of which "Endymion" is the most eminent example should be named, and the poems in which Mr. Lowell has sought for musical effects — a most interesting group to the student of poetry, of which, perhaps, "The Fountain of Youth" is the most remarkable — should not be left unmentioned even in the briefest account of his work. It is not within the scope of this paper, however, to enter upon the criticism of Mr. Lowell's poetry further than to indicate such cardinal qualities as can be brought out by broad treatment of it in the mass; and if the three kinds of verse in which he seems most to excel — the pastorals of his own people in their special language, the poems of patriotism of several sorts, but particularly those in which he employs his peculiar grave and noble style, and the poems distinguished by classic perfection of manner — if these have been discriminated, and in

the course of such remarks the poet's primary instincts
of love of human nature, patriotic passion and faith,
and devotion to the worth and charm of literature in
both its phases of thought and art, have been made
obvious, the little that was aimed at has been accomplished; for it must then appear that in his poetry Mr.
Lowell has really expressed himself with directness and
fullness, and in the best of his work with no more intrusion of the self-consciousness of culture to the
prejudice of the native gift than was necessary to make
his poetry square all round with himself. The fact that
so much of his verse of all sorts has the quality of improvisation is of itself proof of the immediacy of his
method, the genuineness of the impulse, the truth of
his statement somewhere that he has ever waited for
poetry to find him and make itself out of his life. It
results from this that his poetical works are the true
record of that life, — the voice, as has been said, of the
man, and immeasurably more complete as an expression of individuality than the larger body of prose.

If one must pack the description of that body of
prose into a phrase, — and little more is possible here,
— it might fairly be said that (to leave the journals
out of account) the essays and addresses of various
kinds, storing the results of scholarship and reflection,
express distinctively the author's mind. Interesting as
the political papers are, both by their topics and the
special contribution of the author to thought necessarily
more or less shared, they remain subordinate to his
critical work on great authors. It is in the literary
papers proper that Mr. Lowell has hived what he has
gathered of wisdom in his wide range through literature; and though he does not speak more directly in

them than in his speeches or poems, he communicates
more and does it in a more exceptional way. Political
thoughtfulness characterizes many Americans, but one
would hesitate if asked to name Mr. Lowell's equals,
in his time, in acquaintance with literature; hardly any
name but Longfellow's would be offered in scholarly
rivalry with his own on this ground; and he excels Longfellow by virtue of the extraordinary critical power
which he brings to bear upon literature. He is, indeed,
the only critic of high rank that our literature owns,
and the fineness of his quality is obscured by the very
singleness of his position, since there are none to com-
pare him with; nor, if one goes to England for such comparison, is the case much bettered, for he surpasses
his fellows there with equal ease. The critical faculty
is so rare that criticism as an art suffers in repute
thereby, and its results are undervalued; but if one is
willing to learn, there is in the body of Mr. Lowell's
literary papers a canon of pure literature so defined in
intellectual principles and applied with such variety and
fruitfulness as to suffice for an education in literary
taste; and this education is of the best sort since it
teaches how to see rather than how to analyze, is intuitive instead of scientific, and thus follows the method
native to literature and logically belonging to it. The
results of this method in what Mr. Lowell says about
great works of genius are, nevertheless, the main thing,
and the value of them is sufficiently appreciated by
students of literature. It ought to be observed, perhaps,
that the wealth of single thought which has already been
noticed as characterizing his poetry is as strikingly
found in these prose works of every sort. Here, too,
no writer of the time equals him except Emerson; and in

Mr. Lowell's works there is none of that Delphic quality which sometimes renders Emerson's most impressive phrases only an appearance of thought. Just as in all of Mr. Lowell's writings one always seems in direct contact with the man speaking, so his words are always weighted with that sense and common judgment which make them shells so impalpable that one touches the mind through them. In his poetry he gives himself and in his prose he yields up to his wisdom; to do this so immediately that the intervention of the printed page is not felt is the last victory of the faculty of expression in literature, whether it be achieved with the simplicity of genius or by the perfection of art through culture, — nor are the two ways incompatible.

Such, briefly stated, is the impression made by a broad view of Mr. Lowell's various contributions to our literature. Notwithstanding his acquirements in general and the special perfection of his literary culture, which are felt throughout his writings in their mass, it would appear that his self-expression, whether on the more scholarly, or civic, or the simplest human side, has been more spontaneous than is commonly thought. It is true that the spontaneity of a complex mind wears a different aspect from that of a simpler nature, but essentially it is the same, and brings with it the same reality of life, the same genuineness and sincerity, on account of which it is justly thought to be a primary element in the genius of great writers and true poets. The intrinsic worth of Mr. Lowell's works has been purposely subordinated here; but that part of criticism of them is not in any risk of misapprehension or forgetfulness. The simplicity of his nature, as shown in his works, beneath the diversity of his interests and the subtle refinements of his intellectual part, the unity of his life as poet, citizen, and thinker, and the harmonious interplay of his faculties one with another, and especially the directness of his expression in every mode of writing, have not been hitherto so much recognized as was right; and only by attending to these primary traits can one be just to a great writer.

BACON'S ESSAYS

OF the books conceded to be English classics none occurs to the mind more instantly than Bacon's "Essays." It is a small, compact work, and is thought of as a whole, not in fragments, as is the case with many even of the most immortal heirlooms of past time. It is the treasury of a great literary mind, not in one moment of activity or one phase of development, but in mature entirety as it moved through life. From the publication of the first ten of the "Essays" in 1597, when the slim book first "came home to men's business and bosoms," as its author said, it has been universally acceptable. Pure classics are rare, and they do not compete often in longevity with poetic works; but there has never been any wavering in the vogue of this little volume, notwithstanding the fact that it does not interest the young, that it is unsupported by any moral enthusiasm which might enlist the suffrage of older readers, and that, in general, it is destitute of emotional power. Like Burns, like Shakespeare, it is man's meat; and especially it appeals to the hard head acquainted with human nature and the shifts of life as it is led in the world, open to broad views and aware of great elements in the private and public spheres alike, but tangled, nevertheless, in the prudences, the safeties, the necessities of a permanently lower plane of social being. The uniqueness of the "Essays" is to be sought in this direction: they give a grandiloquent voice to the worldly-

wise heart; they mix nobility of intellect with meanness
of action, beauty and charm of language with lame and
impotent conclusions of cynical fact, the greatness with
the littleness of man. Scarcely any other English prose
classic makes so much the impression characteristic of
the ancient writers, as of something concentrated and
old with experience, not to be challenged any more than
proverbial wisdom — conclusions which, whether gold
or baser matter, are the settled dregs of time. Such, in
substance, is the amalgam of the "Essays," lasting in
fame, and obstinate because of the mixed truth which,
like life itself — and therein they represent life — they
contain.

No book could have this power unless it delivered the
total original force of the creative mind that shaped it, all
that was vital in Bacon's knowledge and temperament.
And, in fact, this is readily seen to be the case. The first
edition, comprising ten essays, was published in 1597,
as has been said; the second, thirty-eight essays, of
which twenty-eight were new, in 1612; the third, fifty-
eight essays, of which twenty were new, in 1625. For a
period of twenty-eight years, therefore, the work was
slowly deposited by Bacon's mind, and on each issue
there was revision of the old matter then reprinted. It
appears in yet another way that the volume is representative of Bacon's whole experience, and especially
of his literary genius. The comparative study of the
text reveals the fact that he borrowed from his other
writings both thought and expression which he
apparently regarded as his choicest material, so that
the "Essays" became, in their final form, in some sense
a mosaic of his best passages, a literary jewel-box in
which he stored up the treasure-trove of fancy, reflection,

and eloquence. It is not merely that he repeats himself as one who is always coining from the permanent
bullion of his mind, but he reissues the coinage of other
years.

The "Essays," therefore, show their author at his best;
they exhibit his continuous thought, the fruit of his
meditation, the gathered spoils of his genius. It is true,
however — and it is a fact constantly to be remembered
by a reader — that Bacon does not set forth the principles by which he acted, that he does not support falsely
his moral defaults; in that sense the book is not representative. There is, indeed, something shameless in the
dissociation between his precepts and what his practice
is known to have been. But it is wrong to bring his
character into the question; at least, it is unnecessary;
for the "Essays" express the brain, the worldly intellect
of the man, which does not divest itself of an outward
and seemly virtue, though that virtue must often seem
of lower strain. Within the limits of prudent compli-
ance, however, and this side of actual wrong-doing, the
trend of the "Essays" shows a mind whose main direction by both motive and method was at its best perilously
near to unworthy courses and perhaps incapable of practical nobility. So much of moral autobiography must be
read between the lines, even while we are charmed by
the eloquence of the intellect, the acuteness, the preg-
nancy, the facile and familiar handling of what, however
commonplace, are made to seem great thoughts or wise
counsels.

The element of rhetoric in the general effect is, no
doubt, large. In the "Essays," at all events, Bacon can
only be described as a rhetorician of the school and traditions of Seneca. The word was new, he said, but the

thing was old. The sentence is the 'unit of the style. Each essay, taken as a whole, is a composite of rough thoughts of which each one is stated with a view to its single effect. There is little consecutive development of a theme; the subject, indeed, not infrequently changes suddenly, and the end forgets the beginning. The brevity of statement itself often forces an advance in the thought, and results in surprising transitions and in climaxes of condensation, of antithesis and parallelism. The more carefully the sentences are read, the less of reasonable order is apparent. No attempt is made to exhaust a topic. At the most we seem to get a cluster of valuable notes approximately related to the title. The main purpose of the author is to drive the immediate thought home by some unforgetable phrase, some happy harmony of balanced terms, some perfected clause-structure, just adequate to be packed with the matter. Hence there is no fluency in the manner; but rather something stiff and mechanical, self-conscious, predetermined, artificial, is felt, which wearies the mind in perusal, and oppresses it with the obscure discouragement that lodges in all affectation, all calculated literary effect. That in these points the style of Bacon is touched by the example of English euphuistic prose can hardly be successfully combated. He was not a mere euphuist, like Lyly, nor did he piece his work with the elaborate fashion of the then outworn manner, as Lodge and Greene did in their day; but in the filing of his phrase, in the blocking of his clauses, in the effect at clean-cut "wit" in the old sense, by the medium of a certain grammar and rhetoric which were ready molds of pithy expression, it is plain that he echoes the "fine style" of the preceding generation and found something in his literary taste and love of stylistic displays sympathetic with these first "refiners" of the English tongue. The rhetoric of humanism was still strong in his handling of the language. Without sweetness, without subtlety, such as Sidney had, without the clarity of Shakespeare's prose, Bacon's style is yet retentive, at its best, of a dry, noble light, a cadence almost scriptural in high passages, and at the lowest is skillfully ornate. In the history of English style, however, students of the "Essays" cannot ignore the kinship of the school of Lyly to this greater master of artifice.

The mark of the rhetorician is not confined to the style. The substance itself is sententious. In the development of European literary culture Seneca was only second to Cicero as a model of expression; and Roman emphasis, brevity, and moral commonplace, as they were in the decadence of Latin style, formed an easy pattern to many a writer. There was something in the English love of the didactic, which is a racial trait, that made literature a willing prey to this influence; and sententiousness, under various forms, became almost a vice, fed also as it constantly was from Continental sources in which cognate literary movements had been felt. In the drama the pursuit of the maxim had been marked in early days, and in Shakespeare, where it had been held in due subordination, it had given substance of thought and weight of phrase; but it may well be maintained that the pursuit of the conceit in the Cavalier poets was only another form of the same weakness, which so intellectualized and moralized verse as to denote its gradual extinction on the imaginative and artistic side. The conceit as an image was analogous to the maxim as a thought, and looked to condensation as a means of wit, in the contemporary sense; and the end of this various movement, which was always at bottom the rhetoric of the intellect, was found in the school of Pope, in whose verse, chastened by good sense and freed from fantasy, the literature of sententiousness came to a definite end. From the time of the Senecan drama in England to the romantic age of this century, in one form or another, this classic strain deriving its birth from the Roman decadence was felt, and always in connection with a predominantly intellectual current of English culture.

Bacon's "Essays" remain as the chief prose monument of this long movement, the capital product of the English liking for sententious speech.   The author was a natural hoarder of thought and phrase, as has been noticed, and the quality of both was of the best in this kind.   General truths and specific applications of them to life are the necessary subjects of such writing, which is either philosophic or moral, and sometimes touches on the satirical as its form of humor; and thus, as one looks into the themes of Bacon's meditations, it is found that the best of them are concerned with the world, and with those aspects of life which are most suggestive of advice, of moral principle, of individual utility.   The "Essays" "came home to men's business and bosoms" because they were practical and dealt with personal and almost intimate worldly interests; they contained the lessons of prudence, the cold results of observation, the things often that one feels shame in acknowledging to be true; they are, one might almost say, counsels of imperfection, and those to which this description most justly applies are the most characteristic, effective, and convincing.   In those of the "Essays" which deal with matters of state and policy there is less value, partly from a change in our knowledge and ideals, but also because Bacon handled those themes with less depth, with a feebler comprehension, with the bad fortune of having turned out to be in the wrong. He knew his own and other men's bosoms, and within the limit of that circle he could interpret best, though not often to the credit of mankind; in the larger world of the true greatness of kingdoms and of commercial and military policy he was not in advance of his time; and now, so far as he is read for the substance, he is read as a moralist.

In fixing on this as the main matter, it is not intended to set aside or ignore the fine phrases of his philosophy, the excellence of some flashes of imagination, or the grandeur of a few isolated passages. These have great effect. The luster, the success, the lofty ease of the style obscure the less noble matter much as the greatness of his name atones in men's minds for the facts of his career. The grandiloquence of the work as a whole, its assumption of experience and knowledge, its self-esteem, its seeming mastery, are perhaps the most lasting traits; they were traits of the man himself. How much, too, may be due to the subtle flattery of "men's bosoms," in the immortality of such a splendid excuse for the life of this world!

GREENE'S PLACE IN COMEDY

OF the group of gifted college-bred men who had some part in the fashioning of Shakespearian drama and drew into their mortal lungs a breath of the element whose "air was fame," Greene has long been marked with unenviable distinction. He had the misfortune to try to darken with an early and single shaft the rising sun of Shakespeare; and he has stood out like a shadow against that dawning genius ever since. The mean circumstances of his Bohemian career, and the terribly brutal, Zolaesque scene of his death-chamber — the most repulsively gruesome in English literary annals — have sustained with a lurid light the unfavorable impression; and, were this really all, no one would have grudged oblivion the man's memory. The edition of his collected works, however, which Grosart gave to scholars, has enlarged general knowledge of Greene, and has permitted the formation of a more various image of his personality, a juster estimate of his literary temperament, and a clearer judgment concerning his position in the Elizabethan movement of dramatic imagination; and some few, even before this, had lifted up protestation against that ready damnation which seemed provided for him by his irreverence toward the undiscovered god of our idolatry who, then fleeting his golden days, seemed to this jaundiced eye "an upstart crow beautified with our feathers, . . . the only Shake-scene in a country." Never were more unfortunate words for the "blind mouth" that uttered them. But there is more to know of Greene than this one speech; and though the occasion is not apt here for so complete a valuation of his character and temperament, his deeds and works, as is to be desired for truth's sake, yet it is needful to take some notice of his total personality as evinced in his novels, plays, poems, and pamphlets, in order to determine his relative station in the somewhat limited sphere of English comedy.

Marlowe is commonly regarded as the forerunner of the heroic strain in Shakespeare, with molding influence on the imaginative habit of his younger fellow-workman in respect to that phase of his art; and Greene, who though he will never shine as a "morning-star" of the drama was at least a twin luminary with Marlowe, has been credited with occupying a similar position as the forerunner of Shakespeare with respect to the portrayal of vulgar life. It is hardly to be expected that an antithesis so convenient for the critics should be really matter-of-fact. The narrower distinct claim that the Clown in his successive reincarnations passed through the world of Greene's stage on his way from his old fleshly prison in the Vice of the primitive English play may require less argument; and in several other particulars it may appear that foregleams of the Shakespearian drama are discernible in Greene's works without drawing the consequence that Shakespeare was necessarily a pupil in every school that was open to him. Not to treat the matter too precisely, where precision is apt to be illusory even if attainable in appearance, was there not a plain growth of Greene as a man of letters closely attached to his time which will illustrate the general development of the age and its art, and naturally bring out those analogies between his work and Shakespeare's that have been thought of as formative elements in him by which his successor on the stage profited? The line of descent does not matter, on the personal side, if the general direction of progress be made out.

Greene was distinctively a man of letters. He was born with the native gift, and he put it to use in many ways. He tried all kinds of writing, from prose to verse, from song to sermon, and apparently with equal interest. He was college-bred and must have been of a scholarly and receptive temperament; he was variously read in different languages and subjects; and he began by being what he charged Shakespeare with being — an adapter. His tales, like others of the time, must be regarded as in large measure appropriations from the fields of foreign fiction. Even as he went on and gained a freer hand for expression, he remained imitative of others, with occasional flashes of his own talent; and, dying young, he cannot be thought to have given his genius its real trial of thorough originality. In the main his work is derivative and secondary and represents or reflects literary tradition and example; he was still in the process of disencumbering himself of this external reliance when he was exhausted, and perished; and it is in those later parts of his work which show originality that he is attached to the Shakespearian drama. Slight examination will justify this general statement in detail. It is agreed that he drew his earlier novels from the stock-fiction, with its peculiar type of woman and its moral lesson; and he shows in these sensibility of imagination and grace of style. He was, more than has been thought, a stylist, a born writer; and this of itself would interest him in the euphuistic fashion, then coming to its height

in Lyly; and besides he always kept his finger on the
pulse of the time and was ambitious to succeed by pleasing the popular taste: he adopted euphuism temporarily,
employing it in his own way.   In the drama his play,
"Orlando Furioso," harks back to Ariosto, and it was
when the stage rang with "Tamburlainè" that he brought
out "Alphonsus, King of Aragon," and when "Doctor
Faustus" was on the boards that he followed with "Friar
Bacon and Friar Bungay"; on Sidney's "Arcadia" succeeded his own "Menaphon"; and if "James IV" with
its Oberon preceded "A Midsummer Night's Dream" —
which is undetermined — it was a unique inversion of the
order which made Greene always the second and not the
first.   In view of this literary chronology it seems clear
that in the start and well on into his career Greene was
the sensitive and ambitious writer following where Italian
tradition, contemporary genius, and popular acclaim
blazed the way; and in so doing his individual excellence
lay not in originality on the great scale, but in treatment,
in his modification of the *genre,* in his individual style
and manner and purport — in the virtues, that is to say,
of an able, clever, variously equipped man of letters
whose talent had not yet discovered the core of genius
in itself.

It is observable, too, in the earlier period of his work,
that in his treatment of his material so derived, he displays the qualities of the weaker, the less robust literary
habit; he uses refinement, he is checked by his good taste,
he strives for effects less violent, less sensational, less
difficult in the sense that it requires less of the giant's
strength to carry them off well.   There is little, too, in
this portion of his work which lets personality burn
through the literary mold; that belongs to his late and

stronger time. It is true that his novels have a moral in
them for edification; but, although he had the preacher's
voice, it is not here in the earlier tales that it is heard;
it was the immemorial privilege of the Renaissance tale,
however scandalous, to wear cowl and cassock. In the
cardinal point of his delineation of female character, for
which he is highly praised because of the purity and
grace of the womanhood he presented, he follows the
Renaissance convention, as it seems to me, but with
refining and often true English touches — that ideal of
Italian origin which is, on the whole, one of outline, of
pale graciousness, of immobile or expressive beauty, pictorial; these women seem like lovely portraits which
have stepped down out of a frame, and have only so much
of life as an environment of light and air and silence
can give them. Are they not, for example, as truly like
Spenser's women — except where Spenser's are differ-
entiated by doing "manly" parts — as they are prophetic
of Shakespeare's simpler types? Greene, no doubt, incorporated in this ideal something of his own experience
of noble and patient womanhood, possibly as he had
known it in his wife, as Shakespeare embodied eternal
reality in his creations; but it would not occur to me
to believe that Shakespeare found a model for Ophelia
or Imogen in the Lady Ida and Dorothea, any more than
in Una and her sisters. All these before Shakespeare
are of one family — they are the conventionalized Renaissance ideal variously modified and filled with richer
artistic life; but in Shakespeare they pass into that
clear luminous air where art and humanity are one
thing. Greene should have our admiration for his sensibility to the type, for the appreciation with which he
drew it, for the charm he thereby clothed his pages with;

but as to there being a line of descent, that is altogether another thing; and in respect to Greene himself, his special female characterization imports the elements of refinement in him, the trait of the less robust literary habit just spoken of. Similarly, he was of too sound taste to be long content to speak in the cut phrase of euphuism, and he soon laid the fashion off; and, in his afterplay on the "Tamburlaine" motive, it is a matter of debate whether he was parodying or rivaling Marlowe's large-languaged rhetoric, and, whichever he was doing, he was hampered by a better taste than his model, either laughing at it, or else without the giant's strength to succeed in the worser way; and to "Doctor Faustus" and "Friar Bacon and Friar Bungay," so far as they are compared, like remarks apply. Greene has his own virtues in all these instances, but they are not those of originating power, of creative overflow, of genius of the Elizabethan stripe; they live within the narrower circle of improvement through refined taste, or else of satirical protest or comparative failure due to the same trait.

The thought of refinement in connection with Greene, the stress laid upon it here, has not been commonly prominent in writings upon him, and is out of harmony with our traditional impression of him — the envious and dying profligate in his misery. Yet it is to be found not only in his early portraits of womanhood of the pure type (he afterward presented a baser one), nor in the fact often noted of the marked purity of his works; but more pervasively in his continuing taste, in those habits and choices in the literary field, those revolts and reforms, which show the steady rightness of the man in his self-criticism and his criticism of current successes. I seem to feel this innate refinement in the limpidity of single

lines; but it is plain to every one in the lovely lyrics
which have sung themselves into the hearts of all lovers
of our poetry, those songs, found in all anthologies of
English verse, which bear Greene's name. He was a
gross man, living grossly, as all know; but it sometimes
happens that in such fleshly natures — as, every one will
at once think, in Ben Jonson — there is found this
flower of delicacy, the very fragrance of the soul; and
so it was with Greene, and the lyrics are the mortal
sign of this inward grace. It belongs with this, as has
been observed by several writers, that of all the men
who preceded Shakespeare, Greene most lets the breath
of the English country blow through his pages, and likes
to lay his scene in some rural spot. He loved the country; and yet, here too, protest may well be made when
it is said that in this he led the way for Shakespeare;
surely all country paths were open to the Warwickshire
lad in his own right; nor need the difference be allowed
that the forest of Arden is a conventionalized nature,
as one critic maintains, while Greene's is of the soil —
that is to mistake art for convention; but to say even this
one word in passing in behalf of Shakespeare's nature-
reality is superfluous, except that it suggests the different
road by which Shakespeare here, as well as in his dealing with madness, witchcraft, and fairyland (in all
of which Greene is said to have taught him), went his
own ways, irrespective of comrades of the time. In
this love of the country which Greene had lies the key
to the better man in him and to his own native distinc-
tions. Beneath his literary temperament, which seems
an educational and professional veneer that should finally
drop away, is his genuine nature — the man he was;
and, life going on to imminent wreck, it became clear in

his later works that he was more and more engaged in
contemporary life, in what he saw and knew, and that
he took his material from these; he had written auto-
biographical sketches and accounts of low life and its
characters, and he had displayed certain tendencies
toward preaching and sympathies with the unredeemed
masses of humanity, all somewhat miscellaneously, and
without any other art than a strong prose style; but,
at the end, is it not manifest that he had grown into
realism as his material, and into an attitude of moral
denunciation and popular sympathy in dealing with it,
and is not this the significance of his collaboration with
Lodge in "A Looking-Glasse for London and England,"
and of his own unique "George-a-Greene"? All the
earlier work seems to end, and new beginnings appear
both in his renderings of contemporary realism, and in
his most imaginative and various play, "James IV."

The gradual substitution, then, as Greene came to his
time of strength of frank English realism for cultured
Italian tradition and contemporary vital literary example,
seems to be the true line of his growth. It shows distinctly in his choice of the English subject of Roger
Bacon in place of Doctor Faustus, in his satire of certain
aspects of court life, when he translated an Italian plot
of Cinthio into apocryphal history as "James IV," in
his presentation of the state of London in collaboration
with Lodge, and in the half-rebellious play of "George-a-
Greene." This is the imaginative and artistic side of
what is practical in his pamphlets of personal repentance
and cony-catching. Personally I seem to detect Puritanism morally in the one half, and Puritanism politically
in the other half, of this late dramatic work; but it cannot be maintained that the case is certain. Apart from

that, Greene was — what so few ever are, even in an Elizabethan environment — a humorist; and he used the old English comedy tradition as an element in his purely English work. The matter is so plain and comparatively so slight as to require the fewest words. In comedy specifically he gave examples, which he may be said to have first given in the sense that he gave them in an original or a developed form, of the court fool in Ralph, of the country bumpkin or crass fool in Miles, of the highly developed and wholly humanized *Vice* in Adam, of a special humoristic type (aptly characterized as the ancestor of Andrew Fairservice) in Andrew, otherwise not born till Sir Walter Scott's day, and of the true Shakesperian clown, the unmistakable one, in Slipper. Such was his definite service to comedy in respect to type; and criticism can only point it out, because the substance can be given only by reading the characters attentively. In regard to humor at large, it appears to me that in his hands, apart from linguistic felicity and wit, he presents a humor of situation tending toward pure farce, and a humor of intention tending toward pure satire of the social variety, and a humor of manners tending toward pure pleasantry as in the "Vail Staff" episode. The single link binding him with Shakespeare, in comedy is through the character of Slipper; and yet here, as in the other instances of female type, love of country scenes, and also in madness, witchcraft, and fairyland, I cannot believe that Shakespeare may not have arrived at his end — in this case, Launce — without necessarily being obliged to Greene for assistance. The bent toward contemporary realism, toward a well-languaged and winning clown, toward Englishry, which is another name for nature in human life and its setting, is plain in Greene;

this was the running of the stream; but no larger inference follows from it in my mind than that Greene had worked out his growth, as Shakespeare in his apprenticeship also did, in similar directions, but that Greene had done it on national lines, whereas Shakespeare did it on universal lines, that Greene had done it in a practical, whereas Shakespeare did it in an ideal way, and that Greene had done it largely under personal conditions, being at war with his fate as a mere man, whereas Shakespeare did it as a human spirit above the reach of material vicissitude. What one owed to the other is an insignificant detail at best; what is important is to observe in Greene the advancing movement of the drama in moral intention, in higher characterization, in original phases of humanity, in humor of more body and intellect, in comedy and fantasy approaching the goal of the Elizabethan spirit. Greene, it must be acknowledged, opened some veins that no one followed up; some of his characters and much of his sympathies were his own in an unshared way; but his work of all kinds ended with him, and, so far as he was an explorer of the way, he was most like one who, in our own time, may be an experimenter in some new force — his name is not associated with scientific history, with new invention, with discovery, but such success as he had was because his eye was on the element which men of his craft were working out more thoroughly than he himself.

It is pleasant to close this brief note on one of the most unfortunate of men whom our literature remembers, with a kindlier appreciation of him than has hitherto obtained. The mere volume of his writings indicates great industry; the criticism of them witnesses our respect for his endowments, his taste, his fundamental manhood; the analysis of them shows improvement in himself, and the power of mastery over the material given him in the direction of the true progress of art in his day; the very violence of his fate or of his repentances suggests that the nature so ruined may have been of finer and better metal than those who died and made no such sign of conscious self-obstruction: there remain the ideal women, the clear-cut comedians, the lovely lyrics, to plead for him as an accomplisher of art; and, in view of this, may we not forget the unhappy incident that has made him like the flitting bat in the slow dawn of our golden poet, and remember the much that he, dying so young, at thirty-two, accomplished before the day of his disappointment, the night of his deserted solitude, and the tragic ignominy of his death?

THE BRONTË NOVELS

In the continuing multiplication of novels, and the apparently vast success of new examples of the art which characterizes the day, it is a remarkable tribute to the greatness of the earlier masters of the century that the public still finds them supereminent, and edition after edition fails to exhaust the perennial demand for their works. Something like abiding fame seems assured to them, and not only to the greatest, but to the less powerful and various also. The Brontës were hardly more than amateurs in the profession, yet their reputation remains side by side with Jane Austen's, for example, and shows no sign of waning, whether judged by the number of reissues or by the diversity of critical minds which give attention to the substance of excellence in the work and the idiosyncrasy of character in the authors. Genius of an extraordinary kind is acknowledged on all hands to be theirs; and in the annals of biography merely the entire family has taken a place of a really unique kind, with many of the elements and attractions usually associated with the imaginary world of romance, tragedy, and pathos. It is easy under the circumstances to seek for the spell of the Brontë novels in the psychology of such a family, and to reach with facile handling a conclusion that it is personality, the realism of individuality amid a peculiar and arresting environment, the Brontë spirit and the Brontë fate, which constitute the fascination of the books. Certainly the biographical interest shows as little indication of exhaustion as the literary interest itself, as such studies as Mr. Clement Shorter's have proved a generation after Mrs. Gaskell's first vivid presentation of the story. But the novels had power and vogue before the lives of the Brontës were known, and still have mastery over readers who will never know more than a bare outline, if so much, of the matter. The reflection of a later time, too, may place the novels in a historical perspective with reference to the development of fiction and its currents, but this is also outside the appreciation of any but students and, though interesting is incidental — a part of the critical enginery rather than of the criticism itself. The object of public interest, the ground of lasting fame, is aside from biography or movements of literature, and lies in the novels alone.

Mrs. Humphrey Ward, who wrote introductions to the several novels in the new edition of the Brontës, came to a well-worn topic, upon which both the eloquent and the acute have had their say. Effusion and analysis have preceded her pen, and even the story of the life of the Yorkshire cottage, which offers rare material to a practised hand in fiction, has already been told and retold, as a whole and in episodes and on every scale, by many a writer. Yet her introductions are far and away the best criticism, the most broad and enlightening, at once the most impartial and appreciative, that the Brontës have received in the whole half-century of their praises. She does not confine her views too narrowly within any one of these papers, but exhibits different phases of the subject, as it lay in her mind, in each of them; and she cleverly reserves her summaries for the most effective point. Here it is the "personality,"

spoken of above, that, appealing to her own prediction
for psychology, seems the prominent and one thing necessary; then it is not so much this personality as the race
instincts basal in it — the Celtic romance, pride, shyness,
poetry, endurance, melancholy, wildness; and again it is
not only this racial germinal temperament, but its
fecundation by the books of French romanticism which
Charlotte read, or by the tales of Hoffman in Emily's
case, that places the Brontës in the stream of European
and cosmopolitan rather than of home-bred English
literature. These are general considerations. The detail is not less deep-searching in criticism and wide-
sweeping in appreciation. As a novelist acquainted with
and interested for her art, Mrs. Ward grants and illustrates the obvious crudities and the ineffective or
ludicrous attempts that the tyro makes much of in de-
preciating great books, and brushes them aside as, in
this instance, "unconcerning things," with an ease and
decision that only the master-talent knows in dealing with
the amateur of genius; but she lays her finger on the
truth struck in essentials, and gives her heart to the
flow of impassioned power ever fuller and ampler as
novel succeeds novel; she recognizes the two elements —
the amateurishness due to lack of knowledge and experience, and the tide of genius, not to be withstood, which
bears all these things like the waste drift upon its flood.
And similarly Mrs. Ward is alive equally to the sharp
realism of life bitten into the work, and to the poetizing
idealism which flows round and through it like an atmosphere, pervading scene and character and feeling, as
weather permeates the story of "Wuthering Heights."
The real difficulty has thus been easily met and overcome with generous victory — the difficulty that lies in

the fact that the work of the Brontës, and especially
Charlotte's work, is such a blend of elements — to use
Mrs. Ward's arrangement of them — of Celtic, Puritan,
and French, of satire and pathos, of truth and caricature,
of energy and tenderness, of the poetic and the actual;
indeed, the facets are numberless. Emily's work was
simpler by far, as it was more intense in imagination,
more disinterested in artistic impulse, more something
visible and acted, and only that, than Charlotte's complex
and self-conscious creation. The third, Anne, is a pale
sister beside these two, and her work is perhaps outwardly more near to life than that of the others, and
inwardly less spiritually formed.

The constituent parts of genius and its works, though
the critic is always fond of dabbling in them, may be
traced and catalogued, and the coin of panegyric be
struck in honor of each, without thereby affording the
public much knowledge of its own liking, of those reasons
for its instinctive acceptance which should interpret the
public's response. If the author of "Jane Eyre" herself
was not aware of its crude elements in plot and description of manners, for example, it is conceivable that a
large part of the readers are as blissfully ignorant of
these improprieties and as little affected by them. The
accidents of events and behavior — for all kinds of
events, and all kinds of behavior also, do come to pass
in the world of men — do not matter much to the mass
of the public, so long as the tale goes on with illusion.
What is important is the kind of life represented, and
the bearing of the people in its working out. It may be
that, as Mrs. Ward represents the objector as saying,
an English love of the pathetic, picturesque, sentimental,
has some share in the appeal the Brontë novels make;

but these qualities, so stated, are shallowly grasped; they are in the work, but they are embedded in a conception and presentation of life itself as far removed from the Celtic temperament as the storms of autumn are from an April shower, in a setting forth of life as a thing to be endured; and it is the relentless and bitterly iterative way in which this view is persistently held up and borne in upon the reader which characterizes all the works equally and is central in the Brontë genius. It is not an original view, certainly, but its statement is attended by originality. For instance, one ranking trait in the novels is that the life thus to be endured is illustrated and embodied often in lonely and sometimes almost helpless creatures, and particularly in souls that seem to be reservoirs of confined and compressed life-power — great souls, so to speak, in small circumstances, souls of passion in *culs-de-sac* of existence. Struggle is the law of their being, suffering is its condition, and the quality evinced is the power of the will. Nothing could be more English than this apotheosis of the will as the guide of life, and this demonstration of the earth as a place of endless probationary capacity; and in the atmosphere of scene and action in which it is set, in the conflict with disease, with society, with untoward passion, this theme of the power of the will has a grip on the attention and the respect of the English race which cannot relax except with the race itself. What is Heathcliffe in "Wuthering Heights" but the will turned to evil with a concentration of hate, of intelligence, of patience unrivalled in black monotone? It is the same will in his world of the fiend as the will of Jane Eyre or of Moore in their worlds of dependence and ambition. The passion with which it is presented adds to its fascination and impressiveness; its rude physical analogues, in such characters as Rochester even, help, being in the same sympathetic tone; and the despondencies and despairs, the sufferings and groanings of the spirit, which come into the various stories, are the same subject-matter given in reverse.

This is the permanent basis of the different plots, the changing groups, the social background even; humor and satire may play over it; morality and philanthropy and history may be intermixed with it; but the note of passion, of reality and power, is always the same, and wherever struck emits intensity and dominance, and charges all things, even the landscape, and all characters, whether masterful or delicate, with its profound feeling and truth.   Naturally, solitude, disease, helplessness, are important matters to it; and the countenance of these grim things was, no doubt, learned by the Brontës from their own hard lives.   They became interpreters of such moods, Charlotte using her own experience directly, Emily projecting life into the realm of imagination. Heathcliffe, certainly the most marvelous creation, is as solitary a being as is known in literature; but his is the same solitude that occurs in "Shirley" and "Villette," except that it is of the imagination instead of the memory. Despite the profound difference between the work of these two sisters, their genius was from one root, and the consanguinity between them includes much more than the Yorkshire type of landscape and man.   Mrs. Ward possibly diverts attention from this common element of struggle in adversity, and of the momentousness of the lives of unimportant persons in the region of their own feelings, by the careful regard she gives to the element of love, in the psychology of which she apparently thinks women are more versed than men. But it is not essentially as love-stories that any of these novels have won their place in English literature, nor is it as love-stories that they are thought of. Character, fate, and passion, of which love is only one form, are planted in the works with a genius almost independent of its materials, stamping life into them with a wholeness that belongs only to its own prerogative. It is because life is thus deeply felt in ways consonant with English experience and preconception, almost with the English prejudice in its higher forms, that the Brontë novels appeal and endure.

In addition to this substance of reality and passion which would have shone with a mighty light through much worse errors of construction, portraiture, and taste than are to be found in the Brontës' handling of their materials, through much greater coarseness, flimsiness, and falsity as some call it, there is, besides, the power of a unique and victorious style to be reckoned with. The writers had been fed on old English, and had been practising with its words and cadences from childhood; and the result is a definition, a concentration, and a flow which of themselves might chain the mind without the magical touch that at special points seems to evoke all the "charm in words." In the landscape descriptions — renderings they really are — one notices this more readily because the mind is less engaged with character and thought; but in the dialogue and soliloquy, and in the expression of moods, the same noble and convincing diction, the same imaginative lift of the mere speech, reaches the poetic elevation that belongs to the things of passion. It may seem super-abundant at times, or over-Scriptural, or fail to carry with those who remember the Covenanters on the one hand and the

rhapsodies of De Quincey on the other; but they will
not fail with the mass of readers who are less conscious
of literary habit; and, for the most part, the style has at
its exalted moments the great qualities, rugged, clear,
magical, that seem delegated from nature and passion
themselves. Such works are sheet-anchors of English.
While they continue to be reissued, the tongue of the
people will remember at least the clear strength of its
early greatness, the sound of its original music, and its
large tradition; and when, in addition to its own treasure,
such an edition as this is so well furnished with sympathetic and frank criticism, and with the complete biographical narrative which enhances the interest of the
stories themselves, the best has been done for works which
at least constitute one of the distinctive expressions of
English representative and creative genius in the nine-
teenth century — perhaps more enduring than has been
realized as yet by those who cast up the gains and
losses of the precarious fames that made it illustrious in
literature.

SHELLEY'S POETRY

Shelley's poetic genius was complex. It found expression in narrative, dramatic and lyrical verse and ranged over a wide diversity of themes; its literary sources, owing to his scholarly habits, were uncommonly various. He is, consequently, in his work, taken as a whole, a difficult poet. The lyrical impulse was, nevertheless, predominant in his genius, and modified even its narrative and dramatic expression. It belongs to the lyric to be plain in meaning, direct in address and spontaneous in origin; it is an effusion of emotion, and emotion is simpler than thought. The power of Shelley is thus most felt in his plainest verse when the emotional impulse is controlling, the lyricism most pure, his touch with life most immediate, his expression most unconscious; and his poetry has these traits when it is most brief, most personal, and is most engaged with idealities of beauty, love, truth. Shelley, however, freed his genius but slowly from other elements of his life; it gradually took pure form; it was with difficulty subdued to artistic aims. He was, in particular, strongly under the sway and influence of his political interest, that "passion for reforming the world," which he owned to be his and which was anterior in his life to poetic ardor; he was also much occupied by his intellectual interest, a metaphysical impulse in the main, which was the companion of his genius and forged a group of poetic ideas whereon much of his poetry was articulated, as it were, and given mental structure. There was thus in his verse a substratum of political and philosophical thought, such that the reader must often be acquainted with certain radical ideas in politics and social theory, and with certain transcendental ideas in philosophy, before he can either understand or appreciate the verse. The history of Shelley's mind, in other words, is involved in an adequate appreciation of his poetry; and for this reason much of it remains ordinarily out of general touch. It is only that part of his verse in which the political and intellectual interests are absent, or are present only as the human passion for ideal ends such as universal love, beauty, truth, that makes a wide appeal.

It will be useful, however, even in dealing with this portion to glance briefly at the history of Shelley's poetic career. He was a born writer, and from boyhood wrote both prose and verse; but he was a good prose writer before he was a poet. In verse he was cradled in that school of German ballad romance, whose crude Teutonism he long kept traces of; in prose he began with its mate, the German tales of wonder and horror. But it was in his serious writing that he formed his admirable style. He displays in his boyish romance and balladry the imaginative excitability of genius; in his tracts he shows its mental excitability. He fed himself on Hume, on such philosophy as is found in Baron d'Holbach's "Système de la Nature" and on the ideas of the English radicals headed by Godwin; and he wrote, under the impetus of this reading, tracts for reform both speculative and practical. Though a youth he was very serious in this early proselytism, and became, in fact, a political agitator. He was, nevertheless, born a poet, and he condensed and precipitated

these ideas in "Queen Mab," his first true poem, uncommonly well written verse. It is noticeable as con-
taining a voyage and also a view of the universe scien-
tifically conceived, which remained fixed themes of his
imagination; but it was essentially a didactic poem.
Shelley's idea was to employ his poetical powers, such
as they might prove to be, in the service of reform.
"Queen Mab" is also noticeable as the only poem written
by Shelley in a condition of happiness. It was composed
before any tragic circumstance arose in his life. Five
years later he published "The Revolt of Islam." The
step of progress is that he had eliminated a direct didactic method. But he could not give up the matter of reform; that was still the text. Shelley was always fond
of a story; his first work had been a romance; and he
took to narrative naturally. He was not, however, content with mere narrative; it must have a secondary
meaning and intention of thought; consequently he made
his narrative an allegory of world-reform. "The Revolt
of Islam" is a poem seldom read. More than for its
revolutionary substance it is memorable as the first English poem in which the modern ideal of woman in her
freedom is presented, of which Tennyson's "Princess,"
so different in treatment, is the second. In this poem the
womanly character is given in Laone, the heroine,
plainly an ideal deriving from Shelley's wife, Mary, and
fitly so since she seems the heiress of her mother, Mary
Wollstonecraft, the first English advocate of women's
rights. The poem is noticeable, too, for the frank disclosure of Shelley's willing dependence on the great poets
of the world — a trait constant in his career, and
whether derogatory to his original genius I leave others
to determine. He was content, perhaps proud, to at-

tempt to compose in his own way scenes and effects of
the great classical tradition, as in the account here given
of the plague after Lucretius. Thirdly, the poem pro-
claims, not violence, but passive resistance as the means
of victory and affirms the doctrine of the triumph of
good over evil by love only.

It is plain that Shelley's poetic faculty had developed
even while dealing with a didactic theme however disguised by the method of narrative. He had been, however, before composing "The Revolt of Islam" profoundly
discouraged by misfortune in his private life and had
become fully aware of the futility of the practical attempts he was making for the public cause he sought to
advance. It was inevitable, it was the native drawing
of his genius, that he should feel the impulse to follow
ideal beauty and leave the world to its ways. But he
believed that man is bound, as he said, to serve his
fellow-men; and hence that to let the world go by, to
follow the gleam, was a fatal error, and that isolation,
whatever ideal might be there pursued, must end in destruction. Under the mastery of this idea he had already
written his first poem, free from the political motive,
"Alastor," in which he depicted a youth so destroyed in
his ideal pursuit. The poem is, as it were, a protest and
a warning against his own necessary fate. He had
turned to the long labor of "The Revolt of Islam" in his
old spirit of service to the cause; but against his will,
as it might seem, it was to a detachment from life in
society and to absorption in the ideal that he moved on.
The poetic element in him had received an im-
mense impetus. A great change had occurred. He
had previously been fed intellectually from English, Latin and French sources of poetry and

philosophy. He now became deeply engaged in Greek studies, and the change in his poetry was like breaking a chrysalis, like entrance on another kind of being. The Greek tragedies loosed his lyrical, one may better say, his choral power, the most marvelous of his gifts which made him the first English lyric poet, and Plato unfolded in his mind its instincts toward the supernal and inducted him into the mystical sense of beauty and love, which was to be his touch with the divine. It was a reincarnation of his poetic life. Shelley, however, did not lay his old nature off; there was only transformation in the change. Rapt as he was into the great creative world of art, he was only filled with a deeper, a more intense passion for human welfare; the two elements blended and gave out his great work, the "Prometheus Unbound." As it had been but a step from story to allegory, it was now but a step from allegory to symbolization; and, adopting that artistic method, Shelley symbolized his political and philosophical ideas in the drama, setting forth the Promethean ideal of patient suffering in love for all things and the millennial ideal of the golden age as the final state of mankind on earth, while from another part of his mind he figured in "Asia" — the companion of "Prometheus" — the spirit of nature, visible beauty, the emanation of the unknown and unsearchable power which is the source of all being. Without entering on any analysis or description of this choral drama, it is obvious that Shelley had now freed his poetic genius from the rivalry of either politics or philosophy, and had subdued them to poetry as materials for its creative hand; they are present, but they are present under imaginative and impassioned forms and harmoniously with artistic aims.

Shelley, however, had by no means integrated his genius into a power of pure imagination either lyrically or dramatically; there was still implicitly in it a practical aim — to serve man's welfare though by ideal means. He was too strongly built, too integral himself, to break suddenly with his past. His faculty, too, was fecund, and was always bursting into new modes of expression. His poetic tale, "Rosalind and Helen," had been merely a pendant to an earlier stage of thought and belongs by its story, style and characterization with "The Revolt of Islam." In "Julian and Maddalo" he had opened that vein of familiar verse in which he is without a companion in English literature; but in later years he continued the style only fragmentarily. He had now, however, conceived his career definitely as lying partly at least in the world of pure art, and he undertook a masterpiece of objective drama in "The Cenci"; extraordinary as was his success in a form of writing seemingly so little natural to him, he did not entirely free himself from his own world of thought in the attempt. In his artistic growth his studies of Greek imagination continued to support him most, and aided him to give mythic form to nature in his lyrics and also plastic form in his classical hymns. The symbolic mode of art dominated him in these and, with a closer touch of allegory, in "The Sensitive Plant," while in his simple love lyrics he began to find that immediate outflow from his genius, in forms seemingly unconscious of all art and free from any ulterior purpose, in which his supreme appeal as a universal poet is lodged.

There was one region of his mind, however, which lay somewhat apart. In it grew and flourished his doctrine of love, a mystic and suprasensual theme. He had early formed the ideal conception of love as the divine principle of the universe, and he approached it by the way of its incarnation in transitory beauty; and it is noticeable that from the first he described this as intellectual beauty. The study of Plato, and also the study of Dante and the Italians, developed this germinal idea. It gave out in succession, like blossoms on a spray, separate conceptions. These were not organized in any system of thought, nor were they final or in any way very definite conceptions. He distinguished between the love of the higher and the lower; he kept in mind the Platonic notion of gradual purification in love through attachment to beauty in an ascending series of its manifestations; he brooded much on the drama of the struggle of the higher and the lower love for the body and soul of a youth, whom he named Prince Athanase but whose tale he left untold. He also worked out in his mind other lines of Platonic theory, such as the doctrine of the anti-type, or companion soul, of which the soul itself is in search. These various mystical conceptions were not philosophically related in his mind; they merely existed there like wild seed that had been sown and had come up flowering in confusion but with a life of nature. An accident — his meeting with an Italian lady whose misfortunes and beauty touched him — set these various ideas in commotion; and out of it came the rapid improvisation of "Epipsychidion," in which, variously intermingled and with obscure allegoric relations to his own personal history in love, these ideas were not so much given expression, as made the spring and source of the verse. The poem, highly wrought in imagery and in a mood of ecstasy, is difficult; he himself hoped for but few who should give it fit entertainment; but, since "Prince

Athanase" was never written, it remains the premature and fragmentary expression of his doctrine of love, and is the climax of the philosophical element in him as "Prometheus Unbound" is of the political element, both being poetically rendered. Both, it may be noted, end in a Paradise, a mood of ecstasy, a dream of perfection, in the one case for mankind, in the other for the private life.

Shelley's idealization of women was an important and constant element in his life and thought. He was always a lover; but he had early come to live mentally in the ideal doctrine of love and had developed it variously under the influence of the thoughts of Plato and the poets. What "Laone" had been to the sphere of his revolutionary thought, an ideal of enfranchised woman, that the lady of the "Epipsychidion" was to the sphere of his lover's thought, an ideal of mortal love. The sphere of love, however, was that of his private self, and only at times of discouragement and pain did it at all usurp on the main business of his life which was poetic creation in the large — tale or drama or revolutionary ode. In Italy he was happily removed from near and constant excitement of his political enthusiasm; yet whenever the occasion arose he became the poet of the cause. If workingmen were shot in Manchester, he was ready with "The Masque of Anarchy." If a revolution broke out in Spain or Italy, he welcomed it with an ode of triumph and incitement. If Greece rose against the Turk, he sang a new drama of the "Persæ" in "Hellas"; and his heart was in all these doings. It is noticeable that he retains his gospel-truth of the supremacy of love, patience and kindness, as the method of regeneration for society; but he also rejoices in the victory of bloody arms. His

ideal of the perfect state was one in which government
should be no more; that is, it was an anarchical ideal of
peace on earth, good-will to men, in which there would
be no place for king or priest, for court or prison, for
war foreign or domestic — a millennium; but he accepted
revolution in the making, and bade the fighters godspeed. In "Hellas," nevertheless, close as it is to contemporary things, the artistic element prevails. The
lyric opening has a beauty all its own; the speculative
theory of "Ahasuerus" is a passage of ideality not specifically related to the theme of Greek liberty; the great
choruses are generalized economiums of the glory of
Greece, the march of liberty, the universal hope of the
world. In other words, the political motive laxly controls the drama, for the sense of art had become primary
in every expression of the poet's genius, whatever of
practical occasion and current fact might blend with the
work.

The "Adonais" was the most purely artistic poem of
Shelley. It was related to life, as the larger part of his
verse always was closely bound in some way with things
actual. The elegy was occasioned by the death of Keats.
But if there be any of the longer poems which exists in
the realm of pure art and is the work of the imagination
working solely to artistic end, it is this. It is full of
personal pathos, of meditation on life, of divine philosophy, but all is held within the bounds of beauty and
moves under the spontaneous and unreflecting impulse of
poetic passion. The willing dependence of Shelley on
old writers is noticeable here at the close of his life as
at the beginning; he had, in the works already noticed,
written under the shadow of the glory of Æschylus or
Shakespeare or Plato, and now under the shadow of

the beauty of Bion and Moschus. He had, too, entered the sphere of Calderon, "the light and odor of the flowery and starry 'Autos,'" as he described that lyric world. It seems likely that the works he meditated, of which least is known and of which none was written, such as "The Creator," might have been related to Calderon as the earlier choral dramas to Æschylus; and that in these, and the dramas of which the fragmentary Indian play is an indication, his artistic power would have reached its climax and consummation. The attentive student of his drama can hardly refrain from believing that Shelley was on the eve of naturalizing the Spanish drama in English. The fate of "The Creator" is unknown; like "Prince Athanase," like that longer poem to which, Shelley said in his preface, the "Epipsychidion" seemed to be merely an introduction, like "Charles the First" and "The Triumph of Life," these works were not to be. What is plain is that, on the verge of his thirtieth year, Shelley's poetic genius, subdued to the elements it worked in, had become a pure power of art.

In this rapid view of the history of Shelley's mind it is easy to perceive the close connection and intertexture of his poetry with the realities of his time and his own life. Unreality is the fault most alleged against him; yet as one reviews the successive poems, the basis of reality in them seems large. In his more familiar verse many passages recur to the mind which are but little removed from the actual scenes of life; such, for example, are the sail on the Serchio, the ride with Byron, the letter to Mrs. Maria Gisborne, the pine-forest at Pisa, the anecdote of the Aziola, the day in the Euganean Hills. In observation of nature he was minute and accurate; the description of the skylark is singularly truth-

ful, to name an instance, and so is the broad scene of
the lines on the bridge at Pisa. The scenes of pure
nature are clearly memories of particular moments of
grandeur or beauty, as in the case of the wonderful sky
scene, of which he is fond, disclosing a dawn or a sunset
pouring through a mountainous chasm of cloud, or as
in the many forest scenes. It is noticeable, also, to
what an extent he was dependent on the external stimulus
of an occasion or a person to rouse or to unlock his
mood. With the exception of the "Ode to Liberty" all
his later political verse was occasional, the response of his
heart to current events in England, Spain, Italy and
Greece. The "Epipsychidion," abstract as it is in one
sense, would not have been written except for the accident of his encounter with Emilia Viviani. The "Ode to
the West Wind" and "To a Skylark" were personal experiences. His love poetry, even more exclusively than
his political verse, was incited by persons; there is no one
of them, however universal in appearance, that has not the
stamp of personal experience. Love was for him an
ideality in all its forms, whether divine, humanitarian or
personal; but in each form it was realized in the visible
beauty of nature, in the cause of liberty and in the women
whom he knew and loved either actually and simply or
under one or another form of feigning. In his life woman
was real, love was passion; and in its moods of restraint,
denial and despondency, it was still actual experience.
In no part of his verse is there more reality blended of
many elements than in the final group of love poems commemorating the last year at Pisa and Lerici. The poetry
is not unsubstantial, either as a scene of nature, a revolutionary theme or a personal history. In it Shelley
dealt with known objects, actual events and real persons,

in large measure, and threw over them the veil of his words.

The sense of unreality in the verse, which is commonly strongly felt on the first reading, is in part due to his use of images "drawn from the operations of the human mind," as he himself notes. He shared something of that quality which he imputed to Coleridge whom he described as a "subtle-souled psychologist"; and this tells in the verse as an initial obstacle to most readers. It is also in part due to his use of imagery from the atmospheric elements — light, wind, color, cloud, motion; and in general from the scenery of the upper air — mountains, glaciers, vistas, sunrise, tempest, space, darkness in flight, mists, splendor. The intensity of this imagery, perhaps more than its novelty and rapidity, confuses the unaccustomed mind, nor is any poetry better described as blinding with "excess of light." If the reader should attempt Calderon, he would have a very similar experience at the outset. To this trait is to be added the presence in the verse of a finer sensuousness than is commonly the lot even of sensitive men, and which is as "blood within the veins." It was Shelley's idiosyncrasy to be more a creature of nature than most men, and his language comes from a primitive world; his imagination lives in an outdoor dominion, where he himself had his own familiar life. No English poet ever lived so much in the open air. He had English tastes, in that respect, and from boyhood he indulged them, being born to leisure and never confined by any employment any more than Virgil. He boated and rode, he shot and climbed; he moved easily about with the command of travel; he had the natural habits of a high-bred English youth. It is easy to trace in his earlier works the scenes that he saw

— the spire disappearing among the stars, the heath and the Welsh hills, the western ocean of the Irish seas. The river voyage he never forgot; it was always an ideal felicity for him. He wrote "The Revolt of Islam" floating in his boat on the Thames or walking along the chalk hills; he composed "Alastor" in the shade of the oaks of Windsor Park. His first visit to Switzerland and the Rhine gave exaltation to his landscape and a new sense of majesty. After he settled in Italy there was no longer any occasion for housing himself, and he lived constantly in the outer world, composing in the summer-house at Este, among the baths of Caracalla at Rome, in the Pisan pine wood, by the torrent of Lucca, on the waters by Lerici. He evidently was drawn ocularly to the atmosphere; he watched the heavens; and this appears in his remarkable knowledge of the clouds, which he rendered as no other poet has ever done. If he used the imagery of the atmosphere, it was because he knew it. It was not only this outdoor life that molded his poetry, but the subtle spirit within him feeling every impulse of sense inhabited his verse. It is difficult even to indicate this. It is seen, perhaps, in his constant reference to the state of the air; there is no poetry with so much temperature in it. It is hinted again by the faintness that would from time to time overcome him; even in the open air fragrance would so affect him. Its sign and proof is the recurrence in his verse of the state and phenomena of ecstasy, which he describes over and again and which is the climax and sudden fall of many a poem, the "Hymn to Asia," the "Ode to Liberty," the "Epipsychidion," the "Adonais"; in the shorter lyrics it is equally found. There was something idiosyncratic, something that was seated in his genius deep as life, in all this; and yet it is to be remembered that as in his political evangel he was of the radical school of his time or neighbored its writers, so here he was of the romantic school of his age in poetry; the minute observation of nature, psychology, and the mood of ecstasy were traits of romanticism. What distinguishes Shelley, and in a certain sense removes him from English appreciation, is the presence of a foreign landscape and air; he placed the "Prometheus Unbound" in an Alpine setting, and over all his poetry of the last and fruitful years broods the beauty of the Mediterranean world; a beauty exotic, unknown, inconceivable; and this, passing into the verse, transforms it out of the English genius and touches it with alienation while it immortalizes it.

The touch of Italy was also felt by Shelley in the form of his poetry, which, like the landscape, tended to become foreign. It is perhaps not so clearly recognized as is desirable that his greater imaginative work, though it lies in the classical tradition, departs from the English line of that tradition; he owes less to English than to foreign influences. It is true that his contemporaries of the earlier time, Southey, Wordsworth and Coleridge, in particular, affected the formation of his younger verse metrically and gave direction to his thoughts and imagery; but outside of the great writers of England — Shakespeare, Spenser, Milton — Shelley seems to have had no considerable range in English poetry. If there are indications of more detailed knowledge, as when the opening of "Alastor" appears to echo a passage in Jonson's "Cynthia's Revels," they are probably exceptions; such passages, perhaps, as Leigh Hunt might have brought to his notice. In his youth he read more prose than verse, and mostly in the field of phi-

losophy, history, social reform. In Italy he read the
Greek, Italian and Spanish poets. He took the classical tradition by direct contact, and not mediately through
the English. This explains somewhat the singularity of
the impression made by the form of his imagination,
not only in the "Prometheus Unbound," but in a
broader compass. He was especially drawn by the arts
of Italy, and in particular by sculpture and painting
to which he gave much attention; this, without doubt,
strengthened his plastic power of imagination and helped
him to realize the figured impersonations of his lyric
drama. He had a natural bent to allegory and symbolization, as has been said, and this developed in Italy
into a marked predilection for the forms of the masque.
There are signs of this taste in the "Prometheus Unbound"; its choral groups are conceived rather as merely
musical than as pictorial, but the chariots of the Hours
bring in the picture element, and the vision of the spheres
of the earth and moon is pure masque. The second
instance is "The Mask of Anarchy." The reading of
those poems, called in Italian "Trionfi," further developed
the taste and Shelley's last and most obscure poem, the un-
completed "Triumph of Life," is a pure allegorical pageant. Traces of this manner of figuring imagination and
grouping allegorical figures pictorially are not uncommon
in Shelley's later work. The masque form had conquered his imagination, within its own province at least,
and was the consummation of the allegorical impulse in
his genius, so often shown in its lower modes of art.
There was something kindred to this form-instinct in
his impersonation of the characters of "Prometheus" and
"Asia"; but in "The Creator," which was to be built
on the suggestions of the "Book of Job," this method

of construction would have been used in a more comprehensive way, if the "Prologue to Hellas" may be taken as an indication. Just as the powers of nature are personified in elemental yet human forms, such as Apollo, so ideas may be similarly personified in forms of imagination, a feat which Shelley had in fact accomplished in "Prometheus Unbound." The method of the Spanish drama, dealing with the mysteries of the faith and like subjects, is not far removed from this. Shelley was in the direct line to such an intellectual figuration of abstract ideas and principles, in elemental yet human forms, given dramatic life and lyric expression, but rather on the pattern of Calderon than of Æschylus. The pastoral element, also, which enters only slightly into the "Prometheus Unbound" in the faun-scene, had been greatly strengthened by his life in Italy. It is singular that his works show so few traces of any interest in the Italian pastoral drama. Milton's "Comus" appears to have been the literary example of this mode of imagination in his mind. The remoteness of such poetry from actuality, its pure artistic play, especially attracted him; it was in its spirit that he wrote "The Witch of Atlas," and time and again as in "The Sensitive Plant" he had drawn near its precincts. In the fragments "Ginevra," "Marenghi," "Fiordispina" he had entered on more artistic narrative than "Julian and Maddalo," and in the fragments of "Orpheus," and more clearly in the scenes from the "Indian Play," he was creatively working out a new form of pastoral drama. In none of these various developments of his genius, neither in the grand allegorical drama nor in artistic narrative nor in the drama of pastoral setting, was there much forethought or deliberate intention; they were the spontaneous movements of his genius ripening in art; they were all highly romantic, and constitute the extreme accomplishment of English romanticism. The part of Italy in Shelley is plain — landscape, masque, and plastic form, the philosophical comment of love, the *trionfi;* the part of Greece was the form and artistic spirit of the lyric drama and the intellectual interpretation of love and beauty — Æschylus and Plato; the part of Spain was further to nourish him in grandiose lyric conception and that "flowery and starry" atmosphere in which his senses delighted, weaving thereof the veil of his thoughts — a part inchoate and unaccomplished. In the history of Shelley's genius what took place was the growth of a rich and rare form of Renaissance art, freeing itself from the rationalism, speculation and political turmoil of the preceding age, and coming to its golden fruitage under southern skies in companionship with the genius of those climes.

Such, in rapid outline, is the history of Shelley's genius as a great creative power. It is to be observed that, while the elements of passion and thought are permanent in his work, he had little command of the third province of poetry, action. The unreality that has been alleged against him has been already traced, so far as it lies in his method and style; but its chief cause is, perhaps, the lack of action, and the consequent loss of balance in the whole as a complete representation of life. His narrative lacks incident, as in "Queen Mab" and "The Revolt of Islam"; there is in the pictures that the eye forms in both something tenuous, languishing and sentimental in the figures, which recall the canvases of allegorical painters of ideal scenes, like Temples of Fame, or of romantic episodes or of classi-

cal myth. Shelley's imagination sympathizes much with
moods of painting; in his earlier works it has the remoteness, diffusion, and lack of firm line that characterize a
sentimental school. In the "Prometheus Unbound" the
lack of action is, it is true, the Æschylean tradition of
the play, but on the larger scale of Shelley it is more
noticeable. The scenes change, but there is no real
action. It is fresco-painting, huge, magnificent, superb
in majesty and loveliness; but it is not dramatic —
rather is it a panorama of ideal scenes. Shelley is a
master of the splendor as well as of the music of speech;
in soliloquy and description, in eloquent bursts of passion, he does not fail; but there is no knitting of the
scenes by action, properly speaking; there is no causa-
tion, humanly speaking, but only a self-executing progress of fate, envisioning the abstract. Shelley was primarily a thinker as well as a poet; and in poetic drama
he dealt with humanity as a statesman deals with it, with
ideas, causes, masses, not with individual fates. This is
the highest reach of thought in art. In the
later work, to this same absence of individual
action, as a part of life, is added the fact that the
emotion becomes ever more high-strung, the thought
more subtle; and with all this the veil of words grows
ever more dense with imagery. In the high creative
part of his genius he becomes steadily more difficult;
his last work, "The Triumph of Life," only a poet can
read easily, that is, one who is as accustomed to think
in images as a mathematician is to think in cryptograms
of space and number. In this part of his work Shelley's
genius is most mediated by conscious invention, symbols
of thought, reminiscences of past literary traditions; it
is least direct, and operates through a high intellectual

and artistic culture; it appeals necessarily to a small circle. The reader consequently takes more pleasure in the less creative work, in scenes of nature directly described and moods of feeling into which no element of philosophy enters. The truth is that poetry is best when it is not mediated at all, when it is not related to life through any event or passion or thought, but is that event, passion or thought — when it is life; genius is most itself when it is unconscious of any intellectual process, any practical aim, any artistic means; poetic genius is most pure when it is the rising up of the spirit of life that clothes itself, as it arises, in the mood, imagery and thought of the passing moment. This was Shelley's way, especially in his short lyrics, which were the effusion of his feelings, or in the odes and other poems which were the expression of a personal experience, generally filled or touched with passion or with that melancholy which is the shadow of passion. In these poems he directly expresses life, as it wells from its inner cells. It is by these poems that he clings to life in others; they hold the heart of Shelley. The longer poems contain his passion for the ideal. Elsewhere will be found his passion for liberty, his dream of the millennial hopes of men, his life with nature, his response to romantic motives found in Italian story. His greatest works were never written — "huge cloudy symbols" they were even to him; but he wrote much that is for all lovers of poetry, and often he poured out his heart "like a tired child," and in these outpourings he most drew the love of men. The personality of genius is more than its works, in lyric art; the ideal impulse that streams from Shelley is his immortal part — from him it comes, from the man, and it is in the poems where the man is nearest that it most flows. The lovers of Shelley will read his greater works, his ideas, his high-wrought and difficult art, his dream; but it is the heart of Shelley — himself, that the world listens to.

SHELLEY'S "CENCI"

THE story of "The Cenci" is a family tragedy. Count Cenci outraged his daughter, Beatrice, whereupon the family conspired together and secured his murder, and in due time suffered execution for the crime. The theme of incestuous passion has been repeatedly treated in literature, and more than once great dramas have resulted; but Shelley veiled this portion of the action. In the play three crimes are linked together: that of Count Cenci, which is the motive of the action; that of the family, or parricide; and lastly the judicial murder, as the execution is here regarded, of the members of the family adjudged to death. Shelley considered that the delicacy with which he had treated the first crime would sufficiently allay natural repugnance to the subject, and the last two he treated with as much power as he was master of. The delicacy of which he speaks is not merely a matter of expression, but involves a radical change in the nature of the theme; he conceived the drama not as one of lust but of hate. To this end he makes the Count's crime the climax of a lifelong persecution of his family with which he crowned up his hatred of them; it is represented not as an act of passion but of long deliberated purpose to degrade, injure and destroy his victims; and lastly, it is important to observe, the Count seeks as the ultimate of his hatred, not the outrage of his daughter, but her consent, in order thus to ruin her soul. The play is, in its first movement, a study of hatred using atrocious means to destroy the victim.

The theme, so conceived initially, is placed in an atmosphere of opinion and social custom drawn from Shelley's idea of Italian society and history. This general environment is less in evidence because the play is for the most part, domestic and interior; but its ideas permeate all the characters and its prejudices are an essential condition of the thought and action. The first element in this atmosphere is the place of religion in Italian life. Shelley himself calls attention to this in his preface, and states that religion is there a devout superstition without any relation to practical life; it is believed, but it does not affect conduct, at least until after the event. Count Cenci and all his family are equally represented as devout and credulous; the presence of priestcraft is also illustrated by Orsino, the priest-lover of Beatrice, the kindly Cardinal Camillo and the inflexible Pope. The play thus takes place in a society in which religion is represented as supreme in civil power and over the minds of men, but without influence on their private lives. The second element is the idea of the *patria potestas*, the patriarchal conception of the family. It is set forth as the principle of Roman society. The father of a family is clothed with despotic power over his own; no one would dare to interfere with a domestic rule or to enter into the affairs of a household; least of all would the children and wife rebel, inasmuch as the father is protected by a veneration not to be overcome in their minds. Parricide, in such a society, is the most unthinkable of crimes. This state of opinion is reflected also in the conception of the Pope as the father of the church and exercising such paternal power, and also in the conception of God, in whose image as the Father of all the Pope is made. In the play, in fact, there is a consanguinity, so to speak, between God, the Pope and Count Cenci, which is very disturbing. It is clear, nevertheless, that Count Cenci in his mere fatherhood affects the persons about him, whether his children or others, as sharing in the divine right of the *patria potestas*, to rebel against which, whether in the family or the state or toward God, was the highest crime. The third element is pride of race, devotion to the honor of an ancient house; and this is represented as influential, not only over the family itself, but over such mere members of the populace as were the assassins. Beatrice sustains herself under torture with this motive, and also appeals with it successfully to the murderer, Marzio. These three ideas — faith divorced from morals, the patriarchal autocracy and family honor — are the elements introduced by Shelley into the general texture of the play as being specifically Italian.

The theme itself is displayed rather through character than action, and in particular through the two leading characters, Count Cenci and Beatrice. Each when present fills the scene, and the interest of the drama is in the conflict of their wills. They are diametrically opposed one to the other; Count Cenci is a devilish incarnation of the principle of evil, and Beatrice a human embodiment of the principle of good. They are opposed in yet another way. Count Cenci is an intensely concentrated character, with such a monotone of villainy that he gains, as the play goes on, only by greater intensity and concentration; he is absolutely solitary. Beatrice, on the other hand, is a character acting by variety and diffusion, changing from stage to stage, and

related by human companionship to every character in
the play. She is the center of its personality, in every
aspect, while Count Cenci is the single malignant and
maniacal force that, unloosed on her, ruins all. In him
is to be noted the presence, as the source of his character, of another Italian trait or principle — the trait commonly designated *virtù*. The most modern name for
what is really one of the oldest of human molds, "the
Superman," describes him. He is, in fact, individuality
let loose and dominant, as in a mad Roman Emperor or a
Rennaissance captain or cardinal. His words, when he
is reminded of God's being — "He does his will, I mine,"
might stand as a motto for this type. He has done his
will, and no one rises up to oppose him. He gives his
history in the first scene of the play, and himself notes
the peculiarity of his nature, as Shelley conceived it, in
the fact that he is an intellectual villain. It is quite
true, also, that no other side of villainy except its intel-
lectuality could have engaged Shelley's sympathy. He
reasons his villainy, and seeks that which the mind's eye
only beholds and rejoices in. This psychological "malady
of thought" is noted as a family trait by Orsino and reflected in Giacomo, the Count's son, whose dramatic
character lies only in its expression. Count Cenci conceives that the true injury lies not in the outrage of
Beatrice, which is simple violence, but in the corruption of her soul—in her consent. It is toward this that he
moves, and at the climax it fills his thoughts. Beatrice,
on the other hand, is from first to last the victim, but
she reacts at every stage of disaster and reveals her
nature in ways that awake increasing sympathy. The
general development of the character is set forth by
Mrs. Shelley, who describes it as "proceeding from

vehement struggle to horror, to deadly revolution, and, lastly, to the elevated dignity of calm suffering, joined to passionate tenderness and pathos." Shelley devoted all his power for dramatic revelation to the delineation of these two characters; but it is plain that both are of such a nature and so presented that a great opportunity is given in the play for silent action beyond the text; so much takes place in the mind of both, for which there are no words, that acting is essential to the integration of these characters and their bodying forth in a personality. Such passages occur in the exit speeches of Count Cenci, and a most notable one in the scene where Beatrice makes up her mind to the murder of her father, and not only resolves it herself but makes her resolution the whole life and strength of the enterprise. It is natural to suppose, therefore, that both characters would gain by being acted, and require action for their complete effect. The other characters are entirely subsidiary, and serve either to link the incidents and manage the detail of the action, to draw out Beatrice or Count Cenci, or to illuminate some aspect of the play in general. Giacomo and Orsino are carefully studied characters; the first, though little effectual in advancing the action, affords the only expression of the guilty sense of parricide, and Orsino, who is more directly engaged in the mechanism of the action, also expands the element of priestcraft and gives colors of subordinate villainy; but neither these nor the other minor characters really do more than fill up the scenes and carry on the necessary progress of the play. They do not interest the reader in their own fortunes. The dramatic fascination is substantially confined to Count Cenci and Beatrice.

The action, as has been stated, is threefold. Count

Cenci is the spring of the crime against Beatrice; Beatrice is the spring of the crime against Count Cenci; the Pope is the spring of the crime against the victims in their execution. The first crime is brought forward in the veiled words of Count Cenci in his first soliloquy in the opening scene, and develops especially in the mad scene (iii, i) and the scene of the curse (iv, i); the second, first suggested by Giacomo (ii, ii), is resolved upon (iii, i) and executed (iv, iii); the third begins in the discovery scene (iv, iv) and fills the conclusion of the play (v). Such is the enchainment of the action. Looked on as one complete action it has its climax in the final speech of Count Cenci, his soliloquy (iv, i) closing the scene. This speech is one of double dramatic irony in that Count Cenci mistakes the drugged sleep that comes on him for the blessed slumber of a peaceful conscience, and also in that he triumphs in the thought of immediate success at the moment that he stands above his grave; it comes after the final and repeated refusal of consent by Beatrice, which is the center of the conflict of their opposed wills; up to that point the action has gone forward; and, immediately after, the consequences simply unroll in the catastrophe — the murder scene, the discovery scene, and the various scenes of the trial.

It is obvious that the action, so described, lags in some scenes and is not materially advanced by others. This results in an immobility in the situations, of which there are three corresponding to the threefold phase of the action, and these scarcely change at all in the progress of the scenes. There is much in the play not necessary to the action narrowly defined, or but slightly related to it. In other words it is not exclusively a play of plot. The first plan of murdering Count Cenci, which failed, and

its dependent scene (III, ii), while giving the opportunity
to display Giacomo's character in his soliloquy and, as
has been said, to illumine the crime of parricide as such
by the state of his mind, might be thought superfluous,
since they do not materially affect the action. The same
might be said of the scene between Giacomo and Orsino
(V, i), though it displays Orsino's character and incidentally dismisses him from the play. In general these two
characters, which Shelley took from the history of the
case, are of slight use to the plot. It must be thought
that the scene between Giacomo and Beatrice (III, i) when
he assents to the murder, though dramatically effective
by the kiss in which they seal the compact, on which
the scene closes, is nevertheless a decline in the interest,
coming as it does after the powerful climax of the resolution of Beatrice to do the act. Orsino, too, is a difficult character to handle. A lover for Beatrice is
impossible; if he were possible, the part of vengeance
belonged to him and not to her; under the circumstances
Orsino becomes an interested accomplice, a broker of
assassins, with the hope of thereby entrapping Beatrice
into his power. He is false to her in the matter of the
petition. The effect of his character is to isolate her still
more in a bad world; but on the play itself, as a chain
of action, Orsino has little concrete influence. The petition, like the first plan for the murder, might be thought
superfluous, though it helps to justify Beatrice. The
fact is she does not need further justification. It will be
seen from all this that Giacomo and Orsino, while they
serve the play, do so in minor ways; so far as the action
is concerned, nothing really depends on them except the
hiring of assassins. Similarly with the other characters,
it is not for the sake of the action that they are present

but for some other purpose. So far as the action is
thought weak in structure, it is for this reason. There
is, too, diffuseness in the conduct of the action; in the
discovery scene, and throughout the trial, this is to be
observed, and it is noticeable generally in the large number of soliloquies and in the number of lines given to
the undramatic characters and episodes. High concentration is marked only in the feast scene, the mad scene,
the scene of the curse, and intermittently in the trial
scenes. It is plain that the weakness of the action,
both in structure and conduct, is a consequence of immobility in the situations, of over-characterization and
of dispersion.

It has been said, to notice the last limitation, that the
interest of the play ends with the death of Count Cenci.
It is true that the theme then changes so much as to
become almost a new play. If Shelley had been interested in "The Cenci" only as a personal tragedy, he
might have listened to the suggestion, which has since
often been made, that Beatrice should have declared and
gloried in her deed. In that case the Fifth Act might
have been saved to these critics, and remained integral
with the rest of the play. It is pleaded, on the other
hand, that Beatrice desired to save the honor of the
house, and was governed by this motive, though un-
availingly. But Shelley, consciously or unconsciously,
was interested in the play as a social tragedy, and the
Fifth Act really moves in a larger world than that of
the fortunes of a family in their private life. Moreover,
Shelley was pledged by his convictions to an ideal of
patient suffering; under the spur of sympathy with Beatrice he defended her parricide, as he defended active
and bloody revolution in politics if it occurred, but his

heart was always rather with the idea of patience than
of vengeance. In the Fifth Act he idealized the sufferer,
and it was more consonant with his genius to do so.
The break in the interest of the play, when it changes
from the domain of tragic vengeance in private life to
that of judicial murder by the most Christian of all
states, is very marked; but it is more just to say that
the theme changes in entering its third stage than that
the play ends in the Fourth Act.

"The Cenci," as is seen from this slight analysis, is not
a playwright's, but a poet's play. It is written under a
more liberal canon than that of stage-craft, under an
older canon — the canon of literature. Whether it be
better or worse for that reason is not the question; it is
in place here only to give a somewhat full exposition
of its nature and contents. In its threefold phases it is
a study of hate using atrocious means, of innocence
driven to desperate crime, and of human fate under social justice organized in established authority. Shelley
endeavored, in this instance, to write with the maxi-
mum of objectivity; but no poet can suppress himself
in his work, and the personality of Shelley pervades
the play. To indicate the ways in which it is related
to Shelley is all that can be attempted here. It is, in
the first place, a play of horror. Shelley was in boyhood initiated into literature by the then popular forms
of German tales and wrote highly sensational romances
in that style. Traces of this crude boyish taste long
remained in his work, and are seen even so late as in a
cancelled stanza of "The Sensitive Plant." Horror, or at
least terror, is one of the constant themes of imagination.
The thrill of it was never far from Shelley; in his last
year at Lerici there were visionary incidents, as will

be remembered; and it is appropriate to recall the fact that Mary Shelley wrote "Frankenstein." "The Cenci" may fairly be regarded as the climax in Shelley's work of this element in his nature. He was of a temperament to be attracted by this subject. It is not less to be observed, that this interest had become very subordinate. He naturally developed in a contrary direction, toward beauty, love, patience in ideal hope. In writing "The Cenci" he found it quite consonant with his natural choice to retire the atrocious crime, which is its principal motive, into the background, to veil it, and transform it into an instrument of another passion, hatred; and also to end the play in a glorification of suffering, resignation to calamity, rather than in an apotheosis of an act of vengeance however righteous.

Secondly, it is not a play of plot narrowly limited to a chain of events, but it is a psychological play; and it develops less by a presentation of action than by that of a series of states of mind in all the persons involved in the story. Shelley adhered very closely to the narrative as he had received it, even in small details; he told a clear and definite tale; but he was engaged not so much in the fatality of what occurred as in exposing the mental states of the actors, and he was as careful to do this for the least as for the greatest. Hence the superfluous scenes were included, and the number of soliloquies, in which internal moods are best shown or at least most clearly and fully stated, is large. The psychological method is one with which his own mind most readily sympathized. It aided him especially in delineating Count Cenci, who however he may seem a monster to us is revealed in his own thoughts as intelligible to himself at least. This must be regarded as a triumph of genius for Shelley, himself so remote from such a world. A passage in the preface shows that his thoughts were mainly intent on the justification of the actors in the crime of parricide, and it was in the attempt to clarify their motives that he was led to excess of justification by including every incident that might palliate the crime and by exhibiting as much as it was practicable to exhibit of the black career of Count Cenci. He seems to have relied on this justification and on the historic reality of the events to remove the prejudice that he foresaw against the treatment of the theme at all. In this he was perhaps mistaken, so far as the actuality of the crime is concerned. The world of poetry is not the world of fact; that is to say, it is not the ordinary moral world; the events of ideal tragedy are viewed not so much as crimes but as things of nature; and it is the world of nature, the eternal process of things independent of man's judgments and expedients, that is the world of poetry. Real events must become tradition before they are fit material for the imagination; reality is rather an added grossness to crime; and it is because no crude sense of reality adheres to the "Œdipus," for example, that it is supported as a tragic theme.

Thirdly, "The Cenci" is a play of womanhood. Shelley was preëminently a poet of womanhood, and this appears alike in his personal and his political verse. The ideal of free womanhood he had presented at great length in "The Revolt of Islam" at the beginning of his career, and in the later work of his genius the presence of woman under one or another form of ideality or of personal experience is constant. He knew women better than he knew men, and his sympathies were more deeply engaged by them. Beatrice seized on his imagination and his heart alike, and he delineated in her every phase of womanly attraction that the situation allowed. Count Cenci is a masterpiece of intellectual imagination; but Beatrice is a greater creation because of the diversity, naturalness and human truth of the representation. She is a woman of power, of courage, of resolve, without losing in the least her femininity and womanly charm; she draws from every character, by the mere magic of her presence and the strength of her nature, the utmost of which they are capable, all the good that is in them; from Cardinal Camillo in the trial scene to the assassins in the murder scene, from the timidly fearful Giacomo to the sly insinuating Orsino, she holds them all up to their best, and while under her influence they live, however briefly and futilely, at the height of their capacity. They all take life from her. On the other hand in her own relations she shows all the sanctities of home affection; with her brothers and Lucretia she sympathizes, consoles, incites, sustains — bears all burdens; and, for what is locked in her own heart, she endures all in a solitude of spirit that is never shared. She helps all, but is helped by none. Beatrice is the single vital character that Shelley drew; here is his conception of a woman doing and suffering in life; and for all the gloom and terror of the tragedy that involves her, it is a picture of such sweetness, dignity and power as to be immortal, a type of ideal womanhood quite alone in our literature.

Lastly, "The Cenci" is a play of protest. Shelley without conscious intention delineates here that world against which he had rebelled; he had not so much created it as found it. This world, in which Beatrice lived, recalls that enclosing prison of Poe's tale, which each day contracted its walls till it became a coffin for the prisoner. Historically, it was a world of law that gave no protection, of government that enforced no restraint on the powerful — law that at the last condemned the sufferer to death, and government that directed and executed the sentence, and called these things justice. Typically, it is the world of organized society, Christian, legal, powerful, in which one is without hope if he be a victim. This was precisely Shelley's idea of human government as he knew it in history and saw it in fact, the league of the oppressors of mankind; and the fate of the family of Count Cenci in the hands of Papal law was a type of the world. The minor incidents of the scene, the rack, testimony based on torture, the judge fixed in cruel purpose, are insignificant, the mind hardly rests on them — in view of the hopeless gloom of the whole process — the world of injustice grimly reigning without appeal and naming itself God, Law, Right. The sense of hopelessness that this sight gives brings to Beatrice the darkest hour of all her sufferings; nor did Shelley ever frame again in such deadly words the cry of despair as in her spoken fear lest evil might be finally triumphant in the infinite —

"If there should be
No God, no Heaven, no Earth in the void world,
The wide, grey, lampless, deep, unpeopled world!"

Shelley could not free himself from what was the lifelong preoccupation of his mind — the Revolution and the modes to bring it about. In "The Cenci" he gives a terrible example of the old régime, its vices, wrongs, cruelties, its social futility. So far as the theme of the play is not personal tragedy but — as the theme of all great tragedy must be — human fate, it is here that it is to be found.

The play is impregnated with Shakespearean words, image and tone, which color the style; and at times it also recalls the dramatic handling of well-known Shakespearean scenes and characters. It was Shelley's habit to incorporate in his verse, after the old tradition of poetic composition, the style and phrase of great poets. In "The Cenci" he used Shakespeare as at other times he used Æschylus or Moschus; but the familiarity of the Shakespearean drama makes the fact noticeable, and impairs the appearance of originality in his work to an unusual degree. It is to be observed that the scenes, characters and lines that he follows are such as belong to the most elementary knowledge of Shakespeare and must have been in his mind since boyhood, and that they affect the play slightly in a constructive way, but are rather the dressings of thought and action; they may readily be recognized by the ordinary reader.

The play is thus veined with Shakespeare, and the language of Shelley is often the mere shadow of Shakespeare's thought.

These borrowings and reminiscences, however numerous, make up only a small portion of the entire text, but they give to it a Shakespearean tone and differentiate the play from Shelley's other works in general style. The play is made of style and diction through which the Shakespearean threads are shot. The debt of Shelley to Shakespeare in the dramatic handling of scene and characters is also superficial. It is confined to the handling and does not affect the characterization itself. It is true that Count Cenci recalls King Richard III by

his blitheness and by the presence of the religious element
(though differently conceived), and also Macbeth by his
invocations, in language, and Lear by the fact and violence of his curse; but he is not a compound of these
characters any more than Beatrice is of Constance,
Clarence, Macbeth and Hamlet, whose words or manner
she employs. Both characters are creations of Shelley,
original and entire, in the combination of qualities that
makes vitality and in the reaction on life that expresses it.
Count Cenci is delineated by three traits, his masterless
will, his loathing for beauty and goodness, and his faith
in a vengeful God. There is no character in Shakespeare in whom any one of these traits is depicted, much
less their combination. Beatrice likewise is a character
who owes nothing to any other in literature and is un-
paralleled by any other; she is a new type of suffering,
mingled with courage, endurance and tenderness, and
expressed in new circumstances of pity and terror.
Camillo is admirably drawn, and Bernardo in the last
scenes is pathetic and real, while Giacomo and Orsino,
though overstudied for the parts they play, are carefully delineated in motive and temperament. The character drawing, in fact, which is the strength of the play,
owes nothing to Shakespeare; neither do the dramatic
climaxes, namely, the braving of Count Cenci by Beatrice,
the opening lines of the mad scene and the silent formation by Beatrice of the resolve on Count Cenci's death,
the speech of Count Cenci — "He does his will, I mine,"
and his exit speech, the slumber of Beatrice in the last act,
and the final much admired exit speech at the close of
the play, which is in the great style of dramatic art.
In all these, which with the characters make the play,
Shelley is altogether himself; no other has any part in

them, constructively or in expression. The Shakespearean element occurs most in the weaker portions of the play and is a source of weakness, except so far as it affords the support of a noble diction where the action lags. Shakespeare contributed to the play general conduct of the murder scene and suggestions for the dramatic exhibition of character in other scenes, mainly in language; and, *passim*, an investiture of phrase or image that supports the style, and more rarely a form of thought for situations that are as old as drama. Such forms of thought can be paralleled from any literature; thus Lewes in noticing Beatrice's reminiscence of Claudio's speech on death refers to Euripides' "Iphigeneia in Aulis." The originality of the play lies in creative power applied to character in a new action; in this the Shakespearean element is subordinate and incidental, and is rather a color of Shelley's mind than a constituent of the play.

SIDNEY'S "DEFENCE OF POESIE"

PHILIP SIDNEY in this brief book shrined up for immortal memory the riches of Italian humanism, at a great English moment, just before the romantic outburst of his country's "breed of men" eternized the late glory of Elizabeth's reign. It contains the meat on which their intellect was fed; their temper breathes from it; and it is a mirror of their literary accomplishment at the instant. Its obscure origin in a Puritan attack on the playhouses by Stephen Gosson in 1579, its composition about 1583, though it was not published until 1595; its being a controversial pamphlet in the passing war of the theater or in the more general contest of the purblind party in Europe against the illumination of the new learning, are bibliographical details, interesting but immaterial; for however fortuitous its birth and particular its aim, it at once disclosed the bright metal of those little "golden" books which are among the rarest products of time. It is the first classic — first both in time and in rank — of English criticism; and, happily, its bygone learning, its stylistic devices and quaint terms are steeped in the personality of the best-beloved child of his age who had himself slept in the Muses' Bower, and breathes the fragrance of one of the choicest spirits of mankind. This golden substance and personal charm united to make it a precious volume to later English poets, one of the few books which it is reasonably certain that they all have read.

[1] Reprinted by permission from the Humanists' Library. The Merrymount Press, Boston. Copyright, 1908, by D. B. Updike.

In England humanism has no other monument so shining; neither has it any example so pure. Sidney's thought is woven, warp and woof, of the classics and Italy. Such assimilation implies an affinity in the thought for the thinker — it was his own before he found it; and in Sidney the mind was humanistic. His nurture had made him almost as much the child of European civilization as he was the son of an old English stock. If Italy threw such graces on Surrey's noble mind that men see in his verse the grey streaks of the new dawn, in Sidney

"Hyperion's march they spy, and glittering shafts of war."

He was as well educated as Milton in the next age, as deeply imbued with delightful studies, though his mind was less richly stored; and Surrey and Milton were the morning and evening star of Italian humanism in England. Sidney was a complete example of its modifying power on the genius of his country. He had his Latin and French by the age of twelve, and by twenty he had almost ended his travels on the Continent, where he had imbibed language, literature and knowledge in many kinds, to return home fitted to become one of the best masters of learning in the kingdom, and well on in the journey. His curiosity was unbounded; he was as inquiring as he was observant; and his mind had singular adhesiveness — everything stuck to it. He had more than intelligence; he was as quick with sensibility and imagination. He was more than assimilative; he was naturally imitative, and a creator in his turn. He was a stimulating presence, an agitating influence; everything where he was became a living question. He was no anachronism lingering superfluous on the Field of the Cloth of Gold; no fading knight, the afterglow of things and ways departed from the stirring world, the player of a half esthetic part. Sidney was a man of power. He showed this in inferior ways; he was proud, quick to rebuke, loud-voiced to fling back an earl's insult; and in superior ways he showed it by the equivalence of really great matters in his thoughts. He was a man of affairs, but he still habitually moved in the whole of life; and to him there was a like importance in the discovery of the Americas, the consolidation of Protestant power, the growth of an English stage or even the refinement of the vernacular so as to make its broad syllables yield up their organ notes and its slight vowels their flute-like movement. His influence was at all points enlivening, and he had Shelley's instinct for putting his first thoughts and new loves to immediate use and practice. So, though young, he expressed himself fully. In the "Arcadia" he unveiled his temperament, in "Astrophel and Stella" he laid bare his soul alike in its mortality and its immortality, and in the "Defence of Poesie" he gave us the clear stamp of his mind.

This is the human and particular interest of this book — that Sidney's mind is here. If to the common imagination of the English race he now seems a pictorial figure, a spirit moving in a remoter air, a legend of mythic beauty; if he inspires an adoring rather than an understanding attitude, this is not of necessity the case. He may be as familiarly known as any other English poet or gentleman who lives by the record of the past. If one reads only these few pages with intelligence and alertness, Sidney soon takes on solidity and definiteness of human character. The "Defence" is sometimes spoken of as if it were a declamation of vague feeling, a shadow and echo of Platonic aspiration, a sounding rhapsody only, or as if this quality characterized it. The light and music of Plato are in it, and in its course there does rise that wonderful English ground-swell whose lofty melody is half in the thought, half in the cadence, both wedded in harmony; but though there is such an accompaniment and occasional overflow of the finer element of all language, as in Milton likewise, the "Defence" to a mind grown familiar with its beauty is most striking for the wealth and precision of its details, the swiftness of its condensed logic, the readiness of its citation of person, fact and thought, and especially for its closeness to actual life. The touch of knightly exercises at the beginning; the range from the arentos of the South American Indians, which Sidney had heard of, to the Hungarian feast-songs, that he had been present at; the marks of Wales and Ireland, with both of which he was personally familiar; and in books — not to speak of foreign learning that he had appropriated, of the Greek which he enjoyed or the Latin which, as Languet in his good advice foresaw, he more used — his knowledge sweeps from Percy's Song and Chaucer's "antiquity" to the latest phase of what was then the elegant modernity of Euphuism, and in every case the stamp of vital experience, of personal contact, is on these literary references. His education was so good, so wisely directed, that it became true experience; his experience in turn became true education, the whole a seamless garment of life. The shirt of Nessus was not closer to the flesh than the examples adduced in the text, and all its feeding matter of fact and authority is to the power of thought. It is this last — power of thought — that most marks the "Defence"; its onward march, rapid and assured, is never checked, not even by those cadenced sentences of wisdom, which are foregleams of Bacon and sometimes make the page a ridged sea of melody; "like as the waves make toward the pebbled shore," they all obey the master-flow of the intellect that streams on in its great argument.

It is here that Sidney's Englishry stands clear of his subject. Truly he did not emancipate himself from that veneration for authority that belonged to his nature and his culture alike; but his mind did not abide in Greek or Latin, or in Italy; he brought his treasures home, and they were his servants. It is said that his matter is Italian: no thought but what may be found in a previous writer, and in fact all the thoughts of the Continent on the topic gathered in one comprehensive creed. Minturno, Fracastorio, Scaliger — his granary is stuffed with their grain. The fact is so. The identification of his sources only shows the perfection of his preparation to write his book. But this marshalling of the whole, rationally, lucidly, systematically, this exposition firm, agile, exact, like fencing, is Sidney's; he brings all to a practical end. The blend of romance and practical is racial in the English; in Sidney it was thorough and gave his life that chivalric quality which makes him an ideal figure. The blend of criticism with practice in a similar way characterizes the "Defence." Just as its text is knitted of living experience, and is the spectacle of a live mind, so its end is conjoined with life itself, and is ethical. There was no need for him to range abroad to learn this lesson. It was in the blood from which he sprang, in his English genius that ever follows this master light. Nor can I except from his Englishry the devoutness of his mind. Here at the core of the work, in the devoutness of the author's mind and the ethical

end of his discourse, are the native forces that preserved
for all time in an English classic what in Italian critics
and philosophers has vanished from men's memories.

The true excellency of the "Defence," which is out of
the range of all its other excellences as an index of
culture and a mirror of personality, is that it contains
the truth about poetry. Sidney boldly put poetry in the
front of all merely human power, the friend and companion of man in the virtuous way, disclosing the ideal
and inciting to its accomplishment, illuminating and
warming the soul at once and urging it on in its career
toward that perfectness, in union with which it finds its
true nature. In this doctrine there was not only the
traditional speculative Platonic vision; there was, as he
handled it, intense moral energy. Here Sidney found
the harmony between his Puritan earnestness and Italian
estheticism, which is most clear in his words about the
Scriptures. The Bible was the omphalos of Protestantism; when states shocked together, in that time, faith
was the force that gave momentum to their massed arma-
ments; men daily suffered and died throughout Europe
for their religion. Sidney's devoutness of mind was
not only a grace of his own soul; it was one with his
earthly loyalty to crown and land. To him there was
such sacredness in divine things that he passed over the
notion of the inspiration of secular poetry as an expression and an idea of too doubtful reverence to be
canvassed. But when he found in the Scriptures themselves the ways of poetry used to reveal and to edify,
and tale and psalm and parable wearing the garment of
ideal imagination, his assurance was complete; his argument was sealed with the seals of the Spirit. This faith,
first put forth by him with such a fund of thought, such

glow of words, such elevation, from which the calm self-possession of assured victory is never absent, has been the food of English poets to this day; in their greater works, in their brief lyrics, in their letters and familiar talk, they repeat the old words over; however they may discuss the lesser matters of topic, technique and taste, as Sidney himself did, the wellspring at the source of all is still that faith that poetry has a permission from the Maker of Heaven and Earth to approach nigh to divine ways by creation within our own world of time and sense, by an intimacy in men's bosoms to draw them to the good, by the noble mastery belonging to essential loveliness to awake affection, imitation, realization in their lives. Forgetful of this faith, English poetry falls to lower levels of a rhetorical expertness or intellectual wit; but, when loyal, it scales all heights from the days of Sidney's own companion, Edmund Spenser, to those of Shelley, his last great disciple.

It was fortunate that a faith so exalted was put forth by one to whose character it was so becoming that its expression is his natural and easy speech. His own nobility seems to certify its truth. This serious-minded youth who was also the "rose of the fair state" was destined to so sweet and attractive a memory, to such transcendent ideality in the imagining affections of future ages, that on his lips the doctrine of the divine sanction of poetry and its rank as the most practical of all arts is a fitting utterance. He is equal to so great a sentence without presumption. It was fortunate also for us that Sidney left, in addition to the imaginative work of still younger years, this record of his graver mind where we may approach his every day life which is otherwise known to us only by the loving tributes of his friends, a few tasks of state worthily accomplished and one fine action. By that action, the giving of the bottle of water to the dying soldier, his mortal shape is now figured in all remembering minds; and, for readers, this book of the "Defence of Poesie" now makes most human and draws within the compass of our understanding that strong and beautiful soul, subduing all the graces of life to practical moral energy, in whom for our love and revering all England was modeled in a little clay.

SHAKESPEARE'S
"MIDSUMMER-NIGHT'S DREAM"

SHAKESPEARE was first a poet, and afterwards a dramatist; the history of his development was the powerful specialization of general poetical faculty. He was a very conscious artist; he came early to hold clearly defined in his mind the matter appropriate to imagination, a method of work and a philosophy — by which I mean a way of conceiving the world — in whose sphere this matter took on intellectual worth, moral order, and sensuous charm, and from whose laws this method proceeded. Life first appeared to him as a lyrical power; in his earlier plays this tone is constant, and often exceeds and impairs their dramatic quality; golden words, the echo of rhyme, the linked melody of stanzaic structure inside the dialogue, the chorus combination of the speeches at marked points, the line for line antiphony of older drama which he inherited, are some of these obvious lyrical traits; and lyricism shows its dominancy also in frequent situations and in soliloquy more deeply imbedded in the drama, and even controls character itself, as in Richard II, Queen Margaret, and perhaps Romeo, in whose career of passion the climaxes of the play are not only lyrical moments but take lyrical form, except in the last act, which is in a greater dramatic manner. This lyricism Shakespeare was slow to disuse, and in his latest work it came back with an autumnal flowering. It was at the first not only youthfully impulsive, but reflective and studious. In "Love's Labour's Lost" may be seen the delight of the young poet conning his art, interested in rhetoric, style, diction; examining, choosing, and refining; concerned with the externals of poetizing. The height of his lyricism is reached in "A Midsummer Night's Dream"; and naturally the same play discloses the completion of his self-education in this direction, when he had left all questions of verbal surface and structure behind and, entering into the inner secrecy of art, saw its essential nature. What Biron had begun, Theseus finishes.

Every play of Shakespeare is unique and has a world to itself. In some of the dramas that other world is so powerfully made, it draws into itself so much of the reality of the interest, that it seems to persist by a being of its own long after its inhabitants have been laid away in the tragic grave or love's felicity, as the case may be. "Hamlet" and "Twelfth Night" have such an atmosphere; but the disclosure is more striking when there is a finer sense of fresh discovery in it. In that age of new geography and England's adventurers taking practical possession of the globe, the inland poet added something to her domain; he found the forest of Arden, the witch-haunted Scottish heath, the magic isle of Prospero, and together with these he entered what was the most marvelous realm of this kind, the fairy world. If "A Midsummer Night's Dream" attended the celebration of some noble marriage, that was incidental; but no setting could be more appropriate to the play than such an occasion where the stately lovers should see themselves mirrored in the Athenian king and queen witnessing a play and spectators besides of the action of that fairy power, in an enchantment of midsummer night, which was also

to invoke blessings on their wedded union. The bride-
bed begins and ends the play; sleep, night, and dream
are its world; poesy — to use the word of lyrical touch
— is its element. The marriage of Theseus is the enclosing frame of all; but in the foreground and center
are the creatures, sports, and affairs of the fairy sphere.
Oberon holds the scepter and is master of the revels; the
Athenian court, except for its wandering lovers, lies on
the outskirts of the scene. Dream is the key-word,
the master note on which the melody is built and to
which through all changes it returns. It is not the old
story how "Life is a Dream"; with greater subtlety and
more philosophical truth, here life is rather a thing that
dreams, and all the scene in its moments of high poetic
relief has the vivid unreality which is the sphere of
dreaming power. But even a dream, for dramatic purposes, must have its own cosmos; and this is supplied
by the fairy world. It is near nature, near mortals, and
fills the visible and known world, but it is isolated from
our world by night, and also by sleep, for it is by the intervention of sleep that the lovers come within its sway;
it is concentrated, for local habitation and a name, in
the enchanted wood. It is, nevertheless, a true world
measured by time and space and action; it has distant
territories and past history, a king and queen and court
with a life of amusement, revels, love-episodes, and royal
vexations, all its own; the Indian boy, whose fragrancy
is only told of, gives substance to its polity and its
affairs. Its function is to organize the dream-spirit of
the play, to give sensuous definition and dramatic opportunity, and especially to body forth in films of reality as
thin as rainbow bubbles that world of glamor in which
Shakespeare will express the essence of the imagination

most fantastically, most lyrically. It is the ethereal substance of the play, that in which all the rest coheres and exists, though when it vanishes it leaves "not a rack behind."

Shakespeare, however far afield he may range for poetical matter and creative atmosphere, nevertheless places the true interest in man's life. "Man is one world," in Herbert's phrase, and the other world, in Shakespeare's dramas, whether natural or demoniac or of the elemental spirits, "attends him." Human life in this play is set forth doubly. The court sphere holds the first place, but so far as concerns the action of its higher figures, it is very subordinate. Theseus is king, with the duty to administer the laws of the state unwaveringly, to do justice by the code; and he discharges this office with a noble dignity of speech. He has, moreover, a paternal solicitude for the youthful lovers, and on the proper occasion an older man's resources to satisfy the father behind the scenes. His is the royal sport of hunting, and the final festivities are for his pleasure. He utters the words of most weight in the intellectual sphere, and gives them authority by his grave character. Yet both he and Hippolyta, who is only a consort, are almost lay figures, decorative with a certain antique severity of outline and pose, the restful part in the general action. To the court sphere belong also the two pairs of lovers, Valentine and Hermia, Demetrius and Helena. The youths are the ordinary gentleman lovers of Shakespeare's early stage, with the behavior and love-psychology belonging to the part. Helena, her pursuit of the graceless Demetrius being granted and her betrayal of the rival lovers' plans being excused, is a more maidenly and attractive character than her schoolmate,

Hermia, who only dotes upon Valentine and displays the shrewish temper that Shakespeare so often depicts as a feminine trait. The human plot lies in these characters; it is slight, and does not greatly interest the spectator in their fortunes; it is conducted with lively incident by the resources of a comedy of errors freshly handled in which a change of parts in the lovers is effected, with surprises for the two maidens resulting in great discomposure for Hermia, and a doubly ironical situation for Helena, wretched in being sought by both lovers, falsely and to her flouting as she thinks. The dramatic action is conventional, yet skilfully contrived, involving the familiar matching of wits, the feminine scolding scene and awaking dream device in Hermia; but freshness arises in the treatment of the old machinery of play-acting by means of the novel environing circumstances. The story of the lovers, nevertheless, has by itself little vitality, and is principally an instance of invention.

The second phase of human life exhibited lies in the clown-sphere of the play, the crew of Athenian workingmen, who in love and duty tender their poor interlude, the first labor of their minds, for the royal pleasure. The humor that flows from their presence is blended from many sources. Bottom, in whom it is concentrated, own countryman of Dogberry, is yet singular in his power to expose himself, laying grossly bare a universal human weakness, in his confident ability to play all parts with the unconscious notion that the use of each is to unlock some talent of his own. There is comic situation in the first contact of ignorance with art, when these rude craftsmen attempt to compass it; in the clinging of their minds to the fact of wall and moonshine, and the ludicrous symbolism of their first essays at representation; in the contrast of their coarse realism with the Thisbe fable, turning it to silliness with a clayey hand. There is also, of course, an abstract humor in that a parody of the old stage is involved, still effective though the special plays and authors aimed at are no longer of importance, if indeed there was any pointed contemporary satire in the piece. The main comedy is in the English characterization, the low life, which is rendered in the usual way of Shakespeare in dealing with the populace. The clown-sphere is, however, not dramatically in contrast with the court-sphere; its points are not worked out with that end. Its true opposition is rather with the fairy world, and comes to its dramatic height in the enamoring of Titania with the "translated" Bottom. The fairy plot, slighter even than the human plot, is worked out by this incident in the course of which Oberon obtains the Indian boy and peace is restored to the fairy kingdom. The comedy is most exquisite at this point in the play, and composed at once so grotesquely and delicately that the scene remains one of the capital memories of literature. Titania passes under enchantment through sleep, as the lovers do; but for Bottom a way more appropriate for his character is found in Puck's mischief-making spell who claps the ass's head on him. Titania awakes changed within by the herb's compulsion; Bottom is externally changed, yet in the change reveals himself in his proper nature — the mask on him is really an unmasking; and his mind is unaffected, but adapts itself at once to his new fairy dignities and services as readily as to the lion's part. Enchantment is at its climax; illusion can do no more; the scene goes on with beauty and humor in one rivalry, and only the merriment of surprised delight fills the onlooker at the masque-like spectacle. The clowns are fled to Athens, and following them there after daybreak Bottom returns to his original world and the task in hand, and they act before Theseus's court. The play within the play now takes the place of the woodland masque; but the same opposition of the crass mind with art is subtly echoed in the enactment of the interlude, and the scene is still illusory, though now with the illusion of art.

Character, plot, incident, situation, dialogue — it is plain that the interest of the play, the charm that has made it a marvel of fantasy and beauty, does not lie in these, but in the diffused dream-atmosphere in which all of life is breathing in the enchanted night. Illusion is the theme to which the play returns in Protean shapes. In its grossest form, the illusion of the senses, which is such a stumbling-block to the hard-headed workingmen of Athens, it is given only by the instrumentality of Puck, the mischief-maker; he transforms Bottom to his marvelous self, the ass-headed one, and he misleads the angry lovers, keeping them apart in the tangled wood. The illusion of the heart appears at every turn and in various disguises; humanly speaking, love is the only interest of the play, and love is the illusion of the heart. So it seems, though obscurely and poetically, to the happy pair of eloping lovers, who in that lyrical part for part chorused dialogue, in which they take up each other's words as in a little song, join in speaking of it, Elizabethan-wise, as

> "Momentany as a sound,
> Swift as a shadow, short as any dream;
> Brief as the lightning in the collied night,
> That, in a spleen, unfolds both heaven and earth,
> And ere a man hath power to say, 'Behold!'
> The jaws of darkness do devour it up."

More clearly to Helena, seeing how love's enchantment
works on the deceived Demetrius disdainfully abandon-
ing her charms for Hermia, its true nature is apparent
as she uses the stock-expression of Elizabethan love-
psychology:

> "Things base and vile, holding no quantity,
> Love can transpose to form and dignity:
> Love looks not with eyes, but with the mind;
> And therefore is wing'd Cupid painted blind:
> Nor hath love's mind of any judgment taste;
> Wings, and no eyes, figure unheedy haste:
> And therefore is Love said to be a child,
> Because in choice he is so oft beguiled."

In the wood the juice of the little flower of lovers,
on which Cupid's arrow fell when he shot harmlessly at
the virgin votaress of the West, distilled on the eyes of
Valentine made him pursue Helena, and with changed
affections call her

> "goddess, nymph, divine and rare,
> Precious, celestial;"

on the eyes of Titania made her wake to mirror the
tender vision of the ass's head, engarlanded with flowers,
curried by the patient Cobweb and Mustardseed, with "a
great desire to a bottle of hay"; on the eyes of Demetrius
gave him back to wronged Helena, never to change more,
the gift of Oberon, gentle to lovers, who took not off
the powerful charm.   The lovers woke deeming Theseus
with his hounds a vision of that sleep-cumbered night,
where, as if it had been Morpheus's own realm every one
fell to slumber with the frequency and inconsequence
of childhood or old age in its neglected corner.   But
the great illusion is the illusion of art.   It is stated with

philosophical precision in the front of the last act, which is its sphere:

> "Such tricks hath strong imagination;
> That, if it would but apprehend some joy,
> It comprehends some bringer of that joy."

It is described as the function of the poet:

> "And, as imagination bodies forth
> The forms of things unknown, the poet's pen
> Turns them to shapes, and gives to airy nothing
> A local habitation and a name."

It is put forth by Theseus as the essence of all art: "The best in this kind are but shadows; and the worst are no worse, if imagination amend them." This is that great shadow-idea, one of the few that are constant in Shakespeare, whose persistence through all his thought is so marked a characteristic. King Richard's mirror is an early example; and here, in this play, Oberon, who is a prophecy of Prospero, is named "King of Shadows." Thus Oberon, who controls the action of the play, is the master spirit of its idea.

Illusion in these various forms, involving the whole compass of life, is strongly supported on all sides by the lyrical element which is also omnipresent. It appears, characteristically, in that opening song-dialogue of Lysander and Hermia; it is the natural speech, song-speech, of Puck and the fairies in the induction to the fairy world; and it governs the close in those songs of blessing which Coleridge thought the English notes of a better Anacreon. But it is more pervasive than this; its pastoralism gives the atmosphere, and detail as well, to the rural description, and absorbs all nature in its own point of view in the account of the blight that had fallen on the land; it yields those idyl pictures of girlhood friendship, Cupid shooting his bolt into the West, Hermia's awaking, the Indian boy's mother, the hounds of Theseus, which enamel the verse; and throughout it inspires the infinite touches of golden word and melodious cadence which make the language of such surpassing beauty and pure vocal charm. It is in such a garment of lyricism that the theme of illusion is clothed, and it is thrown over the humor as well as the beauty of the play. Shakespeare in "the northern island sundered once from all the human race" was the crest of the Renaissance that there and in him reached its climax.

In "A Midsummer Night's Dream," how much there is characteristic of the great Italian mood of Europe, idyllic, pastoral, delighting in beauty, painting the frieze of the world with mingled loveliness and grotesqueness, but on no part of it, however Cupid and monster wreathed, such a twine of delicacy and fun as the creatures and pranks of Oberon's court in the wood!

Many of the plays of Shakespeare appear to be climacteric, and there may be error in ascribing such swift and mighty changes even to the soul most capable of education of all born of English earth. If the view here taken have any color of probability, if it be not in its turn a dreaming of the mind, this play discloses as its main characteristic the ripened presence of the poetical faculty, exceeding in value and power the human material with which the dramatist dealt; here Shakespeare at the height of his lyrical inspiration, at the climax of the modes of power possible to its exercise, has reached for the time being a limit. The eloquence of Richard has become, not the passion of Lear, not the natural elevation of Hamlet even, but pure poetry; here the experimental study of Biron has become the mastery of the nature of art in its substance beyond the form; here the handling of the dramatic means of earlier comedy and history has become so habitual that it ceases to occupy any special place or prominence. A supremacy of power in many ways has been achieved. But the sign and proof of excellency in the poetical faculty, which is here to the fore, is the temper of grace by which humor itself is transformed. Bottom, even, in his adornments of flower and leaf, with the doting fondness of the queen of the fairies and the ministries of the sweet winged courtiers, becomes almost poetical. To poetize humor is the last victory of the spirit of the beautiful. Courtesy wins a similar noble triumph in the human sphere, when Theseus lays down its law, finding grace in halting words, and simple virtue in the awkward service of even the coarse-handed and rude-minded craftsmen of Athens turned poet and player in their lowest estate for his sake. The presence of this spirit in both kinds is like the touch of Shakespeare's hand; the man is felt through it, whose wisdom was amiableness in that morning hour. It is a poet's wisdom and fitly crowns him at the moment of his achievement.

The play, too, is throughout a poet's play. It has the fluidity, the brightness, the insubstantiality of a poet's conception of life; for life to him in whose hand it is plastic, contracts plasticity from his hand. Amid such scenes rising in the wakeful fancy life collects enchantment like dew, and seems itself the wood blown through by the breath of the summer night, sleep-heavy, dream-haunted. Then it is nature to use Puck's words, saying, "What fools these mortals be," who take this world for eternal where there is no abiding principle. Art itself is but Hamlet's "shadow's shadow," yet it has more

of eternity in it, and passes not away. This supremacy
of the imaginative view of the world which permeates
the play has made it peculiarly dear to poets, and there
was such felicity in its conception that it has fertilized
their minds, and occasioned a European progeny whose
inhabitancy is in Oberon's world, so real has that world
which Shakespeare evoked become to the imagination of
men. It is true, of course, that historical probability
gives such credence to Oberon as the legend of Troy gave
to Achilles; in an old French poem he appears, and even
the Indian boy in his company; but it is to be feared
that, like Agamemnon, the Indian boy without his poet
would have slipped into oblivion. The issue of genius
is of more import than its obscure ancestry; it is often
infertile; but Shakespeare not only gave the mold of
heroic and romantic human character to the English imagination; he also made it free of his domains, though
it is a daring spirit who ventures to conjure there. The
fairy world, by virtue of some kindness in it, has been
nearer to the poetic mind than Arden or the magic isle,
and more familiarly ranged. A literature, indeed, has
sprung from it trailing a bright track in the world's fancy.
The source, nevertheless, remains shining over all. In
this play — to draw these suggestions to an end — Shakespeare, perfected in poetry, found himself in Oberon
"King of Shadows," lord of the lyrical world of sensuous
emotion and all that there inhabits, even to laughter at
its clownish human visitants. He left this realm of the
gracious comedy of beauty to hold his scepter of illusion
in the human soul, and sway for a season the tragic
world; but in that Buddistic progress he made through
the souls of men, within the limits of one mortal life,
coming to his last transmigration in Prospero, he again

unveiled himself as "King of Shadows," still in the same dream-life that he had first seized in the conception of the midsummer night — the illusory world of art, of life, of all being known to man's consciousness; and wrote the last word of poetic truth:

> "We are such stuff
> As dreams are made on, and our little life
> Is rounded with a sleep."

RUPERT BROOKE

Rupert Brooke was both fair to see and winning in his ways. There was at the first contact both bloom and charm; and most of all there was life. To use the word his friends describe him by, he was "vivid." This vitality, though manifold in expression, is felt primarily in his sensations — surprise mingled with delight —

> "One after one, like tasting a sweet food."

This is life's "first fine rapture." It makes him patient to name over those myriad things (each of which seems like a fresh discovery) curious but potent, and above all common, that he "loved," — he the "Great Lover." Lover of what, then? Why, of

> "White plates and cups clean-gleaming,
> Ringed with blue lines," —

and the like, through thirty lines of exquisite words; and he is captivated by the multiple brevity of these vignettes of sense, keen, momentary, ecstatic with the morning dip of youth in the wonderful stream. The poem is a catalogue of vital sensations and "dear names" as well. "All these have been my loves."

The spring of these emotions is the natural body, but it sends pulsations far into the spirit. The feeling rises in direct observation, but it is soon aware of the "outlets of the sky." He sees objects practically unrelated, and links them in strings; or he sees them pictorially; or, he sees pictures immersed as it were in an atmosphere of thought. When the process is complete, the thought suggests the picture and is its origin. Then the Great Lover revisits the bottom of the monstrous world, and imaginatively and thoughtfully recreates that strange under-sea, whose glooms and gleams and muds are well known to him as a strong and delighted swimmer; or, at the last, drifts through the dream of a South Sea lagoon, still with a philosophical question in his mouth. Yet one can hardly speak of "completion." These are real first flights. What we have in this volume is not so much a work of art as an artist in his birth trying the wings of genius.

The poet loves his new-found element. He clings to mortality; to life, not thought; or, as he puts it, to the concrete — let the abstract "go pack!" "There's little comfort in the wise," he ends. But in the unfolding of his precocious spirit, the literary control comes uppermost; his boat, finding its keel, swings to the helm of mind. How should it be otherwise for a youth well-born, well-bred, in college air? Intellectual primacy showed itself to him in many wandering "loves," fine lover that he was; but in the end he was an intellectual lover, and the magnet seems to have been especially powerful in the ghosts of the men of "wit," Donne, Marvell — erudite lords of language, poets in another world than ours, a less "ample ether," a less "divine air," our fathers thought, but poets of "eternity." A quintessential drop of intellect is apt to be in poetic blood. How Platonism fascinates the poets, like a shining bait! Rupert Brooke will have none of it; but at a turn of the verse he is back at it, examining, tasting, refusing. In those alternate drives of the thought in his South Sea idyl (clever as tennis play) how he slips from phenomenon to idea and reverses, happy with either, it seems, "were t'other dear charmer away." How bravely he tries to free himself from the cling of earth, at the close of the "Great Lover"! How little he succeeds! His muse knew only earthly tongues — so far as he understood.

Why this persistent cling to mortality — with its quick-coming cry against death and its heaped anathemas on the transformations of decay? It is the old story once more: — the vision of the first poets, the world that "passes away." The poetic eye of Keats saw it —

> "Beauty that must die,
> And Joy whose hand is ever at his lips
> Bidding adieu."

The reflective mind of Arnold meditated it,—

> "the world that seems
> To lie before us like a land of dreams,
> So various, so beautiful, so new,
> Hath really neither joy, nor love, nor light,
> Nor certitude, nor peace, nor help for pain." —

So Rupert Brooke,—

> "But the best I've known,
> Stays here, and changes, breaks, grows old, is blown
> About the winds of the world, and fades from brains
> Of living men, and dies.
>   Nothing remains."

And yet,—

> "Oh, never a doubt but somewhere I shall wake;"

again,—

> "the light,
> Returning, shall give back the golden hours,
> Ocean a windless level . . . "

again, best of all, in the last word,—

> "Still may Time hold some golden space
> Where I'll unpaçk that scented store
> Of song and flower and sky and face,
> And count, and touch, and turn them o'er,
> Musing upon them."

He cannot forego his sensations, that "box of compacted sweets." He even forefeels a ghostly landscape where two shall go wandering through the night, "alone." So the faith that broke its chrysalis in the first disillusionment of boyhood, in "Second Best," beautiful with the burden of Greek lyricism, ends triumphant with the spirit still unsubdued.—

> "Proud, then, clear-eyed and laughing, go to greet
> Death as a friend."

So go, "with unreluctant tread." But in the disillusionment of beauty and of love there is an older tone. With what bitter savor, with what grossness of diction, caught from the Elizabethan and satirical elements in his culture, he spends anger in words! He reacts, he rebels, he storms. A dozen poems hardly exhaust his gall. It is not merely that beauty and joy and love are transient, now, but in their going they are corrupted into their opposites — ugliness, pain, indifference. And his anger once stilled by speech, what lassitude follows!

Life, in this volume, is hardly less evident by its ecstasy than by its collapse. It is a book of youth, sensitive, vigorous, sound; but it is the fruit of intensity, and bears the traits. The search for solitude, the relief from crowds, the open door into nature; the sense of flight and escape; the repeated thought of safety, the insistent fatigue, the cry for sleep — all these bear confession in their faces. "Flight," "Town and Country," "The Voice," are eloquent of what they leave untold; and the climax of "Retrospect," —

"And I should sleep, and I should sleep," —

or the sestet of "Waikiri," or the whole fainting sonnet entitled "A Memory," belong to the nadir of vitality. At moments weariness set in like a spiritual tide. I associate, too, with such moods, psychologically at least, his visions of the "arrested moment," as in "Dining Room Tea," — a sort of trance state — or in the pendant sonnet. Analogous moods are not infrequent in the great poets. Rupert Brooke seems to have faltered, nervously, at times; these poems mirror faithfully such moments. But even when the image of life, imaginative or real, falters so, how essentially vital it still is, and clothed in an exquisite body of words like the traditional "rainbow hues of the dying fish"! For I cannot express too strongly my admiration of the literary sense of this young poet, and my delight in it. "All these have been my loves," he says, if I may repeat the phrase; but he seems to have loved the words, as much as the things — "dear names," he adds. The born man of letters speaks there. So, when his pulse is at its lowest, he cannot forget the beautiful surface of his South Sea idyls or of versified English gardens and lanes. He cared as much for the expression as for the thing, which is what makes a man of letters. So fixed is this habit that his art, truly, is independent of his bodily state. In his poems of "collapse" as in those of "ecstasy" he seems to me equally master of his mood — like those poets who are "for all time." His literary skill in verse was ripe, how long soever he might have to live.

To come, then, to art, which is above personality, what of that? Art is, at most, but the mortal relic of genius; yet it is true of it that, like Ozymandias' statue, "nothing beside remains." Rupert Brooke was already perfected in verbal and stylistic execution. He might have grown in variety, richness and significance, in scope and in detail, no doubt; but as an artisan in metrical words and pauses, he was past apprenticeship. He was still a restless experimenter, but in much he was a master. In the brief stroke of description, which he inherited from his early attachment to the concrete; in the rush of words, especially verbs; in the concatenation of objects, the flow of things *en masse* through his verse, still with the impulse of "the bright speed" he had at the source; in his theatrical impersonation of abstractions, as in "The Funeral of Youth," where for once the abstract and the concrete are happily fused — in all these there are the elements, and in the last there is the perfection, of mastery. For one thing, he knew how to end. It is with him a dramatic secret. The brief stroke does this work time and time again in his verse, nowhere better than in "at dead *Youth's* funeral": all were there —

"All, except only *Love* — *Love* had died long ago."

The poem is like a vision of an old time Masque: —

"The sweet lad *Rhyme*"——
"*Ardour*, the sunlight on his greying hair"——
"*Beauty* . . . pale in her black; dry-eyed, she stood alone."

How vivid! The lines owe something to his eye for costume, for staging; but, as mere picture writing, it is as firm as if carved on an obelisk. And as he reconciled concrete and abstract here, so he had left his short breath,

in those earlier lines, behind, and had come into the long
sweep and open water of great style:—

> "And light on waving grass, he knows not when,
> And feet that ran, but where, he cannot tell."

Or:—

> "And feel, who have laid our groping hands away;
> And see, no longer blinded by our eyes,"

Or, more briefly,—

> "In wise majestic melancholy train."

And this,—

> "And evening hush broken by homing wings,"

Such lines as these, apart from their beauty, are in the
best manner of English poetic style. So, in many minor
ways, he shuffled contrast and climax, and the like, adept
in the handling of poetic rhetoric that he had come to
be; but in three ways he was conspicuously successful
in his art.

The first of these — they are all in the larger forms of
art — is the dramatic sonnet, by which I do not mean
merely a sonnet in dialogue or advancing by simple contrast; but one in which there may be these things, but also
there is a tragic reversal or its equivalent. Not to consider it too curiously, take "The Hill." This sonnet is
beautiful in action and diction; its eloquence speeds it on
with a lift; the situation is the very crest of life; then,—

> "We shall go down with unreluctant tread,
> Rose-crowned into the darkness! . . . Proud we were,
> And laughed, that had such brave true things to say.
> — And then you suddenly cried and turned away."

The dramatic sonnet in English has not gone beyond that,
for beauty, for brevity, for tragic effect — nor, I add, for

unspoken loyalty to reality. Reality was, perhaps, what he most dearly wished for; here he achieved it. In many another sonnet he won the laurel; but if I were to venture to choose, it is in the dramatic handling of the sonnet that he is most individual and characteristic.

The second great success of his genius, formally considered, lay in the narrative idyl, either in the Miltonic way of flashing bits of English country landscape before the eye, as in "Grantchester," or by applying essentially the same method to the water world of fishes or the South sea world, both on a philosophic background. These are all master poems of a kaleidoscopic beauty and charm, where the brief pictures play in and out of a woven veil of thought, irony, mood, with a delightful intellectual pleasuring. He thoroughly enjoys doing the poetical magic. Such bits of English retreats or Pacific paradises, so full of idyllic charm, exquisite in image and movement, are among the rarest of poetic treasures. The thought of Milton and of Marvell only adds an old world charm to the most modern of the works of the Muses. What lightness of touch, what ease of movement, what brilliancy of hue! What vivacity throughout! Even in "Retrospect," what actuality!

And the third success is what I should call the "mélange." That is, the method of indiscrimination by which he gathers up experience, and pours it out again in language, with full disregard of its relative values. His good taste saves him from what in another would be shipwreck, but this indifference to values, this apparent lack of selection in material, while at times it gives a huddled flow, more than anything else "modernizes" the verse. It yields, too, an effect of abundant vitality, and it makes facile the change from grave to gay and the like. The "mélange," as I call it, is rather an innovation in English verse, and to be found only rarely. It exists, however; and especially it was dear to Keats in his youth. It is by excellent taste, and by style, that the poet here overcomes its early difficulties.

In these three formal ways, besides in minor matters, it appears to me that Rupert Brooke, judged by the most orthodox standards, had succeeded in poetry.

But in his first notes, if I may indulge my private taste, I find more of the intoxication of the god. These early poems are the lyrical cries and luminous flares of a dawn, no doubt; but they are incarnate of youth. Capital among them is "Blue Evening." It is original and complete. In its whispering embraces of sense, in the terror of seizure of the spirit, in the tranquil euthanasia of the end by the touch of speechless beauty, it seems to me a true symbol of life whole and entire. It is beautiful in language and feeling, with an extraordinary clarity and rise of power; and, above all, though rare in experience, it is real. A young poet's poem; but it has a quality never captured by perfect art. A poem for poets, no doubt; but that is the best kind. So, too, the poem, entitled "Sleeping Out," charms me and stirs me with its golden clangors and crying flames of emotion as it mounts up to "the white one flame," to "the laughter and the lips of light." It is like a holy Italian picture — remote, inaccessible, alone. The "white flame" seems to have had a mystic meaning to the boy; it occurs repeatedly. And another poem — not to make too long a story of my private enthusiasms — "Ante Aram," — wakes all my classical blood,—

"Voice more sweet than the far plaint of viols is,
Or the soft moan of any grey-eyed lute player."

But these things are *arcana*. To the world he will be the poet of the youth of England in the Great War, the living voice before the battle, true heir of Taillefer at Hastings.

There is a grave in Scyros, amid the white and pinkish marble of the isle, the wild thyme and the poppies, near the green and blue waters. There Rupert Brooke was buried. Thither have gone the thoughts of his countrymen, and the hearts of the young especially. It will long be so. For a new star shines in the English heavens.